THE MASON'S WORDS

THE MASON'S WORDS

THE HISTORY AND EVOLUTION OF THE AMERICAN MASONIC RITUAL

ROBERT G. DAVIS, 33°, G.C.

BUILDING STONE PUBLISHING
GUTHRIE, OKLAHOMA

ISBN: 978-0-6158538-2-6

Published by:

Building Stone Publishing
Guthrie, Oklahoma 73044

CONTENTS

ILLUSTRATIONS

AUTHOR'S PREFACE

I will never forget it. I was sitting in the northeast corner of the small lodge room above the grocery store in my hometown. The lodge was located (and still is) across the corner from the county courthouse. The Masons had bought the property in 1905, and had built a substantial two-story building on it. As was typical of the era, they leased the first floor for retailing, so the brethren had to use the "back" entrance to attend lodge.

One had to climb a steep flight of stairs to get there. The old men argued about that for 50 years, until an elevator was finally installed–almost too late, because most that needed it had already passed on by then.

But this particular night would be a life-changing one for me. Of course, I didn't realize it at the time, but I was participating in one of the most ancient traditions of manhood. This night would launch me on a new journey. A pursuit of something uniquely different, and yet so universally sound in its application. Something that, over the years, would have an impact that is too profound for words.

On this night, as I was sitting in the northeast corner of the lodge as the youngest Entered Apprentice, I was living a childhood dream. I could not remember a time when I was not going to be a Freemason.

I took the degrees of Masonry during the summer of my twenty-first year. My father served as Master. He conferred all three of the craft degrees on me; just as he had done with my older brother. On this evening, my dad's brother recited the second section lecture and the catechisms. Many of the men whom I had known and respected in my childhood were there. I can't remember when I didn't know them. They were my father's friends. It felt good to be among them.

For the first time in my life I understood why my dad and uncle had come in from their farming and ranching duties early, bathed, put on their Sunday suit, and spent the evening in town.

It was a ritual they would follow every Wednesday for the half century they were Masons. My uncle lived a mile from us. He would come by and pick up my dad, and they would go to lodge together. As a youngster, I would often promise myself I would wait up until dad got home so I could ask him about his special evenings. But I always fell asleep before he made it back. I could tell he loved it. It was important to him. He always looked forward to his night out with his man friends. There was a kind of a quiet contentment in his face on the morning after these special sojourns. And I was bathed in the mystery of it all.

But now I knew. In fact, I knew a lot I hadn't known before that night. I now understood how my dad knew so many people in town, and why he was such good friends with them. I now realized why he was so close to his brother. A special bond existed between them. I recognized why he was concerned about how other people were doing; why he would often call when some neighbor needed help, just to see if there was anything he could do. I also now understood why he was a man with a gentle spirit.

For me, from that moment in the northeast corner of the lodge until he passed to that "house not made with hands," I would love him in a different way than I had before. It is a powerful and magical thing to be able to call your father, your brother. The mystic tie had united yet another son to his father forever. That is the traditional way of Freemasonry.

It is to my father, a good man and Mason, that this work is dedicated.

Robert G. Davis, August, 2013

A special thanks to the Iowa Masonic Library for granting me the freedom to explore its vast stores of knowledge. This library is truly one of the great Masonic resources in the world.

INTRODUCTION

Freemasonry is the pursuit of that which is noble in man. It is a quest for intellectual and spiritual knowledge. It is a journey to become aware of, and be in tune with the inner nature of one's own being. It offers a prescription in how a man goes about finding self-affirmation and fulfillment. It articulates the nature of truth. It urges us to ask the deepest questions about life, to contemplate what is important, and to strive to learn more than we know–and to know more than we think we can. Freemasonry insists that, so long as we never cease asking the questions, then it will not be possible in a lifetime to fulfill its mission with us.

And, there are many questions!

Take the first one asked the Entered Apprentice in the categorical, or testing lecture of the Degree: "Whence come you and Wither Traveling?" Then, think about the answer given.

Now, remember back when you were in the northeast corner as the youngest Entered Apprentice. More than likely, the ceremony in which you were an active participant was the first time you had experienced ritual in a formal sense, outside perhaps your own place of worship. If you were like most, you probably had not been told a thing about what was going to happen. Before that night, you didn't know what a Masonic Degree was. And yet, there you were, the center of attention in a ceremony so beautiful, so unique, so foreign to anything you had ever seen or heard; it was almost too much to absorb in one experience.

What did it all mean? Where did the Mason's 'Words' come from? Who were the authors? How old were the ceremonies of the lodge?

By the time I had participated in all three of the Craft Lodge Degrees, my mind was spinning with these and many more questions. I couldn't wait until I could ask. Were there books I could read? Did every older Mason know all the answers? Was it possible that I could someday know as much as the other men in my lodge? They all seemed so proficient; so exact in the ritual language they had conveyed to me; so knowledgeable in the ways of Masonry. On that first evening as an Entered Apprentice, I was informed I would have a mentor to answer my questions. I couldn't wait until my first "lesson."

But the lessons weren't quite what I expected. The memory work got in our way. Sure, I understood that I would have to commit the 'catechisms' to memory. But I was in college at the time. Memorization was my business; my mind, a sponge. I wasn't concerned with that. What I wanted to know was all that other stuff. I wanted to know about Freemasonry!

In retrospect, I must admit my "teacher" was a patient fellow. In our sessions, I asked more questions than he did. He didn't know the answers to many, but he never got upset. Unlike some I have since been told about, he was gracious in his ignorance. He just explained that the men in the lodge took a lot of pride in knowing the "adopted work." They enjoyed the weekly fellowship. They were good friends. But they were not scholars in Masonry, nor did they know of any in the area. They just loved the degree work and enjoyed performing it. Besides, it was up to each individual Mason to figure out for himself what it all meant. It was a personal thing. The meaning was different for everyone.

At the time, I understood little of what he was saying to me. But I knew there were answers to be found somewhere. So I went back to school and worried about other things for awhile. Two years later, I joined the Scottish Rite, the so called *'Hauts Grades'* or high degrees of Freemasonry which originated in France and introduced to America in the 1760s. Nobody asked me. I had heard it was the college course in Masonic teachings. Once again, I just wanted to do what my father had done. I remember him saying once that he had been a Master Mason nearly 30 years before joining the Rite. His only regret was that he had not done it much earlier.

It was an extraordinary experience for me–the pageantry, the ceremonies, the theatrical settings and effects–the profound lessons. Who penned this stuff? Where did the ideas come from? It was remarkably good.

I resolved then that I would begin my study of Freemasonry. It was too important, too relevant, too sound in its judgments to set aside. It had survived the test of time. That alone gave it much credibility to my thinking. So I "dug in" and joined the millions of others across so many generations who have sought the personal path of enlightenment and in so doing, enriched their lives. I soon discovered that it is indeed the journey itself which becomes the soul of Freemasonry and the longing of every thoughtful Freemason.

The first Masonic book I read was "Morals and Dogma"—Albert

Pike's lectures to the 33 degree system of the Ancient and Accepted Scottish Rite. When I joined the Rite, every Master of the Royal Secret (32° Mason) was given one as he completed his joining experience in that Rite. It was the first and only Masonic book that I owned. In fact, I had long been acquainted with it and had read it several times before I became a Mason. It was a book in my father's library and had caught my attention even when I was in elementary school. While I did not understand eighty percent of what I was reading at that time, I thought it was the most important book I had ever read. It shaped my ideas about what it means to be a moral person at an important time in my young life. It greatly influenced my early perceptions of the ideals of manhood. It broadened my understanding of the significance of religious thought to world history. Of course, had I known then what I know now, I probably wouldn't have attempted to tackle, as my first challenge, the college course in Freemasonry. But, I was naive and wholly curious in matters Masonic. After I joined, I put my mind and heart into what Brother Pike had to say about our ancient and honorable Order. It was a decision I will never regret.

Pike's lectures led me down many paths of Masonic inquiry. I discovered that other books on Masonry and related sciences were readily available. I learned how rich the study of morals and ethics could be. I began to perceive what was meant by the riddle of the *system of hieroglyphics, veiled in allegory, and illustrated by symbols.* I studied what the ancients said of the language of symbolism, pined over the nature of God, and marveled that man seemed to have a universal and ubiquitous determination to interpret and understand the meaning of the universe and his role in it. I dabbled in mythology and tried to acquaint myself with the pragmatism of the Greeks; as we were informed it is to them we owe everything that is judicious and distinct in architecture. I learned about the ancient philosophers, and read about the cultures in which they had lived and learned themselves. I acquainted myself with the Platonic view of metaphysical ideas. I pored over Masonic history, which made me all the more curious about the source and origin of things Masonic. There was much to know--and I knew so little.

But, it was in this process of finding out how ignorant I was in knowledge, history, culture, and the ways of the world, that I came to realize the potential value of Freemasonry and the contribution that it can make toward a man's education, knowledge, and the acquisition of wisdom. There was much here for the thinking man. Its ritual and explanatory structure indeed facilitates the enlightenment of mind and spirit. I must admit that, even to this day, it is one passion I have not been able to subdue. My prayer is that the flame of curiosity it has kindled in me will always be with me.

I have since read many more Masonic books, and held conversations with many Masons. But, in all of the reading and in all the conversations I have enjoyed with learned men (and I have met many!); in all the degrees I have experienced; in all the hours of quiet learning and reflection–the first and enduring question for every Mason remains –*"As an Entered Apprentice, Whence Come You?"*

For purposes of this book, the first question asked of the Apprentice Mason inspires other equally interesting and thought provoking questions which I think deserve an answer early in one's Masonic experience–questions of which I suggest are to most brothers of the ancient craft equally wrapped in mystery and intrigue. Who asked such a question to begin with? Who penned the question "As an Entered Apprentice, Whence Come You?" And, in a broader sense, who authored the ritual language that is in use today in the world's oldest and largest fraternity? Where did the forms and ceremonies of Freemasonry come from? How has the ritual process of becoming a Mason evolved since it began? How far have we wandered in our ritual development? Are there ritual elements that can be considered landmarks? What of importance has been lost through the centuries? Are there answers to these and similar questions?

Frankly, when I made these inquiries of myself, I wasn't sure. But, if there were answers, I wanted to find them. And I believed there to be others who would also find them to be of some interest and benefit. And so, the quest began.

For me, it has proven a journey worth taking, in a subject which was not readily accessible to most students of Masonry in my time. While much is now available through the digital world of information, it always comes in pieces. I hope this written review will prove more extensive and make the path easier for others who desire to know the source, development, and evolution of the Mason's words. I hope the reader finds the journey fascinating and worthy of his own search for light in things Masonic.

This book is about the men and manuscripts that made the Masonic ritual. It investigates the sources of our entering, passing and raising ceremonies; and how the language entered into and influenced the joining process. I discuss the men who penned the ritual of Freemasonry to the extent it is possible to credit them for its various phrases. I review how our Masonic ceremonies have evolved from simple, informal and sometimes jocular beginnings during the seventeenth and eighteenth centuries; to the exact, sophisticated science of words that have become the standard work of our own time.

But it is not intended that this be the definitive text on Masonic ritual. First, it is not written for the scholar, but for the average Mason who wants to have a general knowledge of where our Craft Lodge ritual language came from, how it evolved, and who the principal players were in its development. The research is also limited to a direct path from the Scottish operative lodges through the English ritual system prior to the Union of 1813, to its practice in the American colonies, and subsequent expansion westward with the Grand Lodge lecturer movement.

The work does not trace the ritual on the continent of Europe, in North America outside the United States, or in South America, Asia, or Africa. Nor does it attempt to include the York or Scottish systems of higher degrees, or any of the smaller Christian Orders of Masonry. I am not claiming to be an expert on Masonic ritual.

This project began as a curiosity about the origin of the Craft Lodge ritual in my own jurisdiction. It grew because I had to travel such a long journey from the recent beginnings of Masonry in Oklahoma (Indian Territory) in 1874 back to the true beginnings of Masonry practiced in the guilds of medieval Europe during the 1400s. Through no fault of mine, I had created a mountain from a molehill.

But, then, Masonry is a mountain that must be climbed.

1 The Making of a Mason

It was cold and dark in the ante-room. I could feel the draft from under the door of the lodge room moving across my lower legs, and up under the loose garment I had donned in place of my usual vestments. The kerchief bound around the back of my head had painfully caught a lock of my hair within the knot. I wish now I had said something to my intender. It was uncomfortable.

I almost reached up to adjust it, but my arms felt numb. I suddenly felt tired. I was alone. I wasn't sure what was going to happen. I could only hear the muffled sounds of talk from the other side of the door...

...and wait.

The fellow who had escorted me up the staircase to the small room had opened a wardrobe and provided me a garment for the ceremony. He said it was the same as had been worn by all others before me. After assisting with the blindfold, he led me several steps forward and admonished me to wait silently. He then retired back through a door to the lodge room to inform the members that I was prepared for entrance. I was told there would soon be a knock at the door, and I was to follow my instructor and bear all that was to happen if I truly wanted to become a fellow of the craft of Free Masons.

I could smell the dampness of the brick walls and the oak wood floor. It was an odor close to that found in wine cellars. All the buildings along the riverfront smelled the same. It settled in the porous surfaces of wood and stone from years of humidity, mixed with tobacco and porter.

It smelled familiar. I needed that.

I was admittedly anxious about what was to happen to me, but also did not want to show any fear. Besides, my hesitancy of the unknown was mixed with a good dose of joy and excitement. For me, the moment had come at last to start on a path of regeneration and renewal. It felt good to be connected with other men in a fraternal bond of friendship and fellowship. It was a rite of passage. At least, that was the way it had been described to me. I had been told that the brotherhood would lead me to a virtuous life; that my connection with other men would provide much joy and security.

I was ready.

Suddenly, loud knocks were heard at the door. Someone opened it, and asked me to take a few steps into the room. From somewhere across the darkness, a voice inquired,

"Is it your own free will and choice that you desire to become a Mason?" My reply was firm. "Yes, it is."

The same voice responded, "Let him see the light!" Someone obliged by removing the blindfold from about my eyes. Even with the hoodwink removed, the room was still momentarily dark. When my eyes had adjusted to the different density of night, I glanced about to the light of a single candle set on a table at the far end of the room. I was conducted to the table, upon which rested a bible with a square and compasses upon it. And a human skull. It was a profound sight–the combination of light, God, death, love, hope–surrounded by brotherhood. It was more than I had expected, yet somehow it seemed so right for the idea of re-birth, and a new life.

Behind the dim light, I noticed a tall, slender man sitting in an arm chair that had been elevated on a platform so that his eyes were at the same level as mine. The flicker of the candle cast a shadow below his cheekbones, and set his eyes even deeper into their sockets; giving an appearance of awful solemnity. After a moment, he arose and moved to a position immediately in front and across the table from me. He had a blue ribbon around his neck, from which hung a triangle. He was also wearing a white leather apron which covered his mid-section and the upper part of his legs. His hands were adorned with white gloves.

He raised his head to the light, looked deep into my eyes, and, in a low resonant voice, asked, "For what have you come hither? Why have you, who have not seen the light, come here among these brethren? What do you seek from us? Wisdom, virtue, enlightenment?"

I wasn't sure what to say. Would my answers be judged? Is it possible that I would somehow fail if I answered in the wrong way? I frantically hoped someone would answer for me. But, there was only silence. I suddenly understood the meaning of initiation. If I was to begin a new path to self improvement, it required that I think for myself. The responsibility was mine alone. Why should these men respond for me? Finally, with much difficulty, I uttered, "Yes...I seek...all of these things. I seek regeneration. I seek guidance...I seek the Truth,"

"Very well", the man replied at once, and continued, "Have you any idea of the means by which our holy Order will help you reach your aim? What is your conception of Freemasonry? Why should we accept you into our ancient and honorable Order?"

"You ask much more than I am able to answer," I said. "I imagine that Freemasonry is a fraternity of men who have virtuous aims. I seek your guidance in making me a better man, and can pledge only that I am an honest fellow who is willing to earn the trust of my fraternal brothers." It was the only reply I could frame; however inadequate it may have seemed to the learned men.

"You are seeking for Truth in order to follow its laws in your life. Therefore you seek wisdom and virtue. Is that not so?" said the Master. "Yes, yes," I quickly assented.

"Then I must ask you one more question," he replied. "Do you believe in that which is not of this world, but is Divine, Just, and Intelligent beyond human comprehension; A Supreme Being; the Cause of all that is, and ever has been?"

My response was quick and sure. "I believe in God, and place my trust in his guidance and final judgment over my life."

"Good!" he exclaimed. "Then you are welcome to discover the chief aim of our Order, and, if you find it, you may be admitted into our brotherhood with profit and confidence. But, I warn you now; our mystery is of such a nature that no one can know or use it unless he has prepared for it by long and diligent self-purification. Not everyone can hope to attain it. But, for those who do, the rewards are great and eternal. Are you ready to pursue such an aim?" "I am," I replied, and for the first time I felt a sense of excitement I had not before known. It was an exhilarating moment.

Another brother came forward and said, "You are now entering into a respectable society, which is more serious and important than you imagine. It admits to nothing contrary to law, religion, or morality; nor does it allow anything inconsistent with the allegiance due to His Majesty." He read from what he referred to as the Old Charges and instructed me in the history and virtues of Free Masonry.

I was then conducted to the center of the lodge room, where I was caused to kneel in the usual manner of Masons on the west side of a group of emblems that had been traced onto the floor. Three large candles were lit from the small one that had been carried from the table by one of the officers. The burning candles were arranged in a triangle bordering the drawing board.

The Master walked to the center of the triangle, then knelt directly in front of me; and, causing my hands to be placed around an open bible he had carried with him from the east, he put his hand under my own holding the book; and with the other on my shoulder, reverently administered the oath of a Mason to me, giving me the sign and word, and binding me to the secrets of the fraternity and to the confidences of my brethren.

The members then gathered around the floor drawings, and each took a part in instructing me on the salient truths of the Craft by the use of the symbols and emblems delineated on the floor. It was a system unique to anything I had before witnessed. There was much antiquity in the symbolism, which seemed to make it all the more sound in the lessons it imparted. Everything was carefully explained. I was moved by the simple, yet penetrating wisdom of the several explanations. Then, to my surprise and mild amusement, I was handed a pail of water, together with a mop, and compelled to rub out the drawing on the floor.

The ceremonies concluded, I was removed out of the company with the youngest Mason while the lodge was prepared for the evening feast and lectures. This fellow would be my intender for a period of one year. He was to instruct me in the catechisms, and serve as my mentor, introducing me to the ways of Masonry, as all others had been prepared before me.

I knew then that to be a brother of the honorable company of Masons was a singular moment, a departure with a new chart in the voyage of my life.

2 The Manners and Customs of the Eighteenth Century Lodge

The above outlined ceremony of the "making of a Mason" is strictly hypothetical. It can safely be said that no man has ever been made a Mason precisely in the manner just described.

It represents a vision of what a rite of initiation may have been like during the formative era of Masonic ceremonies. Each lodge was responsible for its own initiatory experience. There was no single, adopted practice. A similar ceremony may have been employed in English and/or French lodges. Indeed, during the middle part of the eighteenth century. Some elements of this fabrication were taken from a compilation of several Masonic manuscripts and exposures published during that period. Of course, by the time Masonry had reached the level of sophistication suggested in this musing, much had already evolved from the simple words spoken in the making ceremonies of the operative lodges.

We know quite a lot about the workings of those early lodges and their descendants. We can trace much of the language that is still used in our lodges today from the early printed catechisms, or questions and answers exchanged between the candidate and his intender. We even know quite a lot about the men who inspired our ritual words. The purpose of this work is to trace the lineage of the words which are used in our lodges today; to discover how the making ceremonies worked, how the lessons were imparted; how and when the ritual as we practice it today in American lodges came to be.

But the language will come a bit later.

Since the Masonic ritual is performed in Masonic Lodges and the two combine to make the experience of becoming a Mason a singular thing in a man's life, the one cannot be discussed without knowing something about the other. Before proceeding then with the development of the language used by our predecessors, we will first step back and offer a "snapshot" of what lodges were like, the kind of men in them, and how Masonry was practiced before it became the great intellectual and philosophical entity that we now know it to be.

There are few Masons indeed who do not know that the governance of Freemasonry today derives from the organization of the Grand Lodge of England in 1717. And, there is also little doubt in the minds of most that some form of Freemasonry was practiced much earlier than 1717 in Scotland, Ireland, and England. How much earlier has been a centuries-old debate. It simply has never been determined with certainty. Nor is it an inquiry that will be made here.

In this writer's thinking, Freemasonry, as it is now practiced in the United States, derives from the Masonic laws or traditions originating in one, or all three of the above mentioned countries. Regardless of the source and origin of its great teachings (and there are many theories of origin), the practice of Freemasonry has evolved from the forms and ceremonies that were followed by Masons during the transition period from the operative craft guilds of the late middle ages to the speculative lodges of the post-Reformation period. The very structure of the craft confirms this. While Masonic scholars have not yet been able to verify the exact connection, or even to confirm that the connection was direct, there is simply too much evidence that the forms and nomenclature of the 'speculative' lodges of Scotland, and the 'accepted' lodges of England derived from the guild tradition. Whether there is indeed a direct tie to the guilds; or the guild system was simply used as a facade to cover the political aims of the fraternity during this period of time may never be known. Still, there can be no doubt that the charges, the transmission of secret words and signs, and the process of becoming a Mason derived from the guilds.

For example, there are at least 11 indisputable Masonic documents and manuscripts of the pre-1717 period that directly ties the lectures of the operative lodges to the speculative lodges. This connection is now affirmed by nearly every writer of Masonic history.

Today the active debate over origin centers around the antiquity of the fraternity, and whether or not the intellectual structure of Freemasonry can be traced to a craft or trade guild, a secret society or mystery tradition, a club, a cabal of individuals, or some other single source. It is impossible for any thoughtful student of Masonry not to recognize and acknowledge the great intellectual antiquity of the fraternity. Indeed, it may well be that the teachings of Freemasonry have evolved from a joining of several ancient, medieval, or renaissance institutions and/or traditions. Certainly, the many branches of knowledge that can be explored in the numerous Masonic Rites and systems can be traced to many different philosophies, religions, esoteric disciplines, and social movements.

But the antiquity or continuity of Freemasonry is one thing. That of the 'Work,' or language of the ritual, is quite another.

Most Masonic scholars who have made a careful study of the craft are in agreement that "Symbolic or Blue Lodge Masonry" came to be during the period of, or as the result of, the transition which followed the operative science of an earlier period.

For the purpose of attempting to identify the form, the ceremonies, the symbolism, the catechisms, and the lectures comprising the degrees of Freemasonry as it has evolved to its present day practice in the United States, we can start by saying that, with the founding of the premier Grand Lodge of England on June 24, 1717, organized Freemasonry was born. In fact, the Mother Grand Lodge was established on a most Masonic of days–the celebration of St. John's Day–by four of the "Old London lodges."

It was the first Grand Lodge in the world, and all others have derived from it.

Of course, this brings up the question of how lodges could have operated prior to 1717 without sanction or authority. In the U.S. today, it certainly would not be legally possible to create a lodge without some constituting authority. What about the lodges in existence before the first Grand Lodge? Where did they get their authority? How could they operate without a Grand Lodge?

The answer lies in an old Masonic term. Those lodges simply came to be by what is known as immemorial right. Before 1717, Masons met together in lodges, clearly without any charter from a higher authority, because there was no higher authority. The practice was common and well documented in Scotland and England, and even the earliest lodges in America were formed in the same way. Freemasonry simply existed before the idea of a Grand Lodge came into vogue. There was little communication or conformity in form of meetings or matters of ritual between lodges. And, as we shall see, the original purpose for establishing the Grand Lodge was very different than that given to every Grand Lodge in the world today.

So, just what kind of an establishment was an English lodge in the first few decades of the eighteenth century? Where did men become Masons before the elaborate edifices of today were built?

It is difficult to say that there was any one particular form because records describing the physical features of early lodges are rare. We do know that during the early days there were no permanent Masonic Halls or Temples. The term lodge meant any building or room where Freemasons met or worked. Masons generally met wherever space was made available, or wherever the inspiration compelled a gathering of the brethren.

As stated earlier, the word lodge is a term that originated much earlier with the builders guilds, and can be found in documents as far back as the thirteenth century. We have acknowledged that, to the operative craftsmen, it meant the workshop or hut that was common to all major building sites in which the masons worked, stored their tools, ate their meals, and rested. We have confirmed that the long term nature of most building projects resulted in an extended meaning of 'the lodge.' It became any group of masons permanently attached to a particular construction undertaking.

But, by the first decade of the eighteenth century the operatives were a thing of the past. The Masons of the new speculative era were men interested more in fraternalism, and in developing social and economic ties with each other. Individual lodges would meet once or twice a month in a private room of an inn or tavern around a lodge trestle table with the Master at one end and the Wardens at the other, with members in between taking their places in order of seniority. There would be symbols of Freemasonry on the table as well as ample wine, punch and ale, tobacco jars and churchwarden pipes. At some point before or after administrative business and catechetical lectures in which the ceremonies, principles, tenets, symbols and emblems of the fraternity were expounded upon, new candidates took the oath of fidelity and secrecy. Once this was over and the masonic items removed, discussion could be less formal and the landlord brought in dinner, after which the lodge closed.[1]

By far the most common places where Freemasons met were indeed in taverns. It was a rare thing indeed for a lodge to own a building of its own prior to 1750. Those that did almost always owned a two or three-story structure. One such lodge for which we have records was Dundee Lodge Number 18 (formerly Number 9) of London. Brother Arthur Heiron gave us a wonderful account of the first one hundred years of this particular lodge in an article he wrote for the Quatuor Coronati Lodge of London in 1924. Information derived from his work, in particular, provides much insight for the Mason curious about this period of the Craft.

The Old Dundee Lodge

From sometime prior to 1717 until 1739, the meetings of Dundee Lodge were held at the Ship Tavern in Bartholomew Lane, London, right next to the Bank of England. Then, in 1739, the brethren purchased a tavern on the Thames, at Pelican Stairs, Old Wapping, London. This handsome structure was situated on Red Lion Street, and was known as a "freehold" premises. The Dundee brethren were proud to say they were "Masters of their own house!" They sub-let the ground floor and basement, reserving the first floor for the purposes of the lodge. A smaller room which adjoined the lodge room was used as a "Making Room," in which the candidates took their obligations and became members. The larger lodge room was used for the purpose of giving Masonic instruction by means of lectures. This was the general custom in those days.

The Lodge Room was an oblong square, much as in the arrangement of today, but the officer arrangement was formed in the shape of a triangle; with the Master in the east and the Wardens

THE OLD DUNDEE LODGE, NO. 18
(CONSTITUTED 1722-23)

The Old Dundee Lodge, No. 18
Tracing Board or "Lodge"

in the West. While this was an unusual arrangement for the lodges, even in this early period, it is likely that the founders of Dundee Lodge borrowed the tradition from the operative fellow-craft lodges. It may have also derived from the mystery school tradition. The triangle was an emblem held in high veneration by the learned men of the Middle Ages. It symbolized the Deity, and was an emblem used in essentially all ancient initiatory rites. The symbol also represents the Trinity, and is still seen in many rituals of the Appendant Bodies. In several of the oldest lodges in Scotland, the Master is still placed in the east, with the Wardens in the west, but the practice is no longer followed in any of the lodges in the United States. The Dundee Lodge was following what it considered to be an ancient practice of the "Moderns," which finally ended with the union of 1813, requiring the Wardens to be situated in the West and South.

In the "Moderns" lodges (those attached to the premier Grand Lodge), an altar of wood, usually painted white, was invariably situated in the center of the lodge room, at which the candidate was placed during a portion of the ceremony. In all lodges in the United States, the altar is still placed in the center of the room. In many of the English lodges, the practice has not been used for many years. The altar, or pedestal as it is generally called, is in the East immediately in front of the Master. As in many other aspects of American Freemasonry, the old customs that have died out in the Mother Country are still preserved; a fact of which those who like to "preserve the traditions" can take much pride.

During the ceremony of "making a Mason," which, in the case of Dundee Lodge was done in the smaller of the two lodge rooms, a picture of the lodge was drawn on the floor. This was a duty of the Tyler. He traced the designs with chalk and charcoal, the floor generally being of clay tile; hence, the reference to chalk, charcoal, and clay in the Entered Apprentice degree. The picture, (or trestle board as it was called), displayed the usual symbols of the Craft, including the two ashlars, and could be seen by all brethren present. On the 'picture' of the lodge also were placed the two columns, seven steps, dormers or windows, flaming star with the letter "G", square, plumb rule and level. After the "Making," it was required of the candidate that he destroy the drawing, with the assistance of a mop and pail so as not to make known to cowans the secrets of the craft.

Of course, drawing the trestle board is another custom that is long obsolete. The work required to re-create the drawing each time the brethren met was burdensome, and it was soon replaced by a tracing cloth. This, in turn, was modified again when templates, made of tin, were cut to the shape of the objects being delineated on the tracing board. This was undoubtedly an invention of the Tyler, and likely much to his relief, since it saved him much time.

When the 'work' was performed in the larger lodge room, as was more typical of the period, the three candles were placed in an equilateral triangle about the altar. Symbolically, this is the most appropriate arrangement. Unfortunately, in some American Jurisdictions the custom is not followed due to its interference with the floor work. To make matters worse, when electricity came in, the Masonic furniture suppliers began constructing the light receptacles in the wood surface of the altar in a right triangle configuration--an innovation in both the arrangement and the placement of the original burning tapers that has largely been ignored in Masonic Jurisprudence.

In the eighteenth Century lodge, two large and imposing columns, representing the two Masonic Pillars, would stand in the west, between the Wardens. Surmounted with globes depicting the universality of Freemasonry, the situation of the columns was said to represent the west gate of King Solomon's Temple. Many lodges today still have columns constructed architecturally in relief on the west wall, thus preserving the theme.

The Master when in open lodge always wore his three-cornered cocked hat (later the conventional silk hat), which was only removed during prayer. All the brethren wore aprons, made of white lambskin, which were kept by the Tyler when the lodge was closed.

After the actual ceremony was over, portable tables were brought in and placed on trestles in the center of the lodge room. The brethren would take their seats about the table. The Right Worshipful Master would take his place at the head, the Volume of Sacred Law open before him, with the usual emblems in place. The Senior Warden sat at the west end of the table. The wine was then served, and the Stewards handed out the necessary papers of tobacco. Next (the punch having already been prepared and ready to be poured), firing glasses would be brought in and supplied to each member and visitor for use during the toasts.

The lodges that met in taverns were allowed not only to smoke in lodge, but also eat and drink; porter being the favorite beverage in the early days (porter was a kind of beer that was brewed from malt charred by drying it at high temperatures, making the beer dark brown in color, and giving it a bitter taste). Refreshments would also be supplied, usually bread, cheese, sandwiches, apples, oranges, etc.

Again, the poor Tyler was given the duty of purchasing the fruit for the members. This hard-working brother was a far more important officer in the early days. It was his duty not only to "draw the lodge" and buy the fruit, but also to issue the letters or summonses, and personally deliver them to the members at their addresses. In addition, he kept the Tyler's attendance book, made various purchases for the lodge, and was responsible to be careful not to admit "spurious Masons" (those not sanctioned to be in the lodge). This duty alone wasn't easy, since many of the 'Ancient' Masons (those working under the separate Grand Lodge established in 1751) wouldn't permit the 'Moderns' into their lodges until the Union of 1813.

When the lodge of Dundee finally gave up its tavern status in 1763, the brethren resolved that "in the future, there will be no eating in the new lodge room, nor drinking porter. We will now have only wine and punch!"[4]

The lodge refreshments created another small problem. The task of purchasing the wine and other essentials was given to different members at each meeting. In too many instances, the brother assigned the duty would charge the lodge high prices for an inferior quality wine. The problem was finally solved by the lodge, however. In an extract of one set of minutes, it was recorded that "On account of the indifferent wine the lodge has been supplied with for some time past, The Right Worshipful Master and Treasurer were directed to buy a Pipe of wine for the use of the lodge."

Working the Lectures. Was It Really Work?

It is easy to reconstruct the lodge lecture scene, again from Brother Arthur Heiron's account. He reported:

> We purchased tables in 1749–having six leaves–which were set out on trestles in the middle of the lodge. At first the brethren were seated on chairs at these tables, but as the membership increased,

> forms were provided in place of the chairs as being more convenient. As our lodge room from 1763 to 1820 was 44 feet long, by 25 feet wide and 15 feet high, there was plenty of room for these tables. Thirty yards of bordered green cloth were purchased to cover them with, and on these tables were placed the bowls of steaming punch, bottles of wine, rum, hollands, brandy, sugar, lemons, nutmegs and glasses, whilst for the smokers the stewards (called churchwardens at the time) provided screws of tobacco, and pipe lights.[5]

It indeed was a place of true fraternal fellowship!

It is interesting also to note that, since matches were not yet invented, the brethren lit their clay pipes from the small candles placed on the table. Spills of paper were used for that purpose.

Finally, when everything was in order and the brethren seated around the tables, the lectures would commence. The 'Ancient Charges' were almost always read to the Initiate from Anderson's Book of Constitutions. Of course, in the early decades of the eighteenth century, monitors had not yet been printed, or even contemplated. The lectures were a matter of each brother's personal knowledge about Masonic history, symbolism, and the virtues. We know from Dr. Anderson's account of a meeting of Grand Lodge as early as December, 1721, that lectures were an integral part of the ceremony. He remarked that the communication "was made very entertaining by the lectures of some old Masons." The early lectures almost always took the form of tests, or a series of questions and answers; likely carried into fraternal practices by an old knowledge of church catechisms.

The Master presided and put his various questions to the Senior or Junior Warden. As lodges had no Deacons until 1810, the Wardens carried the bulk of responsibility for things concerning the rules of lodge, tyling, the care and examination of visitors, and so forth. Sometimes a "round-robin" method of asking the questions was adopted and the queries went round the table, each brother in turn being invited to reply. It should be pointed out that lectures were given every time the lodge met, unless the brethren voted that they be postponed. It is almost certain that Masonic lectures, regardless of the system used in teaching, formed the most important part of the lodge ritual.

But brethren also knew they belonged to a fraternity. As important as the work was, it hardly took a back seat to fraternal fun. While some knowledge was undoubtedly imparted at these settings, there was also much jocularity. It was reported in the minutes of one lodge that "in the intervals between the questions and answers in these Masonic lectures, one of our swarthy sea-members–a foreigner wearing a pigtail–fresh from a long sea voyage, with face tanned by the sun in far off seas, full of fun, and having eaten his orange, threw the peel at members sitting opposite him at the table!"

Horseplay went along with the excitement of being or becoming a Mason. But, on occasion, it became too much a problem, necessitating a law be adopted to control the situation. In the 1764 by-laws of Dundee lodge, a rule was enacted that "any Brother who is a member of this lodge who shall behave anyways irregular on a lodge night shall pay a fine of two shillings for the use of this lodge and make good all damage that he may do or cause to be done to any of the furniture, etc., and such offending brother who may refuse to pay the same shall have no vote for that night, and if they will not comply on the next public night they attend, they are hereby declared to be no longer a member of this lodge."[6] Extracts from the Cash Books of lodges indicate that numerous payments were made for wine, rum, brandy, and liquors, and also for punch bowls and repairs to the same.

In addition to the appetizing aroma of steaming punch, the hearty round of toasts, the lectures, and the humor provided by the brethren, various songs were sung. The favorite being the "Enter'd Prentices Song." Other common songs were the "Master's Song," the Warden's Song," and the "Fellow Crafts Song."

And, as one would expect, it is not unusual to find wine stains and thumb marks on the old song books used in the lodges of this period.

Lodge Discipline

As mentioned above, because some members always had a way of becoming unruly (probably assisted by the spirits offered at the table), lodges were required to institute a system of fines and penalties for misconduct. These were levied for damaging the lodge properties and paraphernalia; for cussing, swearing, or using indecent language, or attempting to sing an obscene song; or for exhibiting behavior considered to be irregular in lodge meetings. Penalties included being reprimanded by the Master, losing the prerogative of voting for the evening, making good for any damage, being fined a few shillings, and, being expelled from membership.

Once the system of discipline was in place, penalties also applied to milder infractions, such as not attending lodge. This particular practice may have derived from the old London trade companies, and adopted by the speculative lodges. For instance, when a member was summoned to lodge by order of the Master and did not show, and then made no excuse for not appearing, he was fined a shilling. He could also be fined for not wearing his jewel, or for being late for the meeting. A brother could even be fined for refusing to accept an office in the lodge.

Although no connection is intended, many of these customs are now commonly employed by civic clubs of the present day in a lighthearted sense to promote fellowship. It is also likely they were enforced in a similar way by the eighteenth Century Master–the one obvious exception being those relating to behavior–wherein the lodge could be quite rigid. In one instance, a Brother Newton was expelled from the lodge "for scurrilous and indecent language, but on making proper concession to the lodge, he was forgiven, and the lodge well satisfied." A brother Robey was forbidden to visit on account of his "speaking disrespectfully of the Craft." Also two visitors were fined two shillings each for swearing in lodge. If a visitor was guilty of misbehaving and did not pay his fine, he was not permitted to visit the lodge again.

Finally, making a man a Mason was one thing, but accepting him as a member of the lodge was quite another. In 1765, a Brother Perry, having been raised a Master Mason, was, on the same night, expelled from the lodge! He apparently was not behaving in a respectful manner, so the lodge "resolved that he should not be a member of this lodge any longer."

All Sorts of Men

Such were some of the ways of the eighteenth Century lodge in England. It was very much a social club, with simple entrance ceremonies, and few 'secrets.' Membership was available, on recommendation, to all sorts and conditions of men–the rich and the poor, the scholarly and the profane, the laborer and the employer, the craftsman and the broker–all men of good repute, sharing the benefits of fellowship and brotherhood together.

One last record of our old Dundee Lodge confirms that the Freemasonry of the era was indeed an institution that promoted equality and fraternity for those desiring to patronize its assemblies.

A list of occupations taken verbatim from the Minute Book reveals the various avocations of candidates who were made Masons in the Dundee Lodge Number 18 from 1785 to 1808:

> Sea captains of all nationalities, doctors, plumbers, sail makers, wine merchants, bricklayers, stationers, surgeons and apothecaries, shoe makers, carpenters and builders, hatters, seedsmen, and florists, gun makers, hosiers, cutlers, grocers, druggists, watch makers, auctioneers, confectioners, cabinet makers, tea dealers. stock brokers, paper merchants, boat builders, sash makers, music masters, shipwrights, carver and gilders, pawn brokers, surveyors, brewers, dancing masters, officers in the British army, engineers, insurance brokers, engravers, tin plate manufacturers, biscuit bakers, undertakers, attorneys, and gentlemen.[7]

Brother Heiron described it as "quite a democratic assembly, for the proctor of doctors' commons had to sit 'cheek by jowl' with the butcher, whilst the surgeon made friends with the slop seller; and the clerk in Holy Orders took a glass of punch with the undertaker!"

3 The Tavern Lodges

It is a bit unsettling to some members of the ancient craft when they first learn that our old venerated institution was born in a tavern. But in actuality, many, if not most lodges in both the mother country and in our own colonies, reached their adulthood without ever seeing the walls of a temple, a meeting house, or any other place commonly looked upon today as a place of dignity and respect.

Indeed, very few lodges that were founded in the seventeenth century, or even in the first half of the eighteenth century, met anywhere except in a tavern. And the Masons of the period would not have had it any other way.

Of course, the tavern had an entirely different reputation in those days. In many instances today, we think of the tavern as generally being associated with the slums of the city, a place where all manner of sins are influenced, if not committed; and where will be found only the lost, the lowly, and the destitute. And there is much truth that those who frequent taverns often lead an unpretentious life.

But, as we shall see, such was not the case in the 1700s. The eighteenth century tavern was an institution in itself. In many respects it was the same sort of place as the commercial neighborhood pub frequented at lunch and after work by the business and professional man today. But, the eighteenth century tavern was a venerable establishment, with a much broader purpose. In fact, considering its influence in establishing connections and facilitating true male bonding, friendship and camaraderie, it is perhaps a sad truth that the world has left it standing in the eighteenth century.

Before our time, the history of any town or village could hardly have been written without making mention of it. By the close of the middle ages, if not before, the tavern was already established as a commercial center for merchants and traders. It was the economic center for overland transport and communications. The tavern was the main staging point for the thousands of carriers who rode the kingdom, distributing commodities and newspapers every week to all parts of the country.[8]

The tavern, or English alehouse, was also a pillar of social activity for the affluent and well-to-do, as well as the laboring man. Each individual tavern had its own clientele, depending on its location and social tradition. But regardless of which class each catered to, by the post-Reformation period, the tavern was the chief meeting place for the country gentlemen, making connections and doing business with the many prominent members of the urban middle and upper classes; and for tradesmen seeking work with employers. The inns were the scene of activity for celebrations, dinners, feasts, balls, assemblies, concerts, recitals, flower shows, literary and debating clubs, book societies, scientific, religious and other lectures, trade association meetings, election gatherings, Whig and Tory clubs, hunt meets, magic shows, traveling exhibitions. And Freemasons Halls.[9]

Their popularity would dwindle significantly with the modern era; but during much of the period that saw the birth and early growth of Freemasonry, the tavern was a handsome establishment, sometimes extravagant, but always equipped to serve the economic, social, political and cultural life of the English ruling and working classes.

Setting aside the informal nature of its ceremony and the jocularity which prevailed at Lodge meetings, it is easy to see why taverns provided an attractive environment for the Masons of the day. The taverns were far more than just drinking establishments. They were substantial institutions in every respect. And they offered commodious space for those requiring assembly and privacy.

The tavern structures themselves were usually fairly large in size. Most had several rooms and large cellars. One in London boasted of "two floors with garrets and 30 seats on each floor." Another had "8 tables, seats and trestles, a large array of pots, and barrels of wine worth in all about 7 lbs."[10] Ten rooms or more were common in London.

Many also had elaborate signs over the door advertising the kind of wine that was for sale inside. Tavern keepers themselves were often prominent figures in the community, holding considerable properties. It was no wonder they attracted the movers and shakers of the day. One Thomas Decker urged any man that "desires to be a man of good reckoning in the city to take his continual diet at a tavern."[11]

Taverns were, simply stated, places where business was done, investments were arranged, lawyers and physicians consulted, and clubs met. In fact, almost every establishment of any repute had its own club. In addition to the Masons' halls, some were renowned for their clubs for poets and dramatists. The Mermaid in Bread Street, for instance, was the favorite meeting place for Raleigh, Shakespeare, Johnson, Webster and Donne. After the Restoration, the influence of these clubs was evidenced by the fact that many tavern scenes were a stock feature of all the best plays.[12]

The Alehouse Guilds

It is also interesting to note that, by the eighteenth century, the alehouses were the primary locations for the members of the London trade guilds to seek and find employment. It was a time when the traditional operative guild system and its controls were in the process of breaking down. The alehouses actually began operating as the replacement of the guilds.[13] The houses were particularly valued by the seasonal trades. As these occupations were usually functioning in a boom or bust environment, the Masters encouraged their journeymen to be available at the public houses so they could quickly retain them whenever an employer was in need of labor.

The alehouses worked very successfully as points of call because they afforded an important rendezvous for the craftsmen. The men would gather and forge social and trade solidarity. They even functioned as benevolent societies, helping each other out through a box of fraternal assistance that was routinely passed to everyone at the establishment, or at the club or lodge meetings.

The setting was certainly favorable for the creation of Freemason's lodges, and the evidence is conclusive that the lodges had a general appeal to the craftsmen of the period. There is little doubt that some lodges evolved directly from the patrons of the alehouse, or the alehouse guilds. And, as it will be shown, there can be little doubt that the ritual of the fraternity is, in part, adapted from the secret ceremonies of the trade guilds.

As the alehouses became more commercialized, and leisure activities grew in popularity, the cohesion of groups became even more strengthened. Voluntary associations became increasingly more prevalent. For the gentleman, there was a club to suit literally any political, antiquarian, musical, moral, or social interest. And for the craftsman, the alehouse offered everything that a man of his stature could want.

We know all four of the London lodges that organized to form the Grand Lodge of England met in alehouses for their own meetings. We are given the names of the taverns in which they met. The Goose and Gridiron Alehouse in St. Paul's Churchyard was the meeting place of what is now called the Lodge of Antiquity Number 2; the lodge at Crown Alehouse (no longer in existence) in Parker Lane; the lodge at Apple Tree Tavern in Charles Street, Covent Garden, now the lodge of Fortitude and Old Cumberland Number 12; and the lodge at the Rummer and Grapes Tavern, now known as Inverness Lodge Number 4. In fact, there were a large group of taverns and coffee houses in Covent Garden that hosted Masonic Lodge meetings. In addition, the first meeting to discuss the creation of the Grand Lodge was held in the Apple Tree Tavern, and the meeting held to organize the Grand Lodge occurred in the Goose and Gridiron alehouse in St. Paul's churchyard.[14]

With one exception, the membership of the four lodges was largely recruited from the ranks of the skilled workers and Masters of the craft guilds. The exception was the Rummer and Grapes Lodge Number 4, an old, established, and active lodge, sometimes referred to as one of the 'Lodges of Antiquity.' It appears to have been a lodge made up of aristocrats and others of social quality, as it had no membership from the mason trade.[15]

But in all four of the founding lodges, meetings were held monthly at the taverns, with an annual feast. And, as has been previously mentioned, the lodges met in special rooms above or connected with their respective tavern. The landlord was usually the tyler or the treasurer. The charge of keeping the box of fraternal assistance generally rested with him.

The tavern was indeed an institution of social progress. It offered a place where the craftsman could emulate the practices of the more

GOOSE AND GRIDIRON ALEHOUE IN ST. PAUL'S CHURCHYARD

affluent. The old trade guilds were rapidly disintegrating and the club offered a means to keep the groups together, and their rituals alive. The skilled craftsmen were enjoying more prosperity, which enabled them to spend more leisure hours together in social intercourse and conviviality. The tavern created a sense of group, or class awareness and identity.

It also made them more aware of the fact that their positions or occupations were fragile. Many of the trades were inclined to injury, and ill health was always a problem. The clubs, or lodges, through their own beneficence, offered some security against these problems.

Finally, the taverns were popular means of making money for the landlords, and thus, new clubs and societies were encouraged. New members were generally required to purchase a quart of beer or more every club night.

Certainly, by the middle decades of the eighteenth century, every larger alehouse had a club or lodge, and each establishment had its own peculiar character. The fact that Freemasonry evolved in this period as a diverse group of lodges with a mix of all ranks and manners of men could well be because of the influence of the taverns and tavern life on the society as a whole.

But it wasn't long before all this would come to an end. By the middle decades of the century, many of the middle and upper classes of men began to take their liquor at home. A growing number of clergy (once frequent tavern patrons) turned to condemning the alehouses. Restraint in public drinking became a popular cause of the religious activists, urging against the bad example it set for the lower classes. Also, the medical community began to announce on the ills of drunkenness, and championing the cause of healthful sobriety.[16]

By 1800, a new class consciousness poured its energy into the development of art galleries, scientific endeavors, literary and philosophical societies. The Hanoverian era had arrived, and social customs began changing rapidly. The artisans increasingly moved to the parlor as a preserve for more respected customers. In London and other major cities, coffee houses began to spread quickly, replacing the old alehouses and public drinking establishments as the place where one could get food, drink, and news of the day.[17]

It was at this time that most of the Mason lodges established their own premises, moving to more commodious structures, sub-letting parcels of property for commercial ventures, and developing a national network of benefits and sociability to its members. The lodge brethren of the late 1700s were undoubtedly caught up in the great wave of Hanovarian Society, where class was important, and the privatization of leisure was realized through the identity of each organization by the real and personal property it owned.

The alehouse, then, was for all practical purposes, short lived as a host for the Masonic institution. But during its peak of activity and influence, it served as a vehicle for cultural transformation. It helped the English society to hold to its traditional values in a period of rapid commercialization and industrialization. At the same time, it provided a way in which the citizenry could adapt to the new tempo of society. Its universal network of communication among the business elite and the working classes made the transition into the modern era one that brought new opportunities to essentially every class of workmen. It helped to ease the turmoil and instability of the dying guild system, and fostered a new society of workmen, with different rules, and the promise of an ever widening circle of social institutions and agencies with which to be involved.

Above all, the tavern and the alehouse facilitated the transition from the operative to the speculative lodge. They indeed served as the birthplace and favorite resort of Masons and Masonry before and during the early Grand Lodge era. The same held true for the beginnings of Freemasonry in the Colonies.

In fact, in the new country, even the tavern names given to the drinking establishments could often be traced back to the old country. Love for the old home and its associations made the colonist like to take his mug of ale under the same sign that he had patronized when in England. In one such favorite resort of the Masonic fraternity in Boston, we find a Brother Like Vardy, as tavern owner, being honored with a poetic squib of the time:

> Twas he who oft dispelled their sadness,
> And filled the breth'ren's hearts with gladness.[18]

This fond remembrance of old brotherly affection is enough to cause the firing glass to be raised once again in toast:

To spend the wealth of light and song,
That makes the lodge a sacred spot;
Oh, be the season ne'er forgot,
That takes us from a world of care
To happy scenes where Masons are!

4 The Early Ritual Practices

"Are you a Mason?"
"Yes."
"How shall I know it?"
"By signs, tokens, and other points of my entrie."

And thus begins the earliest evidence as to the actual contents of a Masonic ritual of which we have knowledge.

It is the Edinburgh Register House Manuscript of 1696. It wasn't discovered until 1930. It was found by a Brother Charles T. McInnes in the Old Register House, Edinburgh, among a number of old documents transferred in 1808 from the Court of Sessions, Edinburgh, to the Historical Department of the Register House.[19] The gild system in Edinburgh began in the 1400s when the individual craft organizations, such as the masons and wrights, combined to form trade associations, called 'Incorporations.' These newly formed incorporations were granted powers of self-government under municipal charters and oversaw all functions of trade control, including what would later become normal lodge functions. The corporations developed lodge organizations within the craft (sometime between 1475 and 1520) for the purpose of controlling wages and working hours, as well as the making of apprentices, the passing of fellows, the settlement of disputes, and so forth.

The catechism found in the manuscript is among a group of four written out by the Masons of the period (1696 to 1714), to be used as aides to the memory work. They represent the ceremonies as practiced at the time. And while they contain little of what we would consider today as the ritual of Speculative Masonry, they very likely inspired the work that evolved in England in the first quarter of the eighteenth century. Together, they form the foundation for the esoteric work as we know it. The four historic manuscripts include:

The Edinburgh Register House MS, 1696
The Chetwode Crawley MS, c. 1700
The Kevan MS, c. 1714
The "Haughfoot Fragment", 1702

These texts consist of the catechisms and the admission ceremonies for the making of Masons during this early period, and almost certainly for some 50 to 100 years before that time. They are all Scottish in origin and all stem from a common source. But they each exhibit different arrangements in their ceremonies and phraseology which indicates they were not copied from each other. They each provide evidence of the practice of Masonry popular at the time they were written. In fact, as best as can be determined, they represent the ritual practice of the operative working lodges in Scotland for some years prior to the time the documents were actually written.

At the center of all early references to Masonic ritual is the *Mason Word*. In England, reference to a Mason's Word can be traced back to 1638 where we encounter it in a poem published by one Henry Adamson, reader and master of a song school at Perth. Titled *the muses threnodie,* the poem itself is dated to sometime between 1625 and 1630 and recites a dialogue between a Mr. Gall, the burgess of Perth and another friend of Adamson's, George Ruthhaven. Within one stanza, we find the following:

...For what we do presage is not in grosse,
For we be brethren of the *Rosie Cross;*
We have the *Mason Word* and second sight,
Things for to come we can foretell aright.[20]

This arcane reference to a secret word, a second sight, and the ability to foretell the future may well have been the catalyst which launched a pervasive public curiosity and fear that Masons possessed secrets, or worse, secret powers, which were intentionally withheld from the public eye. But to the brother today, it simply suggests that there could have been an esoteric side to the craft from its very beginnings. Certainly, Adamson's allusions in his poem imply the Masons or Rosicrucians, whoever they were, were curators of hidden knowledge which was invisible to the uninformed. He likely knew enough about the properties of the Word to know that it enabled Masons to 'see the invisible,' i.e., they could somehow identify each other by means of which they may not themselves understand. To the non-Mason, the power the Mason Word gave was the ability for Masons to identify fellow Masons secretly, and at a distance, without others present knowing how or when it was done.

Setting the magic aside, the man who actually possessed the Mason Word also possessed signs and postures that enabled invisible communication so that the 'second sight' was not as supernatural as the profane might suppose. There is also some practical evidence that the Mason Word was a mantra among operative craftsmen that an apprentice mason who possessed the word was free to work wherever his trade carried him. He had been initiated, proven his skill in lodge, and given the word which properly qualified him to be admitted to work alongside other masons.[21] To what point that such things were commonly known by outsiders is not known, but one thing is certain—the Masons of Scotland had structured forms and rituals, and the *Word* would ultimately become the most sought after icon in Freemasonry.

It can also be observed here that, because the public has always had a fascination (and judgment) about Freemasonry, the craft has had to endure what has been written about it both from within and without the fraternity. One of the cautions researchers in the history of Masonic ritual must confront is the accuracy and validity of the many exposures now extant. Many of the ritual exposures of which we have information were written for profit, or from spite, by those who violated their obligations or felt disenfranchised from the fraternity. The one piece of evidence we have that the above four manuscripts are a valid link to actual ritual practices during the 1696 to 1714 period is the *Haughfoot fragment.* This short piece was taken from the minutes of a non-operative lodge at Haughfoot and provides twenty-nine words which forms the finale to the admission procedure of the "master or fellow craft" under the Scottish two degree system of that time. These words were found to correspond almost identically with the relevant passages contained in the three complete versions identified above. Thus, the fragment, as small as it is, gives us an important link to the descriptions of actual ritual and ceremonies of this early period. It has been confirmed that these four ritual exposures, then, provide the starting point for reliable investigation of later ritual texts.[22]

The Guild System of Operative Masons

While social and political differences between England and Scotland were significant in the post-Reformation period, the English ritual practice that evolved during the first half of the eighteenth century clearly suggests there were many common elements in the Masonic practices of both countries. After all, the economic and industrial history of both was intimately tied to the rise and development of the earlier guild organizations.

In the middle ages, guilds were established under three principle categories. There were merchant guilds which governed trade; religious guilds dedicated to religious and benevolent works; and craft guilds, which were associations of artisans and craftsmen of the building trades. The craft guilds were essentially town organizations which had as their primary function the complete control over everyone who was involved in a craft or trade. They offered employment to those who were in it, and protected employees from "outsiders." They regulated the trades and the training of apprentices in the trades, controlled the conditions and organization of work and wages, settled internal disputes, and protected the consumer from faulty workmanship. They also performed a strong fraternal element to the guild organization by offering many special benefits to their members. They helped members who fell on hard times, provided decent burial services, and supported the widows and children of their members. The guilds also practiced social solidarity by hosting banquets for members.[23]

While most of the guilds operated to control the trades within the towns, the vast majority of masons actually earned their livelihood at the huge building sites away from the cities and towns (castles, cathedrals, abbeys, city walls, etc.). In those days, the vast majority of houses and buildings were made of wood. The castles, abbeys and monasteries were usually situated far from town. Because these masons were not tied to any one municipality, they were usually compelled to travel in search of traveling companies. The late fourteenth century saw a particular boom in the wages of laboring men due primarily to shortages caused by the Black Plague from 1349 to 1370. Market dislocations, increased mortality, and fewer skilled workers in the labor force caused wages to climb abruptly. If a man knew a trade and could stay healthy, he made a good living in the guilds over the next century.

Unfortunately, this economic bubble for the guild workers would not last. Ordinances adopted by parliament in response to high wage rates eventually depressed labor costs. As good as things had earlier been, the economic status of the guilds changed drastically during the late fifteenth through the middle of the seventeenth centuries. Wages declined with inflation caused by an ever increasing money supply, the flow of wealth from the new world into Europe, and the regulation of wages. Stonemasons and other workers experienced earnings volatility on a scale not previously encountered by the guilds. As a result, operative lodges arose within the guilds for the mutual protection and economic benefit of members as well as instruction in the secrets of a trade. In the case of those lodges that were organized by Masons who had been in continuous employment in places outside municipal rule, their mode of operation was governed by what has become known as the "Old Charges."[24]

The Charges were actually manuscript constitutions that established the rules which controlled the guilds working outside the municipalities. In a real sense, stonemasons and construction worker guilds operated as closed shops. These were designed and sustained as labor monopolies. Employing quality control through training and oversight as well as contract enforcement, the guilds imposed and operated strict employment practices. Membership was controlled by limiting the number of apprenticeships and establishing minimum periods for apprenticeships. To preserve the established rules of the trade, fines were levied for infractions. The guilds set prices and protected their own members' proprietary skills and interests, as well as prevented outsiders who were not trained from hindering the quality of construction. In addition, the guilds offered mutual protection, unemployment assistance, health care assistance, funeral expenses and education to members.[25] Once admitted into a masonic guild, the member would progress through three stages of workmanship, from initiation as an apprentice, to craftsman or journeyman status; and finally, to master mason; the latter two being designations for demonstrated proficiency in the trade for which one was employed. The Charges were the governing mandates of all guild members. About 130 versions of the Charges have survived, the oldest being "The Regius M.S." of c. 1390.[26] And while each of the versions offered differences in specific details, they all have the same general form, which consisted of:

(1) An opening prayer.
(2) A reading of the legendary history.
(3) A code of trade and moral regulations
(4) Arrangements for annual (or triennial) assemblies, at which attendance was obligatory.
(5) Provisions for the trial and punishment of offenders.
(6) Procedure for the admission of new members[27]

And they had one other peculiarity. They shared secret modes of recognition as a part of their admission ceremonies. Those admitted were under an oath of secrecy.

The Regius Manuscript is probably the most significant to Masons today because it is the document that provided the first reference to a Mason's oath, and every extant version of the Old Charges proves that it has been the essential element of all Masonic admission ceremonies since. Indeed, it is the obligations one takes in the fraternity that marks his pledge to follow the rules of governance and conduct prescribed by it.

The Old Charges required a mason to love God and the Holy Church, to be a loyal subject, to love his master and fellows, and to be faithful to his trade and its regulations. The obligation he took was a solemn promise indeed. There were no penalties, no furnishings, and very little paraphernalia. In fact, in comparison with today's elaborate ceremonies, the making of a Mason was a simple thing. There is no indication that there was more than one ceremony. This ceremony was for the making of apprentices, and the admission of fellows. The fellows, or fellow-crafts, were men who were fully trained, who had completed their apprenticeship, and were qualified to set up their own accounts as Masters.

The earliest regulations did not mention the word "lodge", and there is no evidence that mason's lodges existed during the 15th century. Lodges were places attached to buildings where men organized work, ate, or slept. But these sheltered premises also provided a secluded environment in which the mysteries or secrets of a given trade could be protected. Knowledge of a trade was closely guarded to preserve quality of craftsmanship and to limit the number of tradesmen who held specific skills.[28] Even the later versions of the Old Charges use the word to imply a place where instruction was received, a kind of workshop for the craftsmen. The function of lodge, or even Grand Lodge, was not needed. The regulations which applied to the craftsmen were enforced by men appointed as overseers of the work. It was their job to guard against faulty workmanship, settle disputes, and examine apprentices for the distinction of "fellows of the craft." Thus, the word "lodge" eventually came to refer both to the place where masons met and the group of masons who were permanently attached to a particular undertaking.

There is no record of a lodge of masons until 1599, when the Schaw Statutes, drawn up a year earlier by William Schaw, Master of Work and Warden General to the Crown designated Edinburgh to be "as of before" the "first and principle lodge in Scotland."[29] From this date, all the work of making masons, conducting trials, and giving examinations was done in the lodge.

So, the Incorporation established in 1475 became an operative lodge sometime early in the 1500s and was formally recognized by the crown in 1599. The Incorporations became the organs of the craft in its external relationships with the world outside, while the operative lodges dealt with its internal affairs such as the entry of Apprentices, passing of Fellows, and the governance of its trades. And it is certain that England had its own lodges during the same period, as evidenced by the "Acception," which will be described later in this text. There are no surviving minutes of lodges in England prior to 1620, but it is probable that they followed the Scottish model.

Again, there was but one other peculiarity which distinguished the lodges from the craft guilds. The masons of the lodges shared a secret mode of recognition which was communicated to them under an oath of secrecy during a brief admission ceremony. In Scotland, this system of recognition was known as the 'Mason Word,' and can be traced to the early 1500's. In England, the earliest reference to secret words and signs among the masons appear within a decade following 1638, and it seems pretty clear the lines of development in both countries were very similar.[30]

FROM OPERATIVE TO SPECULATIVE

It is not difficult to imagine that the guilds developed over time to become influential economic and political units within the areas in which they were employed. Their architects, designers and superintendents integrated easily into civic leadership structures. In London and other principal cities, members were nominated for city council positions. The strong social, financial and political connections which emerged tied the guilds closely to the municipal authorities. Guild membership gradually became dominated by the more affluent artisans and master builders. Such men had similar connections and possessed comparable economic and political interests. The local merchant and artisan groups that had an economic interest in the provincial towns also used the guild system to advance their financial and personal interests. Economist Maurice Dobb posited that the prevailing condition of the parochial markets of the period encouraged exploitation. Monopoly was the essence of economic life... since the municipal authority had the right to make regulations as to who would trade and when they should trade, it possessed a considerable power of turning the balance of trade in its own favour.[31]

Conditions were ripe for the guilds to admit local dignitaries to their ranks. In his recent extraordinary compilation of materials regarding English Masonry prior to 1717, Ric Berman points out that the benefits were palpable. The local Justices' authority extended to setting wage rates and the local politicians, aldermen, sheriffs and mayors were responsible for the grant of guild charters and commissioning civic building works.[32] It was good for both sides. The authorities received the tax revenues and fees from the guild memberships and productivity, and the guilds controlled the availability and output of labor. It wouldn't last, of course, as the guilds came under increasing pressure from political and economic competitors and conspirators during the seventeenth century, who increasingly accused them of being too conservative and stuck in their own ways to advance economic progress. The general claim was that the guild practices seemed too limiting to industrial progress. The organizational leaders and worker units were too limited to their old connections to foster growth. Even if these claims were so much political rhetoric, the forms of the guilds began to change.

It has been widely suggested by Masonic historians that admission of gentlemen into the lodges gave evidence of a more speculative or spiritual interest in Masonry. Peter Kebbel argues that the elite science of Freemasonry had an intellectual attraction for an 'enlightened' seventeenth century audience.[33] This was undoubtedly the case in lodges that were composed of philosophers, educators and clergy, but it is far more likely that political and business connections, along with socializing were just as significant motives for belonging. After all, feasting and drinking had been the chief activity of the guilds during the whole of the middle ages. These regular and convivial gatherings of men had long defined the guilds. It is likely that many gentlemen and other non-Masons entered the lodge during the seventeenth and early eighteenth centuries for reasons which had little or nothing to do with spiritual improvement. It was far more about the enjoyment of the spirit(s). The fraternal and social setting of lodge, accompanied with the occasional feast, was a compelling combination for feeding the male psyche. It remains so today.

Whatever the reason for joining, by the end of the seventeenth century a number of lodges had evolved to comprise a majority of non-operative Masons. The prominence of the non-operative members perpetuated their influence in bringing friends and associates into the fraternity; as well as sustaining family memberships for generations. By the beginning of the Grand Lodge era, Freemasonry had become a social and political club where dining and networking were the principle features of many lodges.

Notwithstanding their social nature, the elements of their traditional rituals and their traditional histories and codes of behavior remained unchanged. They continued to follow the directions of the Old Charges.

It is thus generally agreed that the compilers of the English printed texts from 1723 to 1730 (when Masonry was coming into its full swing as a speculative society), either had access to the four Edinburgh Masonic documents and other earlier manuscripts, or they had a considerable knowledge of the ritual content of the operative lodges, and its connection with the lodges of the speculative period.

The making of a Mason was indeed a simpler and much shorter affair in the "combined" degree system that existed prior to the 1720s. There was a single ceremony for both the Apprentice and Fellowcraft. Distinct and separate Masonic degrees were not conferred prior to 1716. In fact, the incorporation of the Hiramic legend did not evolve until the 1723 to 1729 period.

So, when the Grand Lodge of England was founded in 1717, there were but two classes of speculative Masons–Enter'd Apprentices and Enter'd Fellows.

A Few Historical Notes

The first Grand Master of the Premier Grand Lodge was Antony Sayer, a gentleman who was a member of Apple Tree Tavern Lodge. Little is known about him except that he may have been a book trader by profession and was likely the oldest tenured Mason among the four lodges that established the Grand Lodge. It was an old English lodge custom to place the eldest member in the presiding position. The next year, the Grand Lodge met for their second Annual Assembly and Feast and elected to the Grand East one George Payne, a government official and 'accepted' mason. Payne had more than a passing interest in the history of the guilds and revitalizing its heritage. He was an antiquarian by hobby and he led a strong element within the new Grand Lodge that had an appreciation for the historical aspects of Masonic membership. He compiled the *General Regulations* of the Grand Lodge in 1720. During his year, several copies of the Old Gothic Constitutions were printed and distributed.

More important, the brother who succeeded Payne, Reverend Dr. John Desaguliers, a man of great energy and high reputation, had an influence and interest which launched a new purpose for the young Grand Lodge. It is speculated Desaguliers joined the fraternity sometime between 1712 and 1715.[34] More of a scientist than a theologian, he was well known in scientific circles, was a Fellow of the Royal Society, and was perhaps singularly qualified to experiment with "new" ideas. He immediately favored the idea of instructing men in morality. The Gothic Constitutions gave him his opportunity.

Desaguliers had developed a method of popular instruction in all the sciences that was similar to solving mathematical problems–

Antony Sayer

through a graded progression in which his students would "advance" from "the easiest truths to those more complex." Perhaps he saw a similar progression in the moral lessons taught in the Old Charges. The idea of a graded system of moral education, of 'speculative' Freemasonry, was a logical next step.[35] Desaguliers had made a visit to the Lodge of Edinburgh in 1721 and may well have observed how his vision could be adapted to the ritual ceremonies already in use. He requested a meeting with the Deacons, Wardens and Master Masons and, upon examination as a Mason, was received as a brother into their society. Meeting with the senior officers of a prominent Scottish lodge provided an opportunity for him to discuss face to face Scottish Masonic practices, and, in turn, pass on information about the formation and goals of the newly established Grand Lodge of London.[36]

To the Masons of the day, his joining was a social coup. They elected him Grand Master at the 1719 Assembly and Feast even though there is no evidence that he had ever served as Master of a Lodge, nor possessed any particular Masonic expertise at all. He was selected purely on his association with the Royal Society and his proven ability as a lecturer.

During this year, another brother of the cloth became active. He was the Reverend Dr. James Anderson. Anderson moved in the same circles as Desaguliers, although he was not a Fellow of the Royal Society. Interested in science, history, and genealogy, he was ready to put all of these interests to work in Freemasonry. It was Anderson, a Scot, who introduced Desaguliers to the early ritual workings of the Scottish Masons. Although Anderson's initiation into Freemasonry is not known, he was likely initiated into the lodge in Aberdeen where his father had served as Master. He became an active Freemason in London, and both Anderson and Desaguliers belonged to the same London Lodge.

The association of Anderson and Desaguliers marked a new phase in Freemasonry. Together, they helped rewrite the history of the guilds and rework the content of Masonry in the name of historical piety. Together, they arranged the lectures for the making ceremony (in the form of questions and answers) and penned the ritual that was used in making Masons during the formative years of the Grand Lodge.[37]

Their social ties also caused a schism to form between the old operative lodges, made up of the artisans and the accepted Masons;

Dr. John Desaguliers

Dr. James Anderson

and Desaguliers and Anderson's friends, the social architects of the day--the historians, scientists, and reformers. Given his status, it was a matter of some shock that Desaguliers was not elected the first Grand Master. He was a member of the Rummer and Grapes Lodge, the membership of which comprised distinguished and titled men. He was the expected leader of the new Grand Lodge.

Antony Sayer may have been elected the first Grand Master because he was not a wealthy man. Many of the men in the lodges felt he was one of them. Steven Bullock, in his landmark work regarding Freemasonry's influence on male cultural transformation, wrote: "Masonry's evolution from operative lodges left the door open for humble men. The majority of members after 1717 came from the middling ranks just below the nobility and gentry. Fraternal charity, mutual aid, and economic contacts were more useful to them than to aristocrats. The affiliation linked them to the cosmopolitan world of learning and gentility—and to the highest levels of society."[38] Social position was a real concern. Some of the old manuscripts that had been kept by the operative lodges were even supposedly burnt to keep them out of the hands of the reformers.

But Desaguliers' status could not be overtaken by the working class men in the lodges. It was recorded shortly after he was elected Grand Master that "now several old Brothers that had neglected the Craft, visited the Lodges; some Noblemen were also made Brothers, and more new lodges were constituted."[39] Whatever factions may have existed between lodges were ultimately united by placing an aristocrat in as Grand Master in 1722. The idea was that someone with noble patronage would legitimize the Order. The dispute was settled when the Duke of Montague was elected as Grand Master. The lodges in London doubled, and Anderson was appointed to take the constitutions that Payne had retrieved, and compile them in a new and better method. The noted and widely distributed engraved frontispiece shows the constitutions being passed from the Duke of Montague to his successor as Grand Master, the Duke of Wharton. Behind Wharton are his Deputy Grand Master, his Grand Wardens, and John Theophilus Desaguliers.

Anderson's Constitutions were adopted the following year, in 1723. These would become the basis for a far-flung network of speculative Freemasonry. Only lodges warranted by a Grand Lodge

DUKE OF MONTAGUE

and approved by a Grand Master or his deputy could initiate members. The Constitutions defined the Grand Lodge as a central government responsible for all Freemasonry within its territory. With one stroke of the pen, the function and purpose of Grand Lodge changed forever; from an annual assembly of Masons to that of a governing body of Masters and lodge officers, subservient in a large extent to the judgments and weaknesses of a sitting Grand Master.

Anderson's charges were prescribed for all initiations, and abandoned all references to the regulation of the building trades. The working tools, tenets, customs, and regulations of the operative craftsmen were adapted to the allegorical uses of speculative Masonry.

After 1723, no operative mason held a Grand Lodge office of any importance. Within a dozen years, Anderson's Constitution would be published by Benjamin Franklin in Pennsylvania as the first work guiding the establishment of Freemasonry in America, thus perpetuating Anderson's myth of Masonic history.

Many Masons today claim that the Reverend Dr. Anderson wrote the first history of Freemasonry, taking our lineage all the way back to Adam. This is both not factual and unfair to him, because he was not writing a history–and he never claimed that he was. He was given the task of writing an apologia, simply giving Freemasonry a glorious descent. As previously stated, it was not even an original work. He compiled it from the Old Charges of the Operatives that date back to A.D. 926. Unfortunately, during the twentieth century, few American Masons cared to research the fraternity's past on their own, and many a young brother was told that Masonic history dates to the beginning of the world–clouding its past with much that is hearsay, folktale, and myth. This kind of rhetoric has no place in current Masonic historical scholarship, as the history of both the Scottish and English Craft is well known. There is no good reason for the Mason of our time not to know what is, and is not, factual about our historical roots.

Early Workings

It is interesting to note that prior to the second decade of the eighteenth century there is not a single reference to Masonic Degrees in any minutes of any lodge in existence. The 'making of a Brother', or to 'make a Mason' were the only designations provided for, and all candidates were "entered."

The process of becoming a Mason consisted of what we would think of today as mere remnants of our first section ceremonies, the catechisms or test questions; and the formal lectures delivered in lodge. The ceremony in its entirety remained much less elaborate from the latter part of the seventeenth century until the time when the ritual became more or less standardized by the Union of 1813.

The pattern in the lodges was basically the same. First, the candidate took an obligation on the volume of sacred law to preserve the mysteries of the Craft. The Mason Word and Sign were then communicated, and the Charges, informing the new brother of his duty to God, his Master, and his fellow-men, along with the legendary history, were read.

Again, this ancient and original form of what Masons consider today as the "work of the first section, with the questions," was derived from the catechetical lectures used by the operative masons of Scotland. Whether the English ceremonies initially derived from the Acception Lodge of England (a branch of the Masons' Company of London, c. 1619-20), or were adapted from Scottish workings during the transition period is not yet known with certainty. While many Masonic historians have viewed English Freemasonry as a product of the work of the operative Scottish lodges, some evidence suggests that the inner circle of the London Company of Masons may have had a great influence on its intellectual and 'speculative' beginnings. First, the word Freemason, while dating back to the twelfth century to define the non-indentured stonemasons, did not become recognized as referring to "Free and Accepted Masons" until the 1720-1730 era.[40] Speculative Masonry prior to this time referred only to the theoretical and mathematical aspects of operative masonry. Breman notes that "Indeed, the use of the term 'speculative' Freemasonry was not until the latter part of the eighteenth century in a letter written by Dr. Thomas Manningham, a former Deputy Grand Master, on 12 July, 1767 to a Bro. Sauer at The Hague."[41] Certainly, Freemasonry as we practice it today comes from our English beginnings. But the roots of the ritual language we learn in our lodges are largely of Scottish origin.

The earliest lodge record extant of an initiation of a non-operative Mason occurred at the Lodge of Edinburgh at Mary's Chapel in July, 1634, when Lord Alexander and his younger brother Anthony, along with one Alexander Strachan were admitted.[42] A year earlier, John

Mylne, master mason to Charles I, and a brilliant architect, had joined the lodge and the three brethren were his friends. Another initiation in England bears the date of May 20, 1641, and took place at Newcastle-on-the-Tyne, when certain members of the Lodge of Edinburgh admitted one Robert Moray as a "fellow of the craft."[43]

Robert Moray was a figure of some intellectual importance, having been an active member and first president of the Royal Society of London, although he was from north of the border. This group was very interested in the trades as an applied science, and Moray attempted to write a history of the Masons for the Society. There were also a noticeably high number of fellows of the Royal Society who were members of the London Lodges, adding much evidence to the fact that the guild system was rapidly evolving into a society with new interests during this period. These higher class of gentlemen seemed very much interested in keeping the old traditions and mysteries of the operative guild system, yet adding the interests and values of the educated man into the mores' of the new group. As I have previously suggested, these men would ultimately come to dominate by the Grand Lodge period.

The Mason's Word appears throughout this period in Scotland, it being mentioned in the general assembly of the Church of Scotland in 1649 and 1652 as part of the Church's unsuccessful efforts to suppress the Scottish Lodges since their inception of around 1600. The 'Word' is mentioned in several extant apprentice indentures of this same period, and in the laws and statues of several Scottish odes prior to 1680.

It is interesting to note that the first reference to the Mason Word does not appear in England until 1672, when a pamphlet was published ridiculing a previously published work that was threatening persecution against those who would not conform to the laws of the Church of England. One Andrew Marvell was upset at those bothered by minor differences in men. In making his point about the futility of dueling factions within families, he made reference to those who "have the Masons' Word, secretly discern one another...." He must have thought his readers would make no mention of it. This published document suggests that the Mason's Word may have been commonly known in England at this time.

In any event, in these and all other lodges of the period, both non-operative and operative Masons were members. The lodges functioned as operative lodges up until the 1700s (meaning that trade regulations for apprentices and journeymen were made, fees were collected, and offenders were punished).

Another record of an initiation in England is well known, and refers to Elias Ashmole, who was "made a Free Mason" in a lodge of Free and Accepted Masons convened at Warrington on October 16, 1646, a Colonel Mainwaring, his father-in-law, being the other candidate. They were both known to be Rosicrucians.[44] It is known that this lodge communicated words and signs which were to be kept secret by the members.

In addition to the Scottish working lodges discussed earlier, there is also some evidence that Masons were made in England through the inner workings of the London Masons' Company. The London Masons' Company was the first trade guild of operative Masons in England. It came to be as the result of a dispute between the Mason Hewers (stone cutters) and the Mason Layers and Setters which occurred in London in 1356. The group went before the city council seeking an ordinance to regulate the quality of construction skills in the city. The council ruled that the Company be created to supervise and evaluate the work of all stone masons in the city, and set up a "Code of 10 Rules," one of which established an apprenticeship of seven years. The London Masons' Company formally incorporated in 1411. It was the only mason's guild in England. It was a purely operative organization, but records of the early seventeenth Century reveal that there existed an inner working, called the 'Acception,' which made masons. The records prior to 1620 have now been lost, but an entry in 1620 reveals that fees were regularly paid for the making of masons above that normally charged for the Livery trade. And some of those who were made masons had no relation with the Livery trade. Thus, the Acception Lodge admitted operatives and non-operatives alike.[45]

The term 'Accepted' in our usual distinction as Free and Accepted (or Ancient and Accepted) Masons may well have derived from this idea that there has always been a separate esoteric division within the society of masons that has admitted persons into an inner fellowship of Masonry who were Speculative, as opposed to Operative or Free Masons. Those so admitted were termed Accepted Masons. It would seem that the 'making of masons' was a completely separate function from the trade functions. There are also references that the Old Charges were used in the making process.

ELIAS ASHMOLE

One of the most important differences in English and Scottish workings was that the Scottish initiations were performed in lodges which existed parallel to the guild organizations but were separate from them. In England, the guild itself was the organization which performed the initiations; thus the idea of there being an inner group within the guild which administered the masons' oaths to non-operatives has merit.

And yet another document provides further evidence that Acception Lodges were comprised of non-operative Masons. In 1722, one J. Roberts published a manuscript which provides the earliest record we have of lodges issuing certificates of good standing to its members. The Roberts manuscript reads, in part:

> Additional Orders and Constitutions made and agreed at a General Assembly held at____________on the Eighth Day of December, 1663."
>
> "III. That no Person hereafter which shall be accepted a Free-Mason shall be admitted into any Lodge, or Assembly until he hath brought a Certificate of the Time and Place, of his Acception, from the Lodge that accepted him."
>
> "IV. That every Person who is now a Free-Mason, shall bring to the Master a Note of the Time of his Acception, to the end the same may be enrolled in such Priority of Place, as the Person deserves, and to the end the whole Company and Fellows may the Better know each other.[46]

Perhaps the Acception was a speculative lodge working within the Masons' Company. There is no way to know, but if it was, it would be further evidence of a transitional stage from operative to speculative.

It is also noteworthy to suggest that an annual Assembly of Masons may have been held for years prior to 1717. It appears that Anderson may have copied from Robert's manuscript in printing his own Constitutions. Roberts published the version of the Old Charges a year before Anderson in response to an attack on the Craft that had been published in the London newspaper, *The Post Man*.

In all the above referenced initiations, and in all those subsequent to them, there was but one ceremony, and Apprentices were never excluded because of there being a higher degree. There was no higher degree. Visitations regularly took place between brethren of lodges in England and Scotland, as well as reciprocally between these two countries. So there must have been some common basis for the work.

5 The Early Catechisms

The four catechisms referenced at the beginning of Chapter 4, along with some twelve others in printed or manuscript form used in the period from 1696 to 1730, reveal language that is similar enough to that found in today's rituals to give us an idea from whence our own work came. A sprinkling of excerpts from several of these texts confirms the antiquity and enduring nature of our Masonic ritual language.[47]

The Register House and the Chetwode Crawley Manuscripts are the earliest of the catechism texts, and contain some features not found in later manuscripts, namely, they both reveal words of entry, allusions to frivolity in the making ceremony, references to the Mason Word, and a distinction between those who were made Masons in the lodge room and those who were made Masons in a separate room. Continuing from the Edinburgh Manuscript, we find the following language segments giving the manner in which the word was put between brother Masons which will be familiar to many brothers today:

> "Are you a mason?"
> "Yes."
> "How shall I know it?"
> "By signes, tokens, and other points of my entrie."
> "What is the first point?"
> "Tell me the first point ile tell you the second. The first is to heill and conceal, second, under no less pain, which is then cutting of your throat, for you must make that sign when you say that."
> "Are you a fellow craft?"

> "Yes."
> "How many points of the fellowship are there?"
> "Fyve, viz, foot to foot, knee to knee, heart to heart, hand to hand, and ear to ear."[48]

The manuscript goes on to describe what makes a lodge, how many masons constitute a lodge, how a lodge is situated, where the lights are arranged, the jewels, and the key [secrets] of the lodge. Then, at a place in the ceremony where the candidate was properly in position to do so, he was given an oath, as follows:

> By god himself, and you shall answer to God when you shall stand naked before him, at the great day, you shall not reveal any part of what you shall hear or see at this time, whither by word, nor write; nor put it in wryte at any time; nor draw it with the point of a sword, or any other instrument upon the snow or sand; nor shall you speak of it but with an entered mason, so help you God.[49]

The Chetwode Crawley MS (c. 1700), discovered in an Irish bookseller's shop in 1900, gives the "Jachin" and "Boaz" words for the pillars and provides the following penalty for breaking the mason's oath:

> Here am I, the youngest & last entered Aprentice, as I am sworn by God and St. John, by the square and compass, and common Judge, to attend my Masters service, at the Honourable Lodge, from Monday in the morning, to Saturday at night, and to keep the kyes thereof, under no less pain, than to have my tongue cutt out under my chin, and of being buried within the flood-mark, where no man shall know.[50]

The Kevan MS (c. 1714), found among a lawyer's papers in Berwickshire in 1954, reveals nothing new from the Register House and Crawley manuscripts in regard to ceremonial procedure, but is important because it confirms the evidence of ritual language presented in the first two. Both Crawley and the Kevan make it clear the five points revealed in the Register House text are the points of fellowship. A third catechism known as the Sloane MS (c. 1700) but unrelated to the Edinburgh group also confirms the points of fellowship and adds these are attended with an exchange of words. The Sloane text also changes the five points given in the Register House as "foot to foot, knee to knee, heart to heart, hand to back, and mouth to ear." The Sloane is also significant to the tracing of early ritual language in that we find the oath of a mason, providing a different twist familiar to many twentieth century Brethren:

> The mason word and every thing therein contained you shall keep secrett you shall never put it in writing directly or indirectly you shall keep all that we or your attenders shall bid you keep secret from man woman or child stock or stone and never reveal it but to a brother or in a Lodge of Freemasons and truly observe the Charges in the Constitution all this you promise and swere faithfully to keep and observe without any manner of equivocation or mentall reservation directly or indirectly so help you god and by the contents of this book.[51]

The Sloane MS reveals the Mason's word and describes how it is to be given. It may be the first to include ceremonial procedures of early English lodges. Another interesting feature of the Sloane MS is that, by giving us a narrative which specifically mentions the "Freemason's" word and signs; the document suggests some English influence, although Scottish in origin. The word 'Freemason' was not known in Scotland as a trade designation.

In another Scottish ritual document that belonged to a lodge in Dumfries known as the Dumfries No 4 MS, c. 1710, we find a reference to the seven liberal sciences (with original abbreviations edited for purposes of clarity):

> There are seven liberal sciences. The first is divinity which teacheth the logical virtues, and the 2d is grammar joined to rhetoric which teacheth eloquence and how to speak in subtill terms. The 3d is philosophy which is love of wisdom by which is brought both ends of a contradiction together and crooked things made straight...the 4th is music that teacheth songs harps and organs with all other sorts of vocal and instrumental musick ...The 5th is logick that discovereth truth from falsehood and is a guide to judges and lawyers. The 6th is geometry that teacheth to measure material heavens with all earthly dimensions and all things contained therein. The 7th and last of the sciences is astronomy with astrology that teacheth to know the course of the sun moon and stars ornaments of the heavens.[52]

Early Masonic Ritual Manuscripts And Exposures
1696 To 1730

EDINBURGH REGISTER HOUSE MS	1696
CHETWODE CRAWLEY MS	c. 1700
SLOANE no. 3329 MS	c. 1700
HAUGHFOOT FRAGMENT MS	c. 1702
DUMFRIES no. 4 MS	c. 1710
TRINITY COLLEGE, DUBLIN MS	1711
KEVAN MS	c. 1714
A MASON'S EXAMINATION	1723
THE SECRET HISTORY OF FREEMASONRY	1724
THE GRAND MYSTERY OF FREE-MASONS DISCOVER'D	1724
INSTITUTION OF FREE MASONS	c. 1725
THE WHOLE INSTITUTION OF FREE-MASONS OPENED	1725
GRAHAM MS	1726
THE GRAND MYSTERY LAID OPEN	1726
A MASON'S CONFESSION	c. 1727
WILKINSON	c. 1727

Figure 1

The seven liberal arts have long been associated with Freemasonry. They are mentioned in the Regius MS, c. 1390 and the Cooke MS of 1410; they are included in the Old Charges and in Anderson's Constitutions. In addition to offering us the first glimpse of language we now know to be part of the Middle Chamber lecture, the Dumfries MS provides our first reference to the use of a cabletow wherein the candidate mentions in an answer to the catechism that he was brought into the lodge with a "rope about my neck."

It should be pointed out that the words Fellow-crafts and Masters were used interchangeably in the Scottish working lodges. The Fellows and Masters were one and the same, the distinction being only one of guild standing. In the old operative system, the Master was the guild Master, a man entitled to take contracts and employ the craft, fellows, and apprentices. The word 'Master' naturally stayed with the nomenclature of the transition period. This has caused much confusion among early Masonic writers who concluded there must have been a third degree or ceremony since these early catechisms made reference to a 'Master Mason.' Again, there were only two parts to a single ceremony, and the men were made either Apprentices or Fellow-crafts in the same night. The Master Mason in a lodge was the predecessor of our 'Master' in the chair. Apprentices were full members of the fraternity, and when a brother was made a fellow, he was given what was often termed as the 'Master's' part. Thus, by the days of the Grand Lodge, the second part of the apprentice work was described as giving the rank of Master and Fellow to a brother.

Presently, there have been at least sixteen Masonic ritual manuscripts and exposures discovered which were known to have been printed from the period 1696 to 1730 (see figure 1). Without giving an exhaustive description of the language found in each of these ritual exposures, we can generally state that the manuscripts of this formative period reveal ceremonial elements including the signs and the manner in which the signs were given; the words and how they were conveyed; along with the steps applicable to each degree or ceremony. *A Mason's Examination* (c. 1723) provides the first mention of ashlars and the Orders of Architecture; *The Grand Mystery of Free-masons Discover'd,* (c. 1724) is the first mention of the twenty-four inch gauge; *The Grand Mystery Laid Open* (c. 1726) includes the trowel as a working tool; the *Graham MS* of the same year is the first to reveal that candidates for the admission ceremonies were clothed in a particular manner, being neither "naked or cloathed, shode nore bairfoot." *A Mason's Confession* (c. 1727) also states that one of the legs is made bare as the obligation is given; and that the candidate is required to "deliver up any metal thing he has upon him"--thus the first reference to the removal of metals from the person as a part of the making ceremony. This manuscript also reveals the first time the penalty is placed within the obligation.

In most cases, the catechisms observe that lodges were dedicated to the St. Johns; there were generally three lights, three jewels, and the two pillars. The test questions were ritual in nature, and, on the whole, they were in agreement among all the manuscript sources.

Working Tools

Although the operative Masons used many different tools to aid them in their building projects, there is no evidence in the admission ceremonies for which we have record prior to 1650 that any instruments of building were moralized as part of the making ritual. Again, the admission procedures consisted of reading the Old Charges and administering the oath of fidelity.

The earliest reference to working tools is found in a non-operative text published in 1688 known as the "*Academie of Armory,*" by one Randle Holme. In a brief passage he penned relating to the Freemasons, he observed the use of these several Tools amongst them." He listed these as the shovel, handhammer, chisel, pick and punch.[53]

The first actual mention of tools in Masonic ceremonies was the Register House MS wherein there is a mention that the candidate is "sworn by God, St. John by the square and compass, and common judge..." The common judge was a gauge or templet. Then, in 1723, *A Mason's Examination* includes these tools but adds the astler (square hewn stone) and diamond (possibly a hammer, or a stone). The following year, *The Grand Mystery of Freemasons Discover'd* included the first mention of the 24 inch gauge, along with the square asher (stone), a diamond, and a square. Also, in 1724, *The Whole Institution of Masonry* lists twelve lights of the lodge to include the "Father, Son, Holy Ghost, Sun, Moon, Master Mason, Square, Rule (24 inch gauge), Plumb, Line, Mell (maul or gavel), and Chizzel." This text also mentions having the square and compass placed at the candidate's breast during the taking of his oath. Another text of 1726, *The Grand*

Mystery Laid Open, lists the hammer and trowel, with the candidate holding these in his hands as he takes his obligation. Finally, the 1727 text entitled *A Mason's Confession* lists the five points in the square as a part of the catechism:

> Q. How many points are there in the square?
> A. Five.
> Q. What are these five?
> A. The square, our master under God, is one; the level's two, the plumb-rule's three, the hand-rule's four, and the gage five.

Thus, we can see that, by this point in the evolution of the ritual, the tools are beginning to be moralized as they are presented to the candidate. We will discover in the next chapter that, by 1730, the language of the working tools in Masonic ceremonies had already taken on words which are familiar to us.

It should also be pointed out that the working tools for each of the degrees were not officially sanctioned for use by the Grand Lodge of England until after the Union of 1813. Perhaps it is out of place chronologically to mention it here, but as we are now discussing the tools, it is interesting to add that the trowel is a tool that was imported into the American work by the great American ritualist, Thomas S. Webb, who received most of his work from a student of the English lecturer, William Preston (the contributions of both these men will be extensively covered in later chapters). But Webb did not get this portion of the ritual from William Preston. The trowel came to America by way of one of the oldest English workings called the "Bristol," which is the ritual worked along the west coast of England. It is said that Boston and Philadelphia both derived some of their workings from Bristol. The trowel is a working tool which seems only to appear in the American and Bristol workings. While mentioned in the earliest English exposures, it is not standard to the English system.

The phraseology on the twenty-four hours of the day being divided into three equal parts (which is part of the symbolism related to the gauge) may have come from Hume's *History of England,* wherein he relates, "The most effectual expedient employed by Alfred the Great, for the encouragement of learning, was his own example, and the constant assiduity with which he employed himself in the pursuit of knowledge. He usually divided his time into three equal parts; one was employed in sleep and the refection of his body; another in the dispatch of business; and a third in study and devotion."

The phrase "undiscovered country from whose borne no traveler returns" is from Shakespeare's *"Hamlet, Act 3, Scene One."*[54]

Finally, in England the working tools of the Entered Apprentice also include the chisel. In Scotland, the Mallet is used in place of the gavel. For the Fellow-craft, both England and Scotland use the square, level, and plumbline. And in the Master Mason Degree, England and Scotland use the skirret, the pencil, and the compasses.

Catechisms are the Universal Means of Teaching

One thing more holds true in all the published manuscripts dating prior to 1730: the tradition of examining the candidate. It is as old as the Masonic ritual itself. It was the first and only means of instructing the candidate for many decades. It was the way in which Masons learned and communicated; the means by which they tested their own proficiency in things Masonic. And it was the method in which new brethren learned of the Masonic way of life. It can safely be said that the catechisms are the true foundation upon which the ritual elements of Freemasonry have evolved. A review of the above referenced manuscripts and the printed exposures lay a clear track to the work of the first sections as they are practiced in the Grand Jurisdictions of today. We can safely conclude that the language contained in the Initiation and Passing ceremonies today are but expanded versions of the Scottish operative lodges and the transition lodges of both Scotland and England prior to the organization of the premier Grand Lodge.

And one other observation should be made. Because of this antiquity, Masonic lecturers and Grand Lodge leaders who are inclined to shorten or revise the manner in which Masons are made today should proceed with caution in proposing ritual changes that would significantly alter the substance of the work in our first section, or making ceremonies. In particular, to change the language, the procedures, and the ceremonial form of the first sections would clearly threaten the very fabric of Masonry, and could result in making it something different than what it has always been.

This is not to say that the categorical lectures or tests of proficiency required by the candidates need follow a rigid question/answer format. We must remember that during the first fifty years of Grand Lodge ritual development, the catechisms were informally presented, and were for instructional purposes only, as the table lodge practices suggest to us. Perhaps it is not essential that these actually be learned by those who become Masons. There is a far greater need to develop different tests of proficiency for candidates; tests which will require personal study in a variety of Masonic subjects, including its history and symbolism. Many Grand Lodges are presently moving in that direction. And there are many ways that a candidate can be tested as to his proficiency. Certainly, a different set of questions and answers for candidates can be better employed in the lodges of today, since additional Masonic education is sorely needed during the process of becoming a Mason.

But regardless of what evolves in Masonic practice here, the catechisms which have long been adopted by Grand Jurisdictions should not be removed from the ritual. These should continue to be given as part of the lecture system of the degrees. As has been shown, these comprise much of the language that is original to the Craft.

Out of respect for things traditional in Masonry, the catechisms as have been known and practiced in lodges from time immemorial should not be lost. These are indeed the cornerstones of the Masonic ritual, and are universal to it. They can be considered among the true landmarks of the fraternity.

6 The English Exposures of 1730 to 1764

It has already been shown that the art of memory was an essential feature of Masonic practices during the early Grand Lodge period. As the catechisms grew more lengthy and complicated, however, memorization became difficult. As one brother put it, "every one who is made a Mason, has not a memory to retain every particular contained in long lectures." Therefore, as previously alluded to, a number of printed *"aides-memoires"* or exposures, appeared; and these were purchased by the brethren for use in lodge.

The process of becoming a Mason changed forever, and was described for the whole world in three so-called exposures published between 1730 and 1764.

The earliest, in 1730, by Samuel Prichard, who claimed to be a late member of a constituted lodge, was entitled *"Masonry Dissected."* Another, entitled *"Three Distinct Knocks"* was published in 1760, and a third, called *"Jachin and Boaz,"* was printed in 1764.

These have value today in giving us the manner in which a brother was made a Mason during this period of the eighteenth century, as well as informing us how the ritual may have developed as the popularity of the ritual ceremonies increased. But, as in all exposures, it is wise to remember that these were likely written by profane, if not definitely anti-Masonic hands. In the case of *"Three Distinct Knocks,"* written as a ritual text of the 'Ancients' lodges (the constituent lodges of the 1751 Grand Lodge), it is occasionally very hostile to the Craft. *"Jachin and Boaz"* was less hostile, and was designed to follow the ritual of the 'Moderns' (the constituent lodges of the 1717 Grand Lodge). Today, we would know not to place too much credence in Masonic accuracy from such sources. But, in their time, these exposures were so popular that they were purchased in great numbers by Masons to help them with their work. When considered collectively, they likely represented a reasonably accurate rendering of the actual ceremonies of the period.

There is no question they greatly influenced the development of the ritual finally adopted by the Grand Lodge of England.

Prichard's "Masonry Dissected"

The most successful of these was Prichard's *"Masonry Dissected,"* which ran into four editions the first month of its appearance. The first edition was advertised for sale in the *Daily Journal* on Tuesday, 30 October, 1730. More than thirty editions would be printed. It was translated and embodied in a French exposure, *"La Reception Mysterieuse"* in 1738, and it became the basis for a whole flood of French exposures that appeared from 1744 onwards. It was also translated into German and Dutch. The book was so popular that it attracted the attention of the Grand Lodge, who issued several rejoinders and imitations.

The body of the work was in the form of a catechism and much new and important matter was included. It greatly extended the information derived from the Edinburgh group.

It was the first to reveal that Masonry had been divided into three degrees. The legend of Hiram surfaced, and the catechisms were much longer than in previous printed exposures. The Reverend Herbert Poole wrote that it "probably did as much as, if not more than, the 'rulers of Masonry' to develop and stereotype Masonry in the form in which we have it now."[55]

By quoting directly from the Prichard exposure, Masons of today will be able to discern the similarities and differences in a selected few of the test questions published in 1730 with that of today's catechisms. The author apologizes to those brethren who may find it offensive to reveal the language of any catechism, but it is not considered a violation of one's own obligation to quote from a previously published exposure. And since the mission of this work is to inform the brethren

Ritual Exposures 1730 To 1769

THE MYSTERY OF FREEMASONRY	1730
MASONRY DISSECTED	1730
THE SECRETS OF MASONRY MADE KNOWN TO ALL MEN	1737
THE MYSTERY OF MASONRY	1737
THE MYSTERIOUS RECEPTIONS OF THE CELEBRATED SOCIETY OF FREEMASONS	1737
MASONRY FURTHUR DISSECTED	1738
LE SECRET DES FRANC-MACONS	1742
CATECHISMS DES FRANC-MACONS	1745
L'ORDES DES FRANC-MACONS TRAHI ET LE SECRETS DES MOPSES REVELE	1745
LA MACON DEMASQUE (THE MASON UNMASKED)	1751
THE FREEMASON EXAMIN'D	1754
THE SECRETS OF THE FREE MASONS REVEALED BY A DISGUSTED BROTHER	1759
A MASTER KEY TO FREE MASONRY	1760
THE THREE DISTINCT KNOCKS	1760
JACHIN AND BOAZ	1762
HIRAM; OR, THE GRAND MASTER KEY	1764
SHIBBOLETH, OR EVERY MAN A MASON	1765
TUBAL-KAIN	1767
SOLOMON IN ALL HIS GLORY	1769
THE FREEMASON STRIPPED NAKED	1769

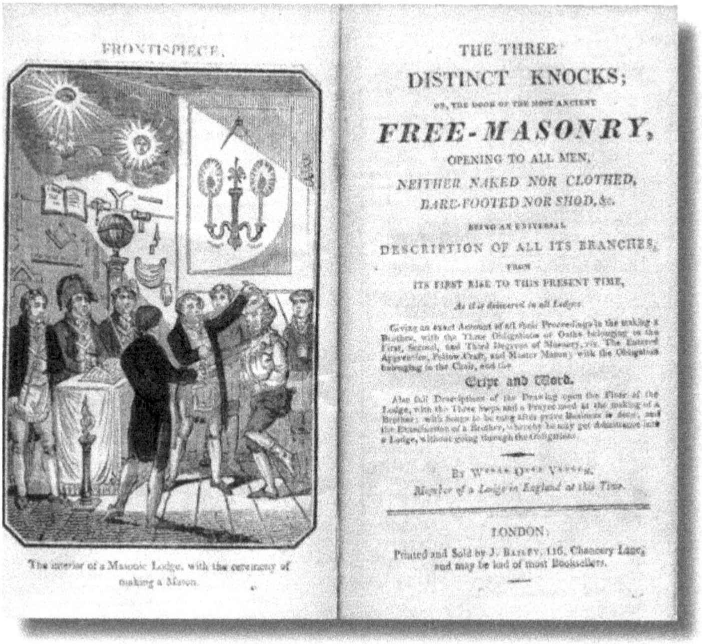

THREE DISTINCT KNOCKS FRONTISPIECE

from whence the ritual came, it is necessary to illustrate a few examples from what we know of the early ritual practices so that we can know something of the age of our own ritual.

A selected few of the test questions from Prichard's exposure of the *Enter'd Prentice's* degree are given here. All of the ritual references quoted below are from the exposure and will not be cited each time.

> Q. From whence came you? A. From the Holy lodge of St. John's.
> Q. What do you come here to do? A. Not to do my own proper Will, but to subdue my Passion still; the Rules of Masonry in hand to take, and daily Progress therein make.
> Q. Are you a Mason? A. I am so taken and Accepted to be amongst Brothers and Fellows.
> Q. How shall I know that you are a Mason? A. By signs and Tokens and perfect Points of my Entrance.
> Q. What are signs? A. All Squares, Angles and Perpendiculars.
> Q. What are Tokens? A. Certain Regular and Brotherly Grips.
> Exam. Give me the points of your entrance. Response. Give me the first, and I'll give you the second. Exam. I Hail it. Resp. I conceal it. Exam. What do you conceal? Resp. All secrets and secresy of Masons and Masonry, unless to a true and lawful brother after due examination, or in a just and worshipful lodge of brothers and fellows well met.
> Q. Where were you made a Mason?
> A. In a Just and Perfect Lodge.
> Q. What do they consist of?
> A. One Master, two Wardens, two Fellow-crafts and two Enter;d 'Prentices.

And we learn the process of entry.

> Q. Who brought you to the Lodge?
> A. An Entr'd 'Prentic.
> Q. How did he bring you?
> A. Neither naked nor cloathed, barefoot nor shod, deprived of all Metal and in a right moving posture.[56]
> Q. How got you admission?
> A. By three great knocks.
> Q. Who received you?
> A. A Junior Warden.
> Q. How did he dispose of you?

> A. He carried me up to the North-East part of the lodge, and brought me back again to the West and deliv'd me to the Senior Warden.
> Q. What did the Senior Warden do with you?
> A. He presented me, and showed me how to walk up (by three steps to the Master.
> Q. What did the Master do with you?
> A. He made me a Mason.
> Q. How did he make you a Mason?
> A. With my bare-bended Knee and Body within the Square, the Compass extended to my naked left Breast, my naked Right Hand on the Holy Bible; there I took the obligation of a Mason.

And, later, the Mason's obligation was repeated, with the following penalty:

> All this under no less penalty than to have my throat cut, my tongue taken from the roof of my mouth, my heart pluck'd from under my left breast, them to be buried in the sands of the sea, the length of a cable-rope from shore, where the tide ebbs and flows twice in 24 hours, my body to be burnt to ashes, my ashes to be scatter'd upon the face of the earth, so that there shall be no more remembrance of me among Masons. So help me God.[57]

The form and direction of the lodge is described from east to west, north to south, and to the center of the earth; and its direction from east to west. The three supports, or pillars of the lodge, are given as wisdom, strength and beauty; and we are informed they are so called because we must have "wisdom to contrive, strength to support, and beauty to adorn." The furniture of the lodge is stated as the "the mosaic pavement, the blazing star, the bible, compass and square;" and six jewels are identified, three being moveable, including the "square, level, and plumb," whose uses are: "the square to lay down true and right lines, level to try all horizontals, and the plumb-rule to try all upright." The three immoveable jewels are given as the "trasel board, rough ashler, and broached'd thurnel (chisel)." The Mason's words (J. & B.) were lettered and syllabled. The principle signs of an Apprentice are also revealed to include the point, line, superfices and solid. The points of entrance were described as the "guttural, pectoral, manual, and pedestal," and these terms explained. The three lights of the lodge are presented as the "sun, moon, and Master-Mason" (Master of the lodge). It is interesting to note that the duties of the Master and Wardens are given as part of the test:

> Q. Where stands your Master? A. In the East.
> Q. Why so? A. As the Sun rises in the East and opens the Day, so the Master stands in the East to open the lodge and to set his men at Work.
> Q. Where stands your Wardens? A. In the West.
> Q. What's their business? A. as the Sun sets in the West to close the Day, so the Wardens stand in the West to close the lodge and dismiss the men from labour, paying their Wages.

In the Fellow-craft Degree, we are informed the candidate receives his wages in the "Middle Chamber," by way of a journey of winding stairs:

> Q. How came you in the Middle Chamber? A. By a winding Pair of Stairs.
> Q. How many? A. Seven or more.
> Q. Why Seven or more? A. Because Seven or more makes a just and Perfect Lodge

The pillars are again mentioned, with names given as "Boaz" and "Jachin." We learn of their height and circumference and are educated that these were adorned with chapiters of five cubits each,[58] along with network and pomegranates. We also find the earliest ritual reference to the Letter G, and are informed:

> Q. Are you a Fellow-Craft?
> A. I am.
> QWhy was you made a Fellow-craft?
> A. For the sake of the letter G.
> Q. What does that G denote?
> A. Geometry, or the fifth Science.
> Q. When you came into the middle (chamber), what did you see?
> A. The Resemblance of the Letter G.
> Q. Who doeth that G denote?
> A. One that's greater than you.
> Q. Who's greater than I, that am a Free and Accepted Mason, the Master of a Lodge?

> A. The Grand Architect and Contriver of the Universe, or He that was taken up to the top of the Pinnacle of the Holy Temple.

A lengthy test was then given to describe the same.

Then, for the first time in any printed manuscript, a description of the Master's Degree was given; again in catechetical form. The story of the Lost Word is described, and the legend of Hiram was narrated. This was called the Master's Part.

But Prichard makes no mention of the Orders of Architecture or the Seven Liberal Arts and Sciences as being a part of the Middle Chamber. The candidate proceeded directly from pillars to doors. In fact, Prichard's version of the Fellow-craft lecture contains nothing of the rich symbolism to which we are accustomed in our current workings. With the exception of the brief phrase regarding the arts and sciences previously given from the Dumfries MS, these themes were simply not fully developed this early in the Fellow-craft Degree. Prichard ignored them. It is likely that the Middle Chamber lecture was added during the latter part of the eighteenth century as the result of William Preston's lectures in the Lodge of Antiquity (which will be outlined later in this work). The ritual exposures of the 1760s mention only the pillars and the letter 'G'.

As previously referenced, the seven liberal arts and sciences, particularly the fifth science, have played a role in the admission ceremonies of Masonry from the earliest of times (*Regius MS,* c. 1390), but it was Preston who first applied the arts and sciences to the seven steps of the staircase.

With this review of the first decade of Grand Lodge development, we can see that the first section or esoteric ceremonies in Masonry as we now know them were developed in all essentials as to language and form during the formative period of the premier Grand Lodge. The *aides-memoires* and published exposures reviewed here clearly show from whence our ritual language has evolved. The language presented in the Masonic craft degrees as practiced in American lodges today is, for the most part, but recitations of words which have enriched the Masonic ritual for 300 years, and more.

Ritual Development from 1730 to 1760

Little is known about the development of the ritual between 1730 and

1760. With only three exceptions, the next set of exposures did not appear in England until 1760. These exceptions included *The Secrets of Masonry Made Known to All Men,* London, 1737 and *The Mystery of Masonry* published the same year. Then *Masonry Further Dissected* appeared in London in 1738. Prichard's work had by far the most significant impact on ritual workings.

Several books were also published by Masons during this period. *Pennell's Irish Constitutions of 1730* was published. It included a two paragraph prayer, the second paragraph of which, in a slightly adapted form, is now almost universally given to the candidate at Initiation. The prayer in its original form is printed here. It is not thought that Pennell actually penned this prayer, but his Constitutions were the first printed source for it.

> Most Holy and Glorious Lord God, thou great Architect of Heaven and Earth, who art the giver of all good Gifts and Graces; and hast promis'd that where two or three are gathered together in Thy Name, thou wilt be in the Midst of them; in thy Name we assemble and meet together, most humbly beseeching thee to bless us in all our Undertakings, to give us thy Holy Spirit, to enlighten our Minds with Wisdom and Understanding, that we may know, and serve thee aright, that all our Doings may tend to thy Glory, and the Salvation of our Souls.
>
> And we beseech thee, O LORD God, to bless this our present undertaking, and grant that this, our new Brother, may dedicate his life to thy Service, and be a true and faithful Brother among us, endue him with Divine Wisdom, that he may, with the Secrets of Masonry, be able to unfold the Mysteries of Godliness and Christianity. This we humbly beg in the Name and for the sake of Jesus Christ our Lord and Savior.

William Preston published this "Prayer at Initiation" in the 1772 appendix of his *Illustrations,* which will be discussed in some detail in Chapter 8. Preston also used the phrase "that, by the secrets of this art, he may be better enabled to display the beauties of godliness, to the honor of thy holy name" in order to make it conform to Dr. Anderson's First Charge in his 1723 *Book of Constitution.* Webb then modified it to read "that, by the secrets of our art, he may be better enabled to display the beauties of virtuousness, to the honor of thy holy name." Jeremy

Cross, another leading American ritualist, changed it to the beauties of "holiness." Like Pennell's version, it appears in Lawrence Dermott's "Ahiman Rezon," fourth edition, published at Dublin in 1780, as "the mysteries of godliness and Christianity." In fact, this variation was the most common of that period.

These and other variations are significant and demonstrate the substitutions and improvements which arise at the hand of those attempting to better define the character of Freemasonry. The language of the Apprentice's Prayer seems to have been intended to convey the thought "that he may, with the secrets of Freemasonry, be able to unfold the mysteries of godliness." Whoever compiled the prayer certainly knew the appropriateness of the phrase; and as the candidate advances in the mysteries of the Order, its meaning and fitness becomes remarkably clear.

William Smith's *Pocket Companion* of 1735 was also published. It gave a short charge to the newly admitted brother, and is the earliest known dated text of the Entered Apprentice Charge (there is at least one other undated two-page manuscript anonymously printed and believed to date from about 1730). Smith's work includes the language known today in regard to our duties to God, our neighbors, and ourselves; our charge as citizens of the State in which we live; the admonition not to let Masonry interfere with our necessary avocations, nor to argue with those who would ridicule it through their ignorance; and, finally, our personal charge in recommending a friend for membership. This was the first of a long series of Pocket Companions which proved very popular among brothers of the eighteenth century. Between the years 1730 and 1800, a number of books were published containing addresses and prayers used in lodge ceremonies. Each individual Master was free to use whatever charges and addresses he pleased. Occasionally, the very best of these would be published in Pocket Companions because of the ease of carrying them. The books usually contained the Constitutions, lodge songs, lists of lodges, and various bits of information useful to the Craft. An Irish edition of Smith's work followed the English edition. It was then adopted by the Grand Lodge of Ireland. The substance of it was once again published in Hutchinson's *Spirit of Masonry* in 1774.

It is not known if Smith authored this language, but it is the earliest attributed printed version of the Charge. Smith also published *The*

Book M in 1736. It repeated the Entered Apprentice's Charge, and the manner in which lodges are constituted, which was taken from Anderson's Constitutions of 1723.

It was during this same period that the ceremony of the Third Degree gradually became a part of the standard work. The old special Master's lodges died out.

Opening the Lodge

Brother James Harvey provided a thorough description of some of the more significant portions of the lodge ceremonies in an article published by Quatuor Coronati Lodge of London in 1964. He described certain elements of the initiation, along with the opening and closing ceremonies as published by the 1760 through 1764 exposures. These depicted English lodge practice of the 1760 period. These exposures were the first to give us the opening and closing ceremonies.

He pointed out that "all assembled at the lodge meetings wore white gloves and white skin aprons, tied with leather strings. Officers wore either square, level, plumb-rule, key, or pens in saltire hung about their necks in triangular blue ribbons; but the Deacons (not known to the Moderns) bore compasses. The Pass (or Past) Master was distinguished by compasses embracing the sun and a line of cords about his neck."[59] The sun was depicted in the central portion of the compasses. The Master of the lodge kept his hat on during all but a small part of the opening ceremony. The Wardens either carried or had their respective Doric or Corinthian columns with them at their stations, and they were used in very much the same way then, as now. The Deacons carried black rods which were seven feet long. In the 'Moderns' lodges both Wardens were in the West, but in the 'Ancients' working they are placed in the same relative positions as commonly found in lodges today.

Three Distinct Knocks (1760) is the first English exposure to give the language of the formal opening and closing ceremonies. Neither it nor *Jachin & Boaz* (1762) gives an opening prayer. Also, no openings are given for the Fellow-craft or Master Mason Degrees. In both exposures, the main work of the lodge ceremonies was the question and answers of the catechisms. *Three Distinct Knocks* splits these into two parts so that each degree is divided into a set of questions and answers relating to the degree ceremony; with another set providing instruction on the symbolism of the degree. The exposure entitled *Jachin and Boaz* (1762) gives the following opening language:

W.M. What is the chief Care of a Mason?
J.D. To see that the Lodge is tyl'd.
W.M. Pray do your Duty.
(The Junior Deacon goes and gives three knocks at the door, and if there is nobody nigh the Tyler without answereth with three knocks). The Junior Deacon tells the Master, and says:
Worshipful, the Lodge is tyl'd.
W.M. Pray where is the Junior Deacon's Place in the Lodge?
J.D. At the back of the Senior Warden, or at his Right-Hand if he permits him.
W.M. Your Business there?
J.D. To carry Messages from the Senior to the Junior Warden, so that they may be dispersed round the lodge.
W.M. Pray where is the Senior Deacon's Place in the Lodge?
S.D. At the back of the Master, or at his Right-Hand if he permits him.
W.M. Your business there?
S.D. To carry Messages from the Master to the Senior Warden.
W.M. The Junior Warden's Place in the Lodge?
S.D. In the South.
W.M. Why in the South?
J.W. The better to observe the Sun, at high meridian to call the Men off from Work to Refreshment, and to see that they come on in due Time, that the Master may have Pleasure and Profit thereby.
W.M. Pray where is the Senior Warden's Place in the Lodge?
J.W. In the West.
W.M. Your Business there, Brother?
S.W. As the Sun sets in the West to close the Day, so the Senior Warden stands in the West to close the Lodge, to pay the Men their Wages, and dismiss them from their Labour.
W.M. The Master's Place in the Lodge?
S.W. In the East.
W.M. His business there?
S.W. As the Sun rises in the East to open the Day, so the Master stands in the East to open his Lodge to set Men to Work.
(Then the Master takes off his hat, which he always has on but at this time, and puts it on again as soon as the lodge is open, but the rest keep theirs off, and he declares the lodge open as follows):
W.M. This Lodge is open in the Name of God and Holy St. John,

> forbidding all Cursing, Swearing, or Whispering, and all profane Discourse whatsoever, under no less Penalty than what the Majority shall think proper. (Then he gives three knocks upon the table with a wooden hammer, and puts on his hat. Then they all sit down and begin their lecture).[60]

It should be pointed out that the author of *Jachin & Boaz* admitted he was never an initiated Mason, but "acquired enough knowledge from the papers of a 'dead relative' to bluff his way into a lodge in the Strand with the result that, in due course, he had the honour of being respected in most of the lodges in London."[61] In all of the exposures of this period, the main business of the lodge was carried out at a table, with the degree ceremonies themselves performed around a floor drawing. Every brother wore a white skin apron.

In the opening ceremonies as revealed in *Three Distinct Knocks* the Junior Deacon is ordered to see that "his lodge is tyl'd." This is the first time this language appears in an English exposure. The officers were also asked their places and duties in turn. No openings are given for the Fellow-craft or Master Mason Degrees. These later ceremonies apparently entered the workings after 1770. In the case of the Fellow-craft Degree, it is likely that no opening would have been necessary, as one was made an Entered Apprentice and a Fellow-craft on the same evening until 1777, when the Grand Lodge ordered that the first two degrees could not be given on the same night.[62]

The Initiation

By the 1760s, the main work in a degree continued to be the questions and answers of the catechisms. *Jachin and Boaz* gave a rather complete description of the process of initiation. A man asked a Masonic friend to join the lodge, and then he was proposed for membership. His qualifications were debated in open lodge and his name was put to a vote. If he was approved, he was ordered to appear with his proposer at the next lodge night.

There was no waiting time for investigation. It was assumed that, if a brother of the lodge recommended a man for membership, he knew the candidate personally and was aware that his record would survive the test of the lodge. It was a time when strangers would not have considered asking, and the brethren of the lodge would not have considered proposing someone whom they did not personally know.

When a candidate arrived for his initiation, he was asked to declare that "he was conscious of having the vocation necessary to be received."[63]

When the candidate arrived, he was taken to a room away from the lodge room, and there asked to wait while the lodge was opened. When the lodge was opened, the Master asked if anyone was in waiting to be 'made.' The wardens and the proposer retired to prepare the candidate. He was taken of his metals, asked some basic questions, such as name, occupation, and place of residence, and then left to his own reflections for at least half an hour (in some lodges, the time was an hour). His proposer sat with him, and he was not allowed to talk. Guards stood near with swords drawn.

While the candidate was in the waiting room wondering what was going to transpire, the lodge set up its trestleboard. As previously mentioned, this was a set of figures drawn into the floor with charcoal and chalk, set in an oblong square. In some lodges a rich variety of symbols were drawn on the tracing board. The number and types of symbols displayed depended on the knowledge of the Master and brethren present for the evening. There was no set lecture at this time; each lodge was left to its own expertise in presenting the lessons of the ceremony.

Typically, the tracing board included the star, the letter G, together with a square, a level, a plumb-rule; along with windows situated east, west, and south as a reminder of the hours in the day; and two columns marked J and B. Some lodges included a ladder, three steps, and candlesticks, set in a triangular arrangement about the lodge.

Brother Harvey stated, "The Master stood towards the east with the bible before him, opened by 'Moderns' at the first chapter of St. John, and by 'Ancients' at the second Epistle of Peter. On the open book lay the compasses, their points covered by a box-wood square that seemed to embrace the Master, while the compasses embraced the brethren."[64]

When everything was ready, the proposer came to the door of the lodge with his candidate and gave the required knocks. The usual question was asked when the door was opened, and the candidate entered "upon the point of a sword or spear, or some warlike instrument" presented to his naked left breast. In the 'Ancients' lodges, the candidate was then delivered to the Master who ordered him to kneel and receive the benefit of prayer. The prayer was omitted in the

'Moderns' lodges. The Master then proposed "In whom do you put your trust?" The candidate responded, "In God," after which he was ordered "to rise up and follow your leader and fear no danger."

The candidate then made three circumambulations about the lodge, ending before the Master once again, who directed him to the Senior Warden to receive instruction. The Warden taught him the steps, and then the Master came toward the west end of the lodge and caused him to kneel (this time within the oblong square before a bible situated on a small table), where he administered the oath of a Mason.

All of the exposures agree on the obligation, which was published in *Three Distinct Knocks* (1760) as:

> I, A.B., of my own free will and accord and in the presence of Almighty God and this right worshipful lodge dedicated to St. John, do hereby and hereon most solemnly and sincerely swear that I will always hail, conceal and never reveal any of the secret Mysteries of Free Masonry that shall be deliver'd to me now or at any time hereafter, except it be to a true and lawful Brother, or in a just and lawful Lodge of Brothers and Fellows, him or them whom I shall find to be such, after just Trial and Due Examination.
>
> I furthermore do swear that I will not write it, print it, cut it, paint it, stint it, mark it, stain it, or engrave it, or cause so to be done, upon any Thing moveable or immoveable under the Canopy of Heaven whereby it may become legible or intelligible, or the least Appearance of the Character of a Letter, whereby the secret Art may be unlawfully obtain'd. All this I swear with a strong and steady resolution to perform the same, without any Hesitation, mental Reservation, or Self-evasion of Mind in me whatsoever, under no less penalty...[65]

Immediately following the candidate's recitation of the obligation (with the help of the Master), he kissed the Volume of Sacred Law and repeated the Latin phrase, '*fune merum Genio,*' which means "pour out good wine for our pleasure." The lodge at that point drank a toast given by the Master to the "heart that conceals, and to the tongue that never reveals." Everyone then drew their firing glass across their throats! Thus we have another indication that wine was very much a part of the lodge customs, and included with even the most solemn portion of the degree ceremony.

The brother was then brought to light by the Master and the brethren, and presented the three great lights "the Bible to rule and govern our faith, the square to square our actions, the compasses to keep us within bounds with all men, particularly with a brother." He was shown the candles, "representing the sun, moon, and Master-Mason; the sun to rule the day, the moon to govern the night, and the Master-Mason his lodge, or at least ought so to do."

The brother was taught the mode of recognition, the signs, along with the emblems within the tracing board. He then was instructed to wash away the floor figures and retire to collect his usual valuables, or be "... invested with that of which I had been divested of... "

On his return to the lodge, he was brought to the northwest corner where he thanked the lodge for admitting him a brother of the honorable society of Masons. He was then conducted to the northeast corner and presented with an apron by the Master, who informed him it was an "emblem of innocence more ancient than the golden fleece or the Roman eagle, more honored than the Star and Garter." In the 'Ancients' lodges, he also received a list of lodges, and then was seated at the Master's right hand, where he was given the lecture on the working tools by the Master. The evening concluded with the brethren all joining together, hands joined crossways in the form of a chain, while singing the Entered Apprentice's song.

After the regular ceremony was concluded, a table was usually put in place of the tracing board, and the members sat around it for the purpose of feasting, toasting, and reciting the Apprentice lecture. Smoking and drinking were permitted, and every brother could propose as many toasts as he wanted.

The lecture was done in a question-answer format, with the Master usually making the queries in a rotational fashion. If a brother did not know an answer presented to him, he would stand up, clap his hands, place his right hand on his left breast, and give a low bow. The question would then be passed to another in the rotation.

The lodge was usually closed in a shorter fashion than it was opened because of the lateness of the hour. The Senior Warden would simply declare that "our Master's will and pleasure that this lodge stands clos'd till the first or third Wednesday in the next month (or according to the nights that their lodge was next held), except a lodge of emergency, and that you shall have timely notice of." Then they removed their jewels and retired to their normal pursuits.

According to Brother Harvey, the above explanation of the working (as described primarily in *Jachin and Boaz)* was the general practice of the lodges in the North of England. It was accurate enough that brethren were encouraged to purchase a copy for their instruction!

Passwords

While the early Scottish catechisms make mention of the Mason Word, and reveal that the biblical names given the pillars at the porch of King Solomon's Temple were part of the Mason Word, there is no mention in any of the Scottish workings that these, or any other words, were actually used as passwords to gain admission into a Lodge. Certainly, apprentices and fellows of the craft were known by the "words and grips" of their particular rank. This practice is recorded as far back as the German *Steinmetzen* guilds in the mid-sixteenth century. But there is no seventeenth century printed reference that any words were required as a test of membership or of gaining admission. The operative Masons universally had secret signals by which they could be known to each other, and the words which were used as a part of this recognition were instructed to the candidates in the entry rituals. But as for the English Masons, there is no evidence that English lodges included passwords in their combined degree system which existed prior to 1725.

The exposure entitled, *Three Distinct Knocks* gave the world the first English printing of the Masonic "Passwords." Again, it was published in 1760. It claimed that the fellowcraft was given a password that came from the 12th Chapter of the book of Judges. It further stated the Master Mason was given a word from Chapter 4 of the book of Genesis.[66]

The first definite mention of passwords in any Masonic work was in the French exposure,*"L'Ordre des Francs-Macons Trahi"*, published in 1745. Since the French Grand Lodge was established in 1726, and received its ritual from England, it is likely that the passwords were either in use in English lodges during this earlier period, or the French embellished the English ritual after they had received it. Brother A.C.F. Jackson, in an article regarding the same subject published in May, 1974, didn't believe the latter was the case. He said, "if French Masons invented passwords about this time, it seems unlikely to have been for reasons of security. The King opposed Masonry and there were occasional persecutions, but there were too many influential Frenchmen and foreigners connected with the Craft for it to be effectively suppressed."[67] Jackson pointed out that the supposed secrets of Masonry had already been published in two earlier French exposures, so there would have been nothing to hide.

Pritchard's *Masonry Dissected* of 1730 did not mention passwords at all. It reveals only the words of the entr'd 'prentice's, fellows and masters. But there was undoubtedly a lot of ritual development during the thirty year gap between this exposure and those of the 1760-1764 period. This is suggested by the extensive information that was made available in the latter exposures that was not covered in the Prichard work, and the fact that the 1760 exposures treat Masonic passwords as normal parts of the work. Further, one can well imagine that had passwords existed in the English workings prior to 1730, Prichard would have included it in his expose'. He would not have left out something as significant as the words required to gain admission into a lodge.

It is likely that passwords were used in the ritual during the 1730-40 decade. There was a French exposure published in 1737 that gave a description of the method of lettering the words. But it is not known if the words so lettered were actually passwords. There is mention in *Three Distinct Knocks* as to how the passwords were communicated, with letter and syllable, but we do not know when these were conveyed. In that exposure, the words appear to be given between the ceremonies. The meanings of the passwords are also given, though not very accurately. It is possible these were given the candidate before he entered lodge, or they may have been given to him by his sponsor between the degrees. Remember, there was a combined degree system in most lodges until well into the latter half of the eighteenth century. Jackson points out that the password was not part of the degree ceremony in the ritual of the 'Ancients' lodge, but a means of entry to it.

It is also unlikely that passwords were in use in the early non-operative lodges. According to Jackson, "Passwords, identifying an individual as a Mason possessing a certain degree, would not have been necessary when there were only one or two degrees; in the case of non-operatives, both usually given on the same night." If his reasoning is sound, it would place the introduction of passwords into Masonic work later than 1725, the earliest year of the tri-gradal system.[68] And, if passwords were used after the third degree was established, then they were most likely introduced into the ritual in the 1725 to 1730 period. But, if this is true, how did Prichard miss them?

It should be pointed out that Prichard published the ceremonies of the degrees that were supposedly being practiced in 1730. He did not include all the work, such as the charges, prayers, or some of the lectures. Since we do not know how passwords were communicated and, if they were given between the ceremonies, they would not have appeared in Prichard's exposure. This could also account for their omission in the early French exposures (prior to 1745), which were all based on Prichard.

It is also possible that the passwords may have originated with the specialty lodges of England, Scotland, and Ireland, who began working the third degree as a separate degree from this period forward. Since all three degrees, when worked, were being worked on different nights in most instances, some system would be necessary to verify the qualifications of those who visited these lodges. Jackson pointed to evidence that passwords may have indeed been introduced and intended for recognition purposes. In a 1742 French translation of Anderson's 1738 Constitutions, one Marquis de la Tierce wrote; "We have secrets; they are figurative signs and sacred words composing a language sometimes mute, sometimes very eloquent, in order to communicate with one another at the greatest distance and to recognize our brothers of whatever tongue ..."[69]

Finally, one other suggestion has been forwarded by Jackson. He reported that Grand Lodge was much disturbed from 1730 to 1739 by the publication of exposures of Masonry. It was concerned that those who were not Masons, armed with Masonic secrets, would attempt to gain access to lodges. Although he does not believe this was reason enough for Grand Lodge to introduce passwords, the exposures did cause the 'words' to be reversed in the first two degrees. It should be noted, however, that this drastic move could just as likely have been dictated by an infiltration of English lodges by Masons from without England. According to Bernard Jones in the *Freemason's Guide and Compendium,* Freemasons from Ireland and Scotland were drifting into England and bringing with them ideas which had grown up not on English soil, but which, nevertheless, were very precious to those who held them. Grand Lodge was probably very worried by the number of unaffiliated Masons coming apparently from nowhere and claiming admission to their lodges.[70]

In any event, reversing the passwords caused so much consternation within the Craft that, even had the Grand Lodge introduced new passwords at this time, the craft would likely have not paid any attention to them. Neither would the other Grand Lodges. They were newly forming themselves. Even when the regular words were switched, the Scottish and Irish Grand Lodges did nothing. Both were in full sympathy with the English craft who had opposed alterations made in the English ritual.

This, along with other peculiarities of governance by the English Grand Lodge (including ceasing to read the Old Charges at initiations, de-Christianizing the ritual, omitting the Deacons as office holders, and neglecting the lectures attached to each Degree), eventually led to the establishment of a second Grand Lodge, called 'the Most Antient and Honourable Society of Free and Accepted Masons' in 1751. The new Grand Lodge claimed it adhered to the Ancient Landmarks of the Order, from which the other Grand Lodge had departed, and thus became known as the "Grand Lodge of the Ancients." The older Grand Lodge was dubbed the "Moderns," having taken upon itself modern innovations to the ancient traditions. This schism within English Masonry would not be settled until 1813.[71]

So, we may never know who invented the passwords for the degrees. However, it is clear that they were either introduced by the English or Irish sometime after the three degree system was established in or near 1725; or they were created by the French as a part of the ritual development that was sweeping continental Europe during that time; or they were copied from the Mason Word taught to the Scottish operatives. For the purposes of the present study on ritual development, it is suggested that our passwords may be considered to have made their appearance into our Masonic ritual about 1725. We know that, by the time the 1760-62 exposes' were published, passwords were treated as if they were normal parts of the work.

Degrees Combined

It should also be pointed out that the Fellowcraft "degree" was not really a separate degree during the early period. In the Prichard exposure, no obligation is given for the second part of the ceremony, thus, one did not "pass" to a second grade as we would think of it today. The Fellow's part was more a re-arrangement of the Apprentice ceremony.

What actually happened in practice was that the Fellowcraft's part was given to the candidate on the same night as he took his first degree. In fact, minutes of lodge after lodge show that this was the regular practice. Most Masons went no further; they remained Fellowcrafts all their days. Not until 1777 was it decided that the first and second degrees must be given on different evenings.

Prior to the mid-1720s, if a third degree was worked, very few brethren knew about it. For years after 1723 (the year of Anderson's Constitution), a great number of the brethren never advanced beyond the second or Fellowcraft degree. In Hughan's "History of Freemasonry in Cornwall", it was noted that one Brother George Bell was only a Fellowcraft when he was Deputy Grand Master. The year was 1751!

There is apparently no conclusive evidence that any changes were made in the established forms of the Masonic ceremonies by the Grand Lodge, either in the way of altering them in substance, augmenting their number, or varying the method in imparting them until the period subsequent to the Constitutions of 1723 and before the year 1730.

The Masonic Penalties

There is probably no other single element in Freemasonry that has stirred more interest or created more misunderstanding and confusion among members and non-members alike than the penalties associated with the obligations. These have been one of the favorite topics of the anti-Masons since Prichard's exposure. They have been viewed with suspect and scorn by both clergy and craft. Indeed, there are few Masons who have not pondered the subject at some point in their Masonic careers.

Since the penalties are very much an eighteenth century innovation of the speculative fraternity, it seems a few words concerning their origin might be appropriate within the scope of this review.

An oath to keep secret what is communicated to him has been demanded of every initiate in every mystery. There is no question the operative masons took such oaths to protect the secret knowledge of their craft. In the medieval era, oaths were nothing more than an appeal to God in support of the truth of something and in witness of a promise to be kept. All craftsmen in medieval days took such solemn oaths.

But oaths differ slightly from obligations. An obligation is a contract, or a binding agreement between two parties. Our operative ancestors took oaths. Today's speculative Apprentices take obligations. It is common for oaths to be validated by a simple affirmation, *viz a viz*, "I make this promise 'without mental reservation or self evasion,' so help me God." Similarly, the Old Charges required an oath to be kept "without any manner of equivocation or mental reservation." This implies the meaning of the oath and its import is tacitly understood by the individual making it. Obligations go a step further by affirming the individual not only knows the intent of his promise, but affirms it is a promise made to others, who themselves, will affirm it when they hear it recited. The penalty, then, applies not only to a breach of that which has been promised, but makes an internal appeal to the conscience that the consequences will be sorely felt within the psyche of the fellow who breaks it. In speculative Masonry, both the obligation and the penalty serve as a binding contract that our fraternal association depends upon a mutual agreement between the fraternity and its members in regard to the laws, regulations, ethical precepts and moral tenets which make us Masons.

It is apparent that only one penalty existed with the obligations of the degrees until sometime after 1730. The Prichard exposure reveals that the penalty for violation of the obligation is given for the first degree only, and it includes all the punishments of the three degrees, at least as Masons would be familiar with them today. The workings of all three degrees were set out in the exposure, but no obligations were included in the second and third degrees. The penalties of the tri-gradal ritual did not become an adopted practice until sometime before 1760, as these were described for the first time in *Three Distinct Knocks*, published in that year.

Penalties for violating obligations are, of course, quite old to ancient craft Masonry. They are found even in scripture. It would be difficult to say where or when these originated. If they were used and adopted by the operative lodges during the sixteenth century, they were likely created as an adaptation of the punishments given of traitors for at least two hundred years prior to that time.

The penalties are important and so often revered in Freemasonry because of their association with the obligations. But they are not indigenous to the fraternity. Those who would oppose their use should recognize they did not originate with the Craft. They were undoubtedly added to the ceremony of making a Mason as a symbolic gesture to convey to the candidate the seriousness with which he should regard the more important ties that he makes to his fellows, and the fraternity, by his obligations.

It should be noted that, for centuries, the obligations were the central theme of admission into the operative lodges. The earliest forms of the obligations most likely derived from the guild oaths, which were simple statements of fidelity to the King, to the Masters, and to the Craft regulations.

In fact, it can be shown that all the craft penalties were either whole or part of those once normally enforced under the laws of England. Again, these originally had no relation to Freemasonry at all, and were adopted by the craft for their symbolic significance alone. The penalties can be traced through the whole period of the medieval era, and were always intended to be those punishments reserved only for the greatest crimes against the state, e.g., high treason.

One can find such in records of the courts as far back as 1283, involving the Prince of Wales; or the Earl of Carlisle, in the reign of Edward II; and of Major General Harrison, in 1660.[72]

Brother Bernard Jones in his "Freemason's Guide and Compendium," even gives an example showing that a penalty very similar to that given in the first degree was common in the Navy from as early as 1375. This may have indeed been the origin of the penalty eventually adopted by the operative lodges. It has assuredly always been puzzling to many land-locked Masons that the ritual refers to such things as the "low water mark", or a "cable's tow length from shore" where the "tide ebbs and flows." Certainly, these terms are not in any way associated with the Mason's trade.

They derive from an ordinance of the Court of Admiralty of the Humbar dating from the time of Henry VI, admonishing the "masters of the quest...if you, or any of you, discover or disclose anything of the King's secret counsel, or of the counsel of your fellows...you are to be had down to the low water mark...and then...executed...hands and feet bound, throats cut,...tongues pulled out, and... bodies thrown into the sea."[73]

We may never know exactly when the penalties actually became a part of the ritual, but we do know that the early speculative lodges had secret forms of recognition. It can be argued that the whole purpose of the Masonic penalty has always been to prevent disclosure of these.

Whether or not penalties also have any symbolic interpretation is a matter for debate to some, but at least one English brother, Bruce Oliver, claims that his Lodge of Instruction, after considerable research, concluded that the Medieval legal penalties were not imposed solely for the purpose of cruelty and revenge, but were based on two age-old beliefs of mankind: that touch or contact was a continuing thing, communicated good or evil as the case may be; and the destruction of the thing which committed the crime not only prevented a reoccurrence, but also expunged the evil created. Hence certain vital parts of the body were selected according to the affectations and passions to be created in each.[74] In all of the Craft degrees, there is a clearly articulated association between that which is being promised and that which is to be taken away with the breaking of the promise. Tim Hogan, a contemporary writer on alchemical symbolism, also suggests that the penalties given in Masonic degrees have specific associations with alchemical processes, and that much of Freemasonic ritual can be traced back to alchemical terminology and practices connected with joining together the physical and spiritual aspects of man.[75] It is certainly easy to uncover the 'elements of the alchemist' in the language of Masonic penalties. Further, the noted Masonic scholar, Rex Hutchens, provided me an extraordinary unpublished manuscript he authored with two others as I was researching this topic of the work. He referenced the elements as described in the penalties and associated these with Carl Jung's symbolic suggestions that water and earth are passive elements; fire and air, active elements. We see the progression from a totally passive to the totally active character that is the goal of every Master Mason. The elements can also be arranged vertically in a kind of natural hierarchy, with earth in the lowest position, followed by water, then air, and finally fire. The two lowest elements are associated with the Entered Apprentice Degree; a mixture of high and low elements with the Fellowcraft Degree and the two highest elements are associated with the Master Mason Degree. Hutchens suggests that the association of the pairs of elements are also related to the powers of judgment, with Earth being associated with experience; Water with opinion, emotion and belief; Air with reason and knowledge; and Fire with faith. He then makes the brilliant observation: "The Entered Apprentice brings to his first Masonic episode whatever worldly experiences he has had. He is presumed to be under the rule of his emotions and is thus early counseled to keep his passions within due bounds and to subdue them. He is totally without Masonic knowledge and is thus tied to mere opinion—a conclusion not based on knowledge. The lesson of the Fellowcraft Degree is knowledge. He is taught to give high regard to the seven liberal arts and sciences so that his experiences may be given a meaning consistent with his new station. Mankind's store of knowledge is built from its collective experiences. The Master Mason is taught the importance of living a well-regulated life modeled after that famous architect whose reason was guided by faith."[76]

As to the transition period from operative to speculative Masonry, there is some evidence that the earliest known obligations contained no penalties. In fact, there is no evidence of penalties being applied to Masonic obligations until the Edinburgh MS, as previously mentioned, was published in 1696, again, of Scottish origin. It is surmised that sometime in the 1720s, when a great deal of Scottish operative material was being introduced into English speculative Freemasonry, the penalties became part of the English ritual. As in earlier times, secrecy became essential to exclude outsiders, and to protect confidences. And thus, the punishment became the corollary of exposure. The symbolic associations as presented here may also suggest that Desaguliers and his esoteric friends intentionally incorporated the penalties into the work as part of the underlying allegorical form intended to keep the profane at bay regarding the real meanings of Masonry.

The severity of the penalties also gave much credibility and authenticity to the antiquity of the Craft, which all Masons of this period genuinely believed without question.

And thus, another Masonic tradition was born.

One other point should be made. There is no evidence that the original penalties were included within (the text) of the obligations, either in the craft lodges or the speculative lodges. In all of the eighteenth century exposures, the penalties were added in the making ceremony at a later time in the initiation or passing than when the obligation was administered to the candidate.

This has major implications for the Grand Jurisdictions today that are considering changes in this particular area of the ritual because it is not considered a violation of the Ancient Landmarks to simply rearrange the work. There are numerous examples of such practices in essentially every Grand Lodge in the world. What is at question, however, is whether or not the penalties themselves are considered Landmarks. If the definition of a Landmark in Masonry is that it should have been in existence before 1723–the year the Constitutions were adopted–then the penalty for the violation of the obligation, of at least the first degree, is one of the old Landmarks.

But, it can also be argued that the penalties for all three degrees are now Landmarks as well, since any Masonic ritual practice adopted by the Grand Lodge of England at, or before, the Union of 1813 would be considered an established Landmark. In any event, Grand Jurisdictions should be very cautious when considering removing the penalties from the 'work.' Responding to recent complaints brought by the Anglican Church upon the affairs of Freemasonry in England, and similar complaints from fundamentalist Christian groups in America, Rex Hutchens, et al, make a compelling observation in this regard. They write, "Any recommendation to remove the penalties implies that they never should have been there in the first place—that our fathers and grandfathers were fools and our wisdom is greater than theirs. We are not here to improve Freemasonry. Freemasonry is here to improve us. We are stewards of ancient wisdom and morality and not purveyors of popular trends."[77]

In leaving this chapter of our story, perhaps it is well to quote from the installation ceremonies of many present day Masonic lodges and Grand Lodges:

> It is not within the prerogative of any Grand Lodge, or Grand Master, or indeed, any brother, "to permit or suffer any deviations from the established Landmarks of the Order."

7 The Master Mason Degree

"Behold! I show you a Mystery..."

It's an old word. In fact, there has never been a time or a civilization when the word was not an operative one in the language. It is found in the ancient religious and philosophic initiations of Greece, Egypt, Persia, and India. In the Middle Ages, it was played in the theatres, in the cathedrals, and in the streets. So long as the basic instinct has been to seek knowledge, there the Mysteries have also been.

The reason is simple. The purpose of the Mysteries was to find and prove good men, and give them instruction in ethics to elevate their soul. It is the reason the classical education of the Greeks is included in the Fellowcraft degree; along with the references to the symbolism of numbers, and the five orders of architecture. These are all part of the knowledge that was hidden in the ancient Mysteries. In Freemasonry, we are indebted to them for the concept of Initiation as a path to knowledge. It is the central theme of the Fellowcraft Degree.

The Mystery Play Tradition

But, there is another kind of Mystery–one that, in its original form, used drama as the means of initiation. These Mysteries were known on the European Continent under the rubric of different kinds of plays. Those that dealt with biblical events were known as Mystery Plays. Those devoted to illustrating the legends of saints and martyrs, the

Miracle Plays; and those used in the service of the Church were called the Interludes. Finally, those which were more of a secular nature, inculcating, for example, the virtues of a better life, were known as the Morality Plays. In England, all of these were generally included under the generic title of the Miracle Plays.[78]

To understand the nature of the Third Degree of Freemasonry, we have to follow a different path than in the preceding grades. The structure of the degree is entirely different. While no one yet knows from whence the Hiramic legend originates, some Masonic scholars believe that the answer most likely will be found by investigating the historical development of these early sacred dramas.

The plays became very popular in the period between the fourth and tenth centuries, primarily because they taught lessons in biblical truth. They were commonly performed by the minstrels and jugglers as a form of recreation in the churches of France and Germany.[79] The Church sanctioned the same, seeing them as an opportunity to teach doctrinal truths to the illiterate (the same Christian Church had condemned and suppressed the earlier Roman dramas). The Plays were a central part of the common man's education for a long while, although they were not native to England. The native Anglo-Saxon speech was not developed enough to include the terms used in Masonry until the thirteenth century, and these were largely adopted from the French. But the conquest of England in 1066 brought many clergy from foreign lands, and with them, new expressions of the life of Jesus.

These representations were also staged in the priories and parishes. It was not uncommon for the younger priests, and even nuns, to act the parts. The dramatic plays were directly based on the bible, or, on stories of the lives of saints and martyrs. The stories eventually became so big, with so many different scenes required to tell the whole story, that all parts of the church were put to use. Stages were literally built around the perimeter of the church and inside, allowing for continuous performance from one stage to the next. The audience would move about the church as the play would unfold.

Before long, elements of comedy found its way into the plays. Laughter was thought to be good for Christians, and the church introduced and sanctioned festivals and special entertainments. Even burlesque and satire made their way as themes that were routinely acted within the walls of the church. After all, should not God's house contain everything? The plays soon became so popular that the buildings could not accommodate the crowds, so the 'miracle' plays moved to the streets of the English towns.

As in most opportunities for expressive freedom, the players took too many liberties with the biblical stories, making them more boisterous and lively as time went by. It was probably good theatre, but it eventually became a bit too noisy (and perhaps uncontrolled) for the sectarian temper of the period.

Finally, the church felt it necessary to remove the story tellers back to the more respected and constrained confines of the church building, and then proceeded to excommunicate the good folks who patronized the outdoor assemblies. Of course, this arrangement once again didn't work. With the return of the play to the church, great difficulty was soon experienced in providing adequate accommodation for the crowd of spectators. The elders began showing concern, morally and ethically, about the growth and popularity of the dramatic and satirical representations of the scriptures within its sacred buildings. The priests were occupying themselves in play-making instead of more sacred pursuits, which resulted in the authorities disassociating themselves from the performance of the plays within the church walls and ordering the presentations to become the responsibility of the townspeople.[80]

Before long, the plays were back out on the street. But not without some revisions; not before the clergy had scribed lengthy additions to the biblical narratives, requiring large numbers to represent the characters in the huge dramas. These more complete plays, along with the minor ones, all became incorporated into the term Miracle Play. The church authorities still thought the "theatre" a good idea in imparting important moral lessons to the ignorant and unschooled.

This is where the Craft guilds came in.

The Guild Actors

The majority of the guilds and trading companies had developed from the religious guilds. They all had their patron saints.[81] It was an easy matter for the church to simply call in the aid of the guilds to mount the productions. And this is exactly what it did. When the authorities mandated the organization and performance of the plays to be the responsibility of the townspeople, the towns, in turn, turned to the guilds. And almost every town had a guild.

It was a real business deal as far as the church was concerned. The guilds would be responsible for paying for and manning the plays, while the church would retain control over the text. Since every town had a guild, the biblical stories could be presented to literally every "ignorant and unlettered bloke" in the area. Almost everyone in town got involved. It sometimes took several days to complete a production.

As for the guilds, they assumed the responsibility of several of the scenes, or sections, of the play. In fact, they became the central element in play production. The guilds were powerful, and essentially all trades, merchants, skilled workers, and apprentices were controlled by them. They covered almost every trade and profession. No cycle of plays could be put together without their crafts, skills, and influence.

By the fifteenth century in London, they had their own halls, held large property holdings, and had set up their own schools and churches. And when the cycle plays were to be performed, they competed with each other in putting on the best show. The more popular the guild, the larger its role in the production. Once the drama left the church, the characters and contents of the plays became less formal. A strong mixture of formal and symbolic representation contrasted with the good humor, local songs, and the native culture of the townspeople. Each scene began to tell a story as simply and directly as possible. As time passed, the guilds began to create their own stories, with a good mix of myth and morality, and a hearty bias toward freedom of expression and thought. Whatever distinctions had previously existed between Mystery Plays and Miracle Plays, most productions simply took on the name of Mystery Plays, and these encompassed almost any story which included some biblical theme.[82]

By the end of the sixteenth century, almost all religious dogma was under pressure of change. The religious dramas were increasingly altered or censored. Professional playwrights, schools and colleges began regularly writing and performing plays based more on classical scholarship. The Mystery Plays took the form of more intellectual entertainments involving instructional moralities, allegories, and rules for the conduct of life. The plays offered a greater freedom for thought along with an escape from religious oversight and politics. The world was rapidly changing to accept new concepts of man with freedoms to explore new ideas and beliefs beyond the rigid structure of divine guidance and order. The mysteries could not be understood through reason and logic alone.[83]

The Mystery Plays continued until about 1600, when James I finally outlawed them. But their popularity cannot be understated. For 300 years they were the chief form of amusement available to the common citizenry. They, perhaps more than any other medium, influenced a better moral and social life of the thousands of folk who gathered together to witness them.

So, what does all this have to do with the Masonic ritual?

Very much, in fact, for a large part of the Master's Degree is a Mystery Play. It is the representation of a biblical situation. It contains a moral allegory. It has all the elements of medieval theatre. It uses symbolism typical of the middle ages. It is not an actual historical event, but a libretto of a religious drama.

And it is possible that the story of Hiram was developed by the Mason guilds as an esoteric play for their membership, performed in an oral tradition during the sixteenth and early into the seventeenth century.

When the Mystery Plays were outlawed as public events, it is logical to assume that the guilds, which had a prominent place in these earlier public presentations, would have been driven to continue the tradition after the action of King James to suppress them. But to have done so would have required them to continue the tradition underground, or in a covert or secret manner.

It is an enticing theory of origin, but the problem is that the actual tracing of the Hiram legend as a guild play has not been accomplished to date. In fact, there is no record of it as a theme among all the known Miracle or Morality Plays that were publicly performed. It cannot be found in any published record of the medieval stage.

There is presently only a small thread of evidence that might suggest a possible link to the Mystery Play tradition. But it is significant, and will take a bit of preliminary explanation.

Was the Master's Degree a Grand Lodge Era Innovation?

In 1726, an advertisement ran in a London newspaper which made reference to the Society of Anti-diluvium Masons (an unknown organization of speculative Masons using the Noah story as the archetype of Hiram). It was a notice of a lodge meeting to be held at Ship's Tavern on Bishopsgate Street. At about the same time, Dr. Anderson published in the Old Charges, a history of Masonry that makes a reference to the fact that a "MASON is obliged by his tenure to observe the Moral Law, as a true Noachida"–suggesting again that there was a Noachic tradition in the fraternity. These two events were likely discounted by Masonic historians as being mere curiosities.

Then, in 1936 an old manuscript was found by one H. I. Robinson that was dated October 24, 1726. Titled the *Graham MS,* it had a profound effect on the attention given to this particular line of inquiry.[84]

The manuscript, probably written some time before the publication date, combined a story about a Noachic legend with that of the legend of Bazalliel, the builder of the tabernacle of Moses. The story evolved around the legend of Noah being raised from the grave by his sons. What is remarkable about the exposure is that it presents almost the exact story as is currently illustrated in the Hiram legend. Of course, it was told of a different character, and on an entirely different occasion, but the details are familiar to all Master Masons. There was a master builder. There are secrets associated with architecture that were shared by three persons and were lost with the death of one of them. A search was made for the body; and, when found an attempt was made to raise it. The fact the word could not be discovered meant that the secrets of Masonry would surely be lost to all future generations. A new name was given, etc.

The Masons of today can readily see the similarities. It is also interesting to note that the first exposure of the Hiramic legend by Prichard came almost immediately after the *Graham MS* was published. Could the Hiram legend have been copied by the Masons from the older Noah Mystery Play and brought into the final version for this new mystery drama (the Third Degree) sometime during the 1717 to 1726 period? It is an even more curious enigma when combined with Reverend Anderson's mention of the *Noachida* in his first of the Old Charges. Could this have influenced Desaguliers to author a similar story as the Third Degree of Masonry? He was the most noted lecturer, writer, and Masonic enthusiast of the Grand Lodge's first decade. He studied alchemy with Isaac Newton, and had a definite interest in 'speculative' Masonry.

In fact, there is at least one possible link to his penmanship of the Third Degree. And it came from an unattributed and undated manuscript entitled *The Secret History of the Freemasons,* published by a fellow named Sam Briscoe. Known as *The Briscoe Manuscript,* it came out soon after Anderson's 1723 Constitutions and purported to be a more accurate history of Freemasonry than that penned by Anderson. The writer of the pamphlet purported to be a serious Freemason who was shocked with certain elements in Anderson's work, principally in its biblical accounts. In challenging Anderson's story regarding the chief builder of King Solomon's Temple, the writer accuses the author of making Hiram Abif a jack of all trades by assigning all manners of skills to the carver in brass. He states: "Thus far the holy Penman, but the most ingenious Doctor Desaguliers, to make this Hiram, who was a Founder, and Carver in Brass, a Stone-cutter, or Free-Mason, ... and has found out the very letter of recommendation which King Hiram sent to Solomon ... sent a cunning man, endued with understanding, skillful to work in Gold, Silver, Brass, Iron, Stone, Timber, Purple, Blue, fine Linnen and Crimson, ..."[85] As this story appears only in the Third Degree of Masonry, the reference at least suggests that Desaguliers was writing about Hiram Abif as a central character in the emerging degree of Master Mason.

Desaguliers and his friends had a fascination with the imagery of King Solomon's Temple. After all, the old Constitutions made liberal references to the use and importance of the operative stonemasons in the temple's construction. Two of the most popular books regarding the spiritual nature of Solomon's temple had been published during the late seventeenth century, and were in the libraries of a number of the founding era Masons.[86] Perhaps Desaguliers used his creative writing skills to adapt the old Noah legend to Solomon and his temple builders.

Bernard E. Jones ("Freemason's Guide and Compendium") suggests that "the medieval operatives knew of King Solomon's Temple and of Solomon's architect; there is a bare possibility that some of them or their priestly scribes might have known the legend of Noah and his son Ham. Some of the Rosicrucians, and other delvers into the mystic who came into freemasonry in the 1700s, were probably aware of the Noah story, and it is not impossible that they gave it a dramatic setting. Later editors, aware of all the foregoing, would be able to introduce the name of Hiram, the biblical character intimately concerned with Solomon's great project. Forthwith Hiram was transformed into an architect, and made the centre of a story that fitted well into the setting of King Solomon's Temple."[87]

And thus the theme of the Third Degree was formed. Could it have been a remnant of an older Morality Play?

We may never know. While the Hiram Legend cannot be found in the list of Mystery or Morality Plays that have survived to our time, still the theme is so typical of this type of play that it cannot be discounted as not having originated from the same tradition. The Morality Plays created by the guilds always represented dramatic struggles. There were good and evil features in every plot. The characterizations were real and sophisticated. A psychological understanding of man is evident.

The Master Mason Degree describes a psychological process similar to that found in many of the moralities--the dramatic struggle of a man who must face himself in the process of his own demise, and assume responsibility for his own life. He experiences the emergence of his real self, he finds his will, and is prepared to surrender it to the Deity in order to preserve some moral principle which he is committed to uphold.

And deep within this process of challenge, struggle, death, and victory are found the true secrets of a Master Mason.

Who Was Hiram?

The central character of the Third Degree theme is another enigma in Freemasonry. There are no less than a dozen different hypotheses as to the origin of the Hiram story. In fact, one of the reasons that it could have likely originated in the Mystery Play tradition is that it cannot be traced to a single historical source. The fact that it cannot be found in any extant document of any secret society (and many exist), or in the records of any one medieval institution, lends credence to it being an allegory handed down from generation to generation through some form of oral communication. Since it cannot be found in any of the manuscripts of the old operative working lodges, it can be assumed that it was brought to Freemasonry from some other medium of transmission.

Still, as was just noted, some scholars have suggested the legend was simply penned by the early Masonic writers sometime between 1717 and 1726 as a creative effort to augment the moral lessons of craft Masonry. Yet, this seems just as unlikely to others, arguing that any freelance effort would have been considered a substantive innovation during this period. Proposed changes of much less import raised opposition that lasted for years. The Masons of England would simply not have accepted a new tradition unless it had already had some history behind it that was somehow previously and intimately connected with the craft.

Many scholars feel, therefore, the eighteenth century is too late a period for the legend to have been born.

Of the many possible roots of the Hiram tradition, there are several theories of origin that have persisted as being the most plausible, or at least, the most popular.

One is that the tradition was carried by some guild of master masons, or operative artisans, who managed the Craft during the sixteenth and seventeenth centuries. In this scenario, the Mystery Play means of transmission is again likely. But who was Hiram? And why would there have been so much secrecy concerning him? Was he really the biblical hero mentioned ever so briefly in Kings and Chronicles? Could he have been a real person; could perhaps an English hero of one of the guilds have been the real Hiram, whose life and death was significant enough to commemorate through the ages? Or, perhaps some intrigue during the Middle Ages made it "politically correct" to veil the truth by secretly promoting a cause that was important to the guild craftsmen. Could the Hiram story be derived from the general background of Medieval or Renaissance magic associated with necromancy; obtaining hidden knowledge from the dead by way of a secret organization? Or, was the Hiram character simply adapted from the older Noah story revealed in the 1726 Graham MS? Was the legend added to Masonic ritual to emphasize the central theme of many forms of initiation, namely ritual death and rebirth? Was Hiram a remnant of an old dying god religious cult?

Again, we may never know. But one thing is certain. If the legend was created to perpetuate a singularly important historical event, it must have been extraordinary indeed so to thoroughly disguise it under the name of a quasi-biblical personage. And it is highly improbable that the character represented in the Third Degree has any real tie to the biblical account. For one thing, the story, in its entirety, has no biblical evidence. Hiram is only mentioned in two chapters. Neither of the versions in the Old Testament of the building of King Solomon's Temple describes Hiram as an architect, nor is there any mention at all of his death. The story cannot be confirmed by any record outside the Craft. The name appears late in the Ancient Charges. For instance, the Charges that were printed between 1583 and 1677 carried the name "Aymon" (meaning "master-builder"), rather than Hiram. And, too, we have always been told the story is an allegory based on a myth or legend. So, if there was some other source of origin intended by the ritual writers, it will have to be discovered from some other line of inquiry.

One such path might be the story of Hermes, a central figure in Hermetic philosophy. Hermeticism was a form of magic that grew out of the Renaissance and spurred interest in Plato and Platonic correspondences, as well as studying works of explicit magic and wisdom from the ancient writings on alchemy and spiritual magic. These traditions were often lumped together under the name of Hermes, reputedly an ancient Egyptian magus who had a precocious understanding of Christianity. Whether or not he was a real personage, Hermes became known to the alchemists as the patron saint of alchemy. Alchemy was a spiritual pursuit aimed at recovering the religious understanding of the ancients and their deep insights into the nature of the material and spiritual world. Such ideas had a close relationship with the theoretical concepts envisioned for the study of speculative Masonry. Hermetic philosophy figured prominently in almost all western esoteric traditions, including Freemasonry, and was a hobby of early speculative Masons, including Elias Ashmole, Sir Robert Moray, Isaac Newton, and John Theophilus Desaguliers. Hermes is quoted in a number of passages of the degrees of the Scottish Rite; and is mentioned in the old Gothic manuscripts compiled and published by brother J. Roberts in 1722, one of the early sources of Masonic ritual inspiration. It has been suggested by more than one writer that the very name of Hiram is a Hebrew version of the Greek 'Hermes.' It is said that Hiram is taken from the Chaldean "Chiram;" that the name Hiram was created by the translators of the bible from "Chiram" by changing the Hebrew letter "Chet" into "He," both being similar letters in Hebrew. Since Hebrew does not use vowels, with a different emphasis on consonants, the Hebrew "Hiram" becomes the Greek "Hermes."[88] This line of inquiry leads one to investigate Hermes's *Emerald Tablet,* which has so many alchemical associations with Masonic symbols that it would be difficult to suggest the legends associated with Hermes had little influence on speculative Masonry and its many ritual themes and symbolic ideas.

The other persistent theory of origin rests with the Crusades. The central idea is that some of the Templars who escaped France and England in the early 1300s to avoid arrest and persecution by Phillip the Fair, fled to Scotland. There, they connected with the Scottish Stonemasons and became cathedral builders in their own right. This tradition suggests that their last Grand Master, Jacques DeMolay, was immortalized by the establishment of a legend whose associated secrets were transmitted to the Gothic masons. This, then, may have finally evolved into the disguised third degree legend picked up by the guilds.

Of course, there is no proof of this line of inquiry. To verify it, one would need to investigate the available records in regard to the Templars of Scotland. There is some evidence to suggest that the knights, or perhaps their serving brethren, may have merged and formed with the Craft fraternities. If they communicated their story to the masons, it is possible that a secret tradition may have evolved from which the Hiram story was the result.

The obvious weakness with this theory is that it is hard to surmise that a burning of a French knight in France would have made an English hero. King Edward was not particularly interested in the Templars, and, in fact, he let them escape England to Scotland rather than be personally implicated with their arrests. There was no political strife between Edward and King Robert of Scotland at the time. So, to the Englishman, there is no real story here upon which to base an allegory.

It may be that the rift between the Stuarts and the Jacobites concerning the suppression of the British monarchial constitution and the death of Charles I was the real story behind the Hiram allegory—the untimely death of Hiram being an allusion to the execution of Charles I and the attempt to raise the Master's body an allusion to an attempt to raise the young Prince Charles from the grave of exile to the throne of England. This would place the Masonic fraternity solidly in the political arena, a fact that has some credence in the 1650 to 1700 period. After all, it was a time of transition. The craft guilds were falling apart, and a socially superior class of members was entering the fraternity as speculatives. Certainly, many of these had political ties to the king and were royalists in every sense of the word. They could have established the allegory as a reminder of the murder of their King, and the role the Royalists should have in the future in preserving the monarchy.

In any event, the Masons of today can be assured that the Hiramic tradition, regardless of its origin, is an allegory of major import. Indeed, the study and contemplation of what lies behind it is one of the great challenges and joys of being a Mason.

But it is far more than just an allegory. For this legend to have been brought into the Masonic ritual at its relative late point in time, and then to have evolved to what many consider the *ne plus ultra* of Freemasonry, cannot lightly be set aside by any thoughtful Mason. It is considered the foundation of Masonic ritual today, and remains the most highly revered instruction in all of Freemasonry's many rites and ceremonies.

It was the Hiram legend that institutionalized Freemasonry.

The Working of the Third Degree

The first minute of an actual working of the Third Degree comes not in a lodge minute book, but in an organization known as the *Philo Musicae et Architecturae Societas Apoloni*, or "the Apollonian Society for Lovers of Music and Architecture"--the members of which were all Freemasons. The society apparently permitted itself to hold an occasional lodge for the purpose of ritual workings. While the practice was irregular, the custom of the group seemed to be that it would initiate and raise its members into Freemasonry. If the music society conducted such Masonic ceremonies, it did so as an irregular lodge as far as the Grand Lodge was concerned. However, as this is precisely the way many unattached accepted Masons had joined lodges for many years before the Grand Lodge came into being, the 'Philo Musicae' Freemasons likely considered they were simply following the old traditions of making Masons.

Regardless of its organizational status, the minutes of the society reveal that on May 12, 1725, one Charles Cotton was regularly passed a Master. There is no doubt about this working of a third degree because records exist which prove Brother Cotton had previously been initiated and passed a Fellowcraft in a regular lodge.[89] The Grand Lodge was concerned enough about Brother Cotton's raising that it dispatched Past Grand Master George Payne to visit the Society and make investigation in September of that year. Grand Master Richmond then sent a cease and desist letter to the Society. The response from the group was that the Grand Master had erroneously assumed for himself a pretended authority; and ignored the order. Interestingly, the Grand Master made no further issue of the situation, probably because of the Philo Musicae's well-connected membership. Not only were its members connected to royalty, several, including Charles Cotton, belonged to the same lodge with Richmond![90]

In November of that same year the Grand Lodge authorized lodges to work all three degrees (there is some evidence that only the Grand Lodge could work a Master's degree prior to this action, or perhaps only a select number of Master's lodges were authorized to do so). When the practice finally came into existence, it was discretionary with each lodge. As change is always slow to catch on at the lodge level, the great majority either could not, or did not, include it in their ritual practices until well into the 1740s.

Those lodges that did choose to work the "superior" degree became known as "Master's Lodges." There were two kinds–those that met on certain nights just to work the degree, and those who assembled only as Master Masons. If a Fellow wanted to advance to the Third Degree, he usually had to find a Master's Lodge, and then be recommended before he could receive the secrets offered by the Third Degree ritual. The Grand Lodge did not formally and officially recognize that Freemasonry was a system of three degrees, and set its seal on the order, until the Constitutions of 1738.[91]

The Prichard exposure of the Master's Degree is also the first reference we have of the actual contents of the Third Degree, as it was being worked in England. As previously mentioned, it is safe to say that this exposure stabilized the practice of Masonic ritual in England. It was the most descriptive and complete of all the manuscripts and catechisms printed from 1696. It verified, or perhaps defined the tri-gradal degree system, and it validated that the Hiramic legend was at least known by the ritual writers as early as 1696 (because of the F.P.O.P in the Edinburgh MS), and thus, the Hiram story was in some stage of formal development up to the time it was first exposed and published in 1730.

The Prichard exposure had a major influence on defining the degree system of the eighteenth century because, during the next 30 years, nothing else important in ritual development in England was published. The thirty editions that were printed clearly attest to its popularity. In fact, so many non-Masons purchased copies that the Grand Lodge panicked, and, as one story goes, ordered that the degree signs and words be reversed in the Entered Apprentice and Fellowcraft degrees (to some purists, a clear violation of the Landmarks). Whether or not this was the real reason for the change has always been debated, as it is more likely that the exposure caused a drain on the charitable funds of the lodges from imposters applying for Masonic relief. But, nonetheless, these, and other elements of the two degrees were changed, and remained thus altered until the Union of 1813. The installation ceremony for the office of Worshipful Master was abolished, the lectures were condensed, some parts of the ceremonies were eliminated, and some of the secrets reserved for the office of installed master were given over to the third degree.[92]

These actions proved unfortunate for other reasons, as the numerical strength of the Grand Lodge waned during the period of the next twenty years. As previously noted, it may have been the tampering with the esoteric work that eventually led to the formation of a second Grand Lodge of England (the Ancients) in 1751.

The period from 1740-1750 was particularly bad for the Grand Lodge. There appeared to be a lack of interest and leadership by successive Grand Masters. The Grand Lodge met in few assemblies, and the proceedings almost invariably reflected business that was routine, with no new focus or energy directed toward progress. Only one new lodge was formed in London during this ten year period (although the rural lodges were expanding), with more than half of the London Lodges losing their charter for non-attendance at Grand Lodge (a requirement of the English system).

Of course, there were outside influences contributing to the decline, as well. A papal bull was issued against the fraternity in 1738. Public ridicule reached new heights in 1742, with the publication of several cartoons making a mockery of the procession of Masons engaged in the Annual Feast. Europe was also at war with the Austria Succession, and France declared war on England in 1744. The Jacobite threat for the throne, pitting the Catholics against the Protestants, became real as the Pretender landed in Scotland, and began marching south.[93]

For a period, English Freemasonry indeed lost its novelty and appeal. The indifference and ineffectiveness of its leaders, the apathy among its own members, and pressure from outside influences may have all contributed to its decline. But the Grand Lodge survived and its authority remained intact. It could well be that the creation of the rival Grand Lodge in 1751 was the tonic that ultimately caused a resurgence in interest, and brought about the revival of Freemasonry.

In contrast, the period from 1730 to 1760 was a period of rapid growth in Masonry in France. In fact, the only ritual exposures (outside of some fourteen Prichard's editions) during this time were the French exposures.

The French Exposures, 1737-1751

Freemasonry appeared in France just about the same time the Third Degree came into Masonic ritual workings. According to Rebold, in 1725 Lord Derwentwater received from the Grand Lodge of London powers to constitute lodges in France. He would eventually become a Provincial Grand Master, but he and two other English gentlemen constituted the first lodge in Paris in June, 1726.[94] While Masonry started slowly in France because of initial governmental opposition to it, by 1737 it had spread widely throughout the country.

There were a total of twelve French exposures from the period 1737 to 1751. All but two of these were penned anonymously and none of them had official sanction. The main interest in these works is that they provide evidence of ritual expansion during the rather dormant English years of the 1740s, particularly in the modes of recognition, floorwork, ceremonial procedures, catechisms and symbolism. Harry Carr concluded that two characteristics of the French exposures deserved special attention because they were of outstanding importance to students of Masonic ceremonial procedures and practices of that period:

1) The highly informative narrative style in the majority of them, which helps to depict the actual movements and procedures so that it becomes possible to reconstruct the ceremonies in real detail. In this respect, they are far in advance of the English texts of 1696-1730.
2) The great emphasis which these documents place on table procedures and toasting routines. These details had never appeared in the earlier English texts.[95]

With the exception of the first five exposures published between 1737 and 1744, none published after 1744 offer anything of interest on the subject of ritual. They are useful, however, because they contain collections of songs and verse which greatly add to our knowledge that music was very much a part of lodge ceremonies.

The earliest French exposure is styled, *Reception d'un Frey-Macon,* published in Paris in 1737. The Initiation ceremony is explained with much detail. The candidate is taken into one of the rooms of the lodge and is deprived of all metals. He is clothed in a particular way and his eyes are bandaged. He spends an hour in the darkened room and left to his own reflections. After the usual knocks are returned, he is led three times about the lodge and placed by special movements between a floor drawing of two columns representing the ruins of King Solomon's temple. At each side of this space, the letters J and B are drawn. In the middle are three lighted candles arranged in a triangle. Gun powder is then thrown on the candles to startle him, and then he is brought to light. He is advanced to the east in front of the Master and made to kneel in the proscribed way. He is given the obligation of the entr'd 'prentice with one hand on a compasses he holds himself against his left breast; the other hand placed upon the volume of sacred law opened to the Gospel of St. John. The penalty of the apprentice, fellow and master are recited. The candidate is then brought to the Master's side and presented with a white skin apron and two pairs of white gloves; one for himself, the other for the lady he most highly esteems. An explanation of the J. and B. are presented, along with the signs and grip. The candidate is then pronounced a brother and the ceremony ends.

The exposure then gives us one of the earliest descriptions of a table board and firing routine. Immediately following the ceremony, all are seated at a table where they drink to the health of the new brother. Each has a bottle before him and when they want to drink, they say "give the Powder" and wine is poured into the glass. All rise and the Master orders all to lay their hands to their firelocks; the toast is delivered and they drink, carrying the glass to the mouth in three movements; after which it is carried to the left breast, then to the right, and then forwards, all in three movements. After three more movements, the glasses are brought down to the table in unison. The brothers clap hands three times and each cries three times *Vivat!*[96]

In *La Reception Mysterieuse,* published in 1738, there are lengthy catechisms for all three Degrees, and each is taken, with some modifications, from Prichard's *Masonry Dissected.* In the Apprentice Degree, the candidate responds to ninety-three questions; in the Fellow-craft, thirty-one; and in the Master's examination, thirty. We learn that seven or more persons are needed to open an Apprentice and a Fellow-craft Lodge; while three Masters are required for a Master's Lodge. In the second Degree, the winding stairs is described and consists of seven or more steps. In the Master's Degree, the legend of Hiram is explained and the 'Word' is revealed to the candidate.

We are also given an interesting explanation of the meaning of the word *Free-mason.* According to the exposure (which again is taken from an earlier English working), the word is comprised of two words, which has a double meaning;

> that of a Mason, which claims to show that this Society is built upon a solid foundation, such as every good Architect or Mason lays down to take the weight of the Building before it is put up; the word Free which precedes it, means that in general the Society always works for the freedom and liberty of the Nation, and that Masons are never tired of working for this object; this liberty lies in the free election of Members of Parliament and the right of every individual to say what he thinks according to Magna Carta.[97]

In 1742, *Le Secret Des Francs-Macons* was published. It was one of the few French exposures whose author, Abbe Gabriel Louis Calabre Perau, was well known. The exposure did not include opening or closing ceremonies, nor was there any information regarding the second or third Degree. The most helpful contribution of *Le Secrets* is the emphasis placed on fraternal cheer and enjoyment. It was observed of Free-Masons' banquets: "they certainly do not exclude all gaiety and enjoyment; their conversations are quite lively, but their principle charm is derived from the tenderness & fraternal cordiality which prevail among them." In addition, Perau was firm in his conviction that a person's character was often manifested by the songs he sang. A typical Masonic meeting included Masonic hymns which were sung for the Wardens, others for the Masters; still others for the Fellows (members). The lodge always finished the evening with the Apprentice's Song. The exposure provided a nice collection of a majority of songs sung in different lodges of the period.

Catechisme Des Francs-Macons was published in 1744 and, though based on Prichard's exposure, this expose' gives an excellent version of the Hiramic legend. While Prichard's account was all in the form of questions and answers, this French work was beautifully narrated and had a much more modern look. The work also provides a complete ceremony for the reception of a Master.

But it's most important contribution to present day understanding of early day practices relates to the fact that it includes two engravings illustrating the floor cloths or drawing alluded to in the earlier English workings. One illustration depicts a drawing of an Apprentice Lodge; the other, a Master's Lodge (figures 3 and 4). These are the earliest known printed illustrations of what ultimately would become our modern Tracing Boards.

Another tidbit from the *Catachisme* is that Prichard's questions and answers are expanded and show a definite growth in symbolic interpretation in the 14 years of ritual development since 1730. In addition, we find that the candidate for the Third Degree is no longer divested of his outer apparel. He is not hoodwinked, nor slipshod, nor deprived of metals. He is free to wear anything he likes for the ceremony and he wears the apron of a Fellow-craft. During the drama portion of the Master's Degree, the candidate physically represents Hiram as in our contemporary ceremonies. Of the French exposures, the *Catachisme* became one of the most popular and was embodied in many later and larger works.

Finally, the fifth of the early French exposures offers little to expand our knowledge of mid-eighteenth century Masonry. Through the use of titles and terms which do not appear in any previous working, it was authored by one who is clearly not a Mason. However, we are given a masterpiece of Masonic philosophy in a Master's address following the catechism of the Third Degree which is profound in substance and worthy of consideration by any Mason of any time:

> The common Profane, who sees in things nothing but the superficial, laughs at our Mysteries, he looks at them with a disdainful air, because of ignoble appearance which seem to confuse us with mercenaries; but Wise Men who have a perceptive vision import a very different judgment to our art; they regard our ornaments, our ceremonies, our mysteries & our language as precious remains of the ancient wisdom, which, like us, had reasons for displaying itself only in

Figure 3

Plan of the Apprentice Fellow's Lodge

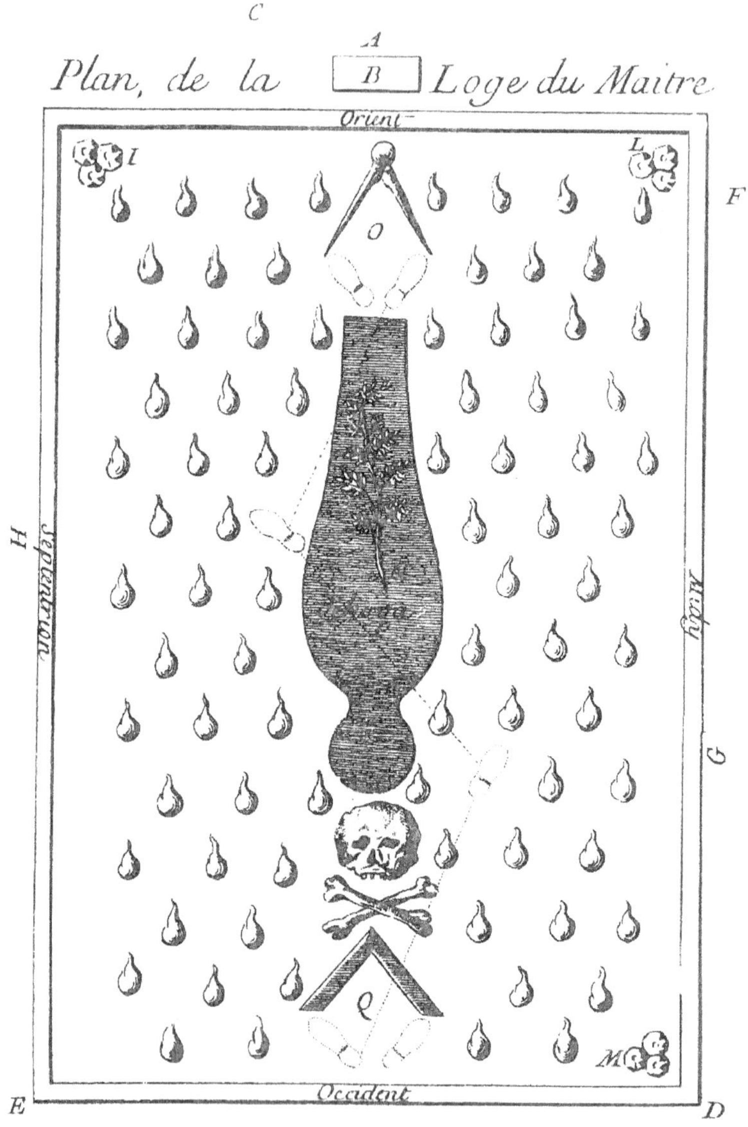

Figure 4

Plan of the Master's Lodge

> Hieroglyphics; these Wise Men, I say, know that we do not bear the name of Mason in vain; in fact we are building the vastest edifice that ever existed, since it acknowledges no other boundaries than those of the Earth itself; virtuous & enlightened men form its living stones which we bind together with the precious Cement of Friendship. We build, according to the rules of our moral Architecture, impregnable Fortresses around the building in order to defend it from the attacks of vice & error. Our occupations also have as their objective the works of the supreme Architect, we contemplate their perfections, & in the great edifice of the Universe, & the admirable structure of all the sublunary bodies, we carry our thoughts from there until we make a dwelling within ourselves for that great Architect, whom the Heaven & the Earth cannot contain. We build for Him, by the hand of virtue, a sanctuary in the depths of our heart. We invite Him with loving cries, redoubled a hundred fold, to come & honour it by His presence; He yields to our prayers, He unites Himself with us, He deifies us. It is thus that the Mason becomes the polished stone of all created Beings. Did you ever think while you were yet a Profane, that our art concealed so much glory, & such grandeur, under such poor exteriors?[98]

Then, in England, a new group of exposures finally appeared in the 1760s These have already been mentioned. The two that were the most successful were *Three Distinct Knocks,* published in 1760 as supposedly the work of the Ancients, and *Jachin and Boaz,* printed in 1762, which claimed to cover the ceremonies of both the Ancients and Moderns. These both ran into many editions, and were extensively used by the Masons themselves as *aides-memoires* until the turn of the century.

These exposures revealed that the ceremonies of becoming a Mason had developed into much more elaborate settings, and that the 'work' of both the Moderns and the Ancients were essentially the same. As symbols easily migrate, it is also possible that some of the work of the French lodges was picked up and incorporated in the ritual language of the English degrees that evolved during this period.

The principle additions to ritual development from 1760 to 1769 were significant, and include:

- the formal opening and closing ceremonies,
- moving to and from labor and refreshment,
- different preparations of the candidates for each degree,
- the Junior Warden was moved to the south,

- a separate obligation for each degree,
- the perambulations,
- first appearance of the passwords,
- the manner of presenting the lesson on charity,
- formal presentation of the apron and the different manner of wearing it in the three degrees,
- the symbolism of the working tools, and
- a full explanation of the Master's degree traditional history.

The exposures also verify that the language used in the degrees is clearly the precursor of that practiced in the lodges today.

Summary of the First 50 Years of Masonic Ritual Development

It is clear that, up to 1730, Masonic ceremonies were formative at best, with the three degree system evolving from the early making ceremonies of the Scottish lodges to the somewhat elaborately defined structure of the English degree system of Entered Apprentice, Fellowcraft and Master Mason. The work of this period culminated with the publication of *Masonry Dissected* by Samuel Prichard in October, 1730. This expose' sustained the English Masonic system between 1730 and 1760, as twenty editions were published. Prichard's exposure not only served as an aide to the memory work of Freemasons, it attracted a good deal of curiosity in the fraternity from the profane. It was widely successful by anyone's standards.

Not a lot was added during the 1730 to 1760 period. One of the most noted being the Apprentice's Prayer, first discovered in Pennell's *Irish Constitutions* of 1730. Smith's *Pocket Companion,* 1735, added a charge to the newly admitted brethren, which became the earliest version of the Entered Apprentice's Charge. The ceremony of the Third Degree grew in stature and prominence among the lodges, and the old Master's lodges went by the wayside. The development of Freemasonry in France was slower to catch on and did not receive the sanction of civil authorities during these formative years. The Craft also saw the beginnings of the Royal Arch Degree toward the end to the era.

The 1760 to 1769 English ritual exposures gave the craft the ceremonies as worked by both English Grand Lodges and created popular aides to the memory work for both the Antients and Moderns.

A final observation of all the early manuscripts, both the indisputable Masonic documents and the printed exposures, is that they all have some vital connections, and yet, not one of them is wholly copied from another. In the points that are in agreement, it can only be assumed that their joint origin must be found in an earlier period than the eighteenth century, and that the Third Degree, while written or developed during the same period, was not conferred until sometime between 1723 and 1729.

We have learned the catechetical lectures were the development of the test questions and answers used in the ceremonies of the operative masons. Since there were no early English sources, we have to rely on the manuscripts that were of Scottish origin, although there is no reason to suppose that English practices were different. The manuscripts I have referenced in the present work show there is a basic similarity in all of them which provides us a certain conviction that together they do represent the catechetical part of the operative ceremonies of the seventeenth century.

The test questions and answers were of two kinds: those that relate to the form of communicating the secrets, and those that are informative and explanatory. Candidates were obligated in an ante room, taken out of the lodge room and taught the proper way to enter a Lodge, and then returned to be examined by the Master and given the word. As lodges lost their operative functions and became more speculative in character, additional explanations were brought into the examinations. The literary tastes of the brethren led to these explanations taking on a symbolic and/or moralizing character which, over time, became incorporated into the body of the original workings.

During the first half of the eighteenth century, these explanations were largely worked as table lodges, after the brief ceremony of admission had been completed. The Master in the East put the questions to either his wardens, or in a circular manner to the brethren present at the board. Tobacco and liquor were available, and intervals were filled with charges, toasts and songs. These table lodges persisted well into the nineteenth century.

For the 'Ancients' the lectures were essential and it was one of their complaints against the 'Moderns' that the latter abolished the old custom of studying geometry in the lodge, preferring the use of knife and fork.[99] It has been shown the art of memory was an essential feature of these exercises. As the catechisms grew more lengthy and complicated, memorization became difficult and *aides-memoires* or exposures appeared and these were purchased by the brethren for use in lodge. Some were published by disgruntled Masons, some by non-Masons who got hold of ritual language; all of them were suspect.

We also know the popularity of Prichard's *Masonry Dissected* of 1730 attracted so much attention that Grand Lodge rejoinders and imitations were issued. The new and important information regarding the division of Masonry into three degrees and the legend of Hiram launched into the form which became widely practiced in the fraternity. Then, from 1760 forward a new series of English exposures appeared which incorporated the more symbolic nature of the French exposures of the 1740s and established the beginning point of the lengthy explanations and moralizations of the lecturers that surfaced in the last half of the eighteenth century, which I will address in the next chapter.

Having put together that which has been made available to the present, the precise origin of all the degrees or ceremonies remains one of the great mysteries in Freemasonry. Was there a formally authorized Masonic ritual before 1700? Who would have authorized it? Was the ritual, as described in the exposures, from the pre-Grand Lodge period? Did the English ritual derive from that of the operative mason lodges practicing in Scotland prior to 1700? Or did the Scottish lodges copy their work after the ritual of the old Acception Lodge of the London Trade Company? Did the Acception Lodge perform the mystery plays after the period these were suppressed? Did the French artisans of the Craft guilds bring architectural symbolism to the ritual language? Did the Masons of the transitional period write the Hiram story? What was the influence of the Rosicrucians? Or was there yet another source of origin of the Freemason's ritual? The ancient and honorable Order never ceases to challenge us with questions.

But that is the way of Freemasonry.

8 The English Lecturers and Their Work

Having attempted to cover the development of the ritual language (that which communicated the secrets) of the Degrees of Freemasonry in the preceding chapters, what remains are the lectures. These consist of the charges to the officers and brethren, the lectures on the tracing boards, the symbolism narratives, and the explanations or moralizations.

As previously mentioned, these were initially communicated at table lodges, where the brethren, having concluded the "making" section, would sit around a table in the middle of the lodge room and, under the direction of the Master, take a turn at answering his questions concerning the history, customs, and practices of being a Mason. With the exception of the reciting of the Ancient Charges, the lectures varied greatly, depending on who was present at lodge and the knowledge of the brethren participating. As the literary tastes of the brethren improved, this part of the lodge business took on more importance, eventually leading to lengthy explanations on the symbolic and moral characteristics of the earlier catechisms. The greater part of a lodge meeting was spent moralizing on the principles and tenets of the Order. Indeed, as the catechisms grew more lengthy and complicated, the *aides-memoires* became more popular.

As previously noted, the 1760s era of the Grand Lodge saw a new series of lectures that were much longer than the earlier ones, having been greatly influenced by the Enlightenment fervor sweeping Europe at the time, and, perhaps to a smaller extent, by the French exposures. Some of the earlier material was replaced by questions and answers more descriptive of the lengthened ceremonies and by expanded passages of symbolism and moralization. The ritual exposures published in 1760-62 were widely used by lodges. I have found a collaboration which suggests the Antients Lodges preferred *Three Distinct Knocks* (1760), while the Moderns favorite was *Jachin and Boaz* (1762), which was influenced by the 1745 French exposure, *l'Ordre des Francs-Masons Trahi* (1745).[100] The problem was that the corruptions of language between the exposes' and the actual lodge practices continued to create a perplexing problem for the Grand Lodge. Lodges were learning the work from the purchased exposures rather than from the oral tradition of the lodge instructors. This was exacerbated by the fact there was no adopted work. No single system of lectures of any kind had ever been adopted or officially sanctioned by any Grand Lodge at this time.

The rule was simple. So long as the Master of a lodge observed the "Landmarks of the Craft," he was at liberty to give the lectures in whatever manner best suited the character of his lodge. Of course, the result was that many of the lectures were quite unofficial and without any Masonic authority whatsoever.

It became clear that some regular or sanctioned system of Masonic lectures would be desirable to protect the fraternity from over-zealous innovation.

Fortunately, the Craft was rescued by three brethren who were each interested in the philosophy of Freemasonry, and who each wrote extensively on the subject. Wallace McLeod said these three men, Wellins Calcott, William Preston, and William Hutchinson, wrote longer charges than anyone before them, and for the first time included something for the mind.[101]

It can truly be said that this trio lifted the institution from a fraternity primarily social in nature to a grand moral science, breathing new life into the great ethical principles popularized by the Reformation. Collectively, they framed the only Freemasonry that Masons of the twentieth century have ever known.

So, who were these pioneers and what contributions did they make to the Masonic ritual work?

William Hutchinson

WILLIAM HUTCHINSON

William Hutchinson was born in Durham County, England in 1732 and resided at Bernard Castle. Of all the Masonic writers of the eighteenth century, there was probably no one who did more to elevate the spirit and character of Freemasonry. A solicitor of the Chancery Courts by profession, he had a gift for oratory. He was also a respected author. As a writer of fiction, he had published four works prior to 1772. He was a writer of plays, and is known to have published three tragedies, at least one of which was successfully performed in several of the leading provincial theatres.

Hutchinson then turned his interests to archeology, and distinguished himself by the publication of three county histories. He became a prominent member of the Royal Society of Antiquaries where, again, he published extensively.

But it was as a Masonic writer that he acquired the most lasting reputation. It can be said that he was of one of those classes of men whose life was influenced by the fraternity. He was the Master of Bernard Castle lodge for a number of years, where he was active in instructing brethren, writing lectures and charges, and providing spiritual interpretations of the degrees. His lectures became so popular that brethren would visit from miles around to hear his discourses and instructions. Some of these proved so popular that he was encouraged to publish them in the form of a syllabus.

He applied for permission to publish the same in 1774, and, having received a favorable response from a Grand Lodge that had a stubborn reputation for refusing to grant such liberties, he gave the Masonic world his first edition of *The Spirit of Masonry, In Moral and Elucidatory Lectures.*[102] After the first edition, the latter part of the title was dropped, and the text became thereafter known as *The Spirit of Masonry*. Five editions of the work would be published during his life.

Hutchinson's work opened new thoughts on the symbolism and philosophy of Freemasonry. It was the first efficient attempt to explain in a rational and scientific manner that Masonry had a philosophy. He was perhaps the first to show that Masonry exists for the enlightened mind, that the fraternity is more than merely a convivial association of men, that it is a great school of philosophy, religious in nature, and veiled in allegory–a true "science of morality."

He wrote eloquently of the cardinal virtues of prudence,

temperance, fortitude and justice as emanating from the blazing star in the east and gave a lofty explanation of each virtue. He opined on the meaning of the mosaic pavement as representing the uncertainty of life, "reminding us of the precariousness of our state on earth" and suggesting that all men, in birth and in the grave are on the level; and while we tread on the mosaic pavement we should act as reason prompts us, but live in brotherly love.[103] He wrote of the furniture and jewels of the lodge, the pillars of Solomon's Temple and the meaning of their names. He gave a lecture on geometry which includes language on its moral advantages that is now included in all lodge lectures. He seems to attribute the authorship of this beautiful monitorial lecture in its entirety to Charles Leslie in an appendix that was added to *The Spirit of Masonry.*[104] He penned several charges to Masters and officers at lodge installation that are now a part of our standard monitorial work.

Hutchinson also proved that any Mason is entitled by the laws of the Order to make his own interpretation of the meaning of its lessons. An ardent Christian, he interpreted the Third Degree to represent the new law of Christ, taking the place of Judaism as the true religion.[105] Of course, this interpretation has no official sanction in most Grand Lodges in the world today. It would be as inadmissible Masonic dogma as making a claim that the legend of Hiram is a symbolic allegory representing the story of Isis, Osiris, and Horus. But Hutchinson's example informs us that each man is free to interpret the meanings of our allegories in the way that means the most to him.

William Hutchinson's lectures matched the attitudes and theories of many of his contemporaries, and his enlarged and elevated views of Masonry as a moral and religious science added immeasurably to the Craft's understanding that there was indeed more than meets the eye in the symbolic structure of Masonry. The merit of his work is that he directed attention to the study of the symbols and ceremonies of the Craft. His interest was primarily the religious and spiritual philosophy of Masonry. He was not particularly concerned with its history; rather, his fascination centered on the need to explore and develop the underlying meaning of its legends, allegories and symbols. Dr. Oliver declared that "Dr. Anderson indicated the mine, Calcott opened it, and Hutchinson worked it. In this book [*Spirit of Masonry*], he gives the science its proper value."[106] Perhaps his greatest accomplishment was that he elevated the craft above the status of a drinking club, and inspired them to know that Masonry had a lofty spirituality.

He died April 7, 1814, at the age of eighty-two. His wife survived him two days, and they were buried in the same grave. He clearly was one of the pioneers of the philosophy of Masonry.

Wellins Calcott

Not much is known about the man who wrote and published the first book of Masonic lectures. He was the son of a town councilman of Shrewbury, England. We don't even know when he became a Freemason. Lodge records indicate that he visited a lodge in Edinburgh in 1761, and registered as the "Right Worshipful Master of the lodge at Holywell, Flintshire." He also served as Master of the Lodge of Regularity in London in 1768. But in 1769 he published in London a book titled *A Candid Disquisition of the Principles and Practices of the Most Ancient and Honourable Society of Free and Accepted Masons.*

As was a common practice of the period, he first secured subscribers, making sure that he would be able to cover his expenses. They paid in advance for the privilege of having their name inscribed in the front of the publication. Of course, to do this successfully required that one get on the speaking circuit to gain a good following. Apparently, Calcott was an accomplished speaker. He traveled extensively in England and Scotland, and even promoted his book in America after the London edition was published. One lodge recorded in their minutes that "Brother Calcott's lecture was the best and most informative ever heard in this lodge." His London edition carried 1,164 subscribers, including the Grand Lodge officers, and twenty-three Dukes, Marquesses, Earls, Viscounts, Barons, Baronets, two royal princes, and sixteen members of parliament! Even Edward Gibbons, author of the "Decline and Fall of the Roman Empire", was a subscriber.[107]

Three years later, when Calcott brought out another edition in America, among the subscribers were Robert Livingston, Dr. Samuel Bard (Washington's personal physician), Paul Revere, and Joseph Warren.[108]

In penning his work, Calcott freely borrowed from the Old Charges, Anderson's Book of Constitutions, the earlier Masonic manuscripts, and the published catechisms, so it is not possible in every case to conclude he was the original author of many of the words that are now so familiar to us. But his book does reveal a number of words, passages, and episodes that have not been found in any preceding work, so we can, at least for now, attribute these to him as the original source.

He is apparently the first to include the phrase "moral and social virtue" in the closing prayer. He discusses the story of the Ephraimites and the river Jordon; he speaks of the world of Pythagoras and the Egyptian philosophers, and he points out that, in all ages the right hand has been deemed "the seat of fidelity," which is "sometimes represented by two right hands joined together, or by two little images shaking each other's right hand."

He mentions the custom that is found in the book of Ruth concerning contracts.

In a charge to a lodge, he admonishes the brethren that, at their meetings, they will "hear no disputes concerning religion or politics"..."no other contention but who can work best, who can agree best." Also, "to subdue our passions, and improve in useful knowledge... are principle duties in the lodge." In the same charge, Calcott writes that "Truth is a divine attribute, and the foundation of all Masonic virtues. To be good men and true is part of the first lesson we are taught....hypocrisy and deceit must be banished from us–sincerity and plain dealing complete the harmony of the brethren."

Calcott writes in a charge given at a lodge Feast of St. John in 1765 that "the internal, and not the external qualifications of a man, are what Masonry regards." He goes on to say that Masons should be careful to justify themselves by a behaviour; "to superiors, submissive; to equals, courteous and affable; to inferiors, kind and condescending."

And in a charge to a newly admitted brother, he says that "You are now admitted....a fellow of our most ancient and honourable society; ancient as having subsisted from time immemorial, and honourable, as tending in every particular to render a man so, that will be but conformable to its glorious precepts...The greatest of all ages have been encouragers of the royal art...not thinking it any diminution of their...dignities to level themselves with their brethren..." Calcott further adds, "There are three great heads of duty, which Masons ought always to inculcate, viz. to God, our neighbors, and ourselves. To God, in never mentioning his name but with that reverential awe which becomes a creature to bear to his creator; and to look upon him always as the summum bonum....to our neighbors, in acting upon the square, or doing as we would be done by. To ourselves in avoiding all intemperance's and excesses, whereby we might be led into a behaviour unbecoming our laudable profession."

Calcott's charge as a citizen of the state is equally familiar, and the Mason is exhorted that "he is not to neglect his necessary avocations for the sake of Masonry, nor to involve himself in quarrels with those who through ignorance may speak evil of, or ridicule it." Calcott was also the first to publish a justification for the lodge officers; "Such is the nature of our constitution, that as some must of necessity rule and teach, so others must of course learn to obey."

Finally, the opening prayer of lodges in many Grand Jurisdictions can be attributed (in part) to Brother Wellins Calcott's additions to Pennell's earlier writing. It reads;

> Most Holy and glorious Lord God, thou architect of heaven and earth, who art the giver of all good graces: and hath promised that where two or three are gathered in thy name, thou wilt be in the midst of them: in thy name we assemble and meet together, most humbly beseeching thee to bless us in all our undertakings, to give us thy holy spirit, to enlighten our minds with wisdom and understanding, that we may know and serve thee aright, that all our doings may tend to thy glory, and to the salvation of our souls: And we beseech thee, O Lord God, to bless this our present undertaking, and to grant that this our brother may dedicate his life to thy service, and be a true and faithful brother among us: endue him with divine wisdom, that he may, with the secrets of Masonry, be able to unfold the mysteries of godliness and Christianity.[109]

There is no doubt that we owe a debt of gratitude to Brother Wellins Calcott for perpetuating, by his publication of the *"Candid Disquisition,"* and through his own eloquent phraseology, a significant portion of the lecture language that is in use today. Knoop and Jones thought he was "probably the first writer to endeavor to explain the symbols of the Craft."[110] In a text of only sixty pages, it might be argued whether he was attempting to explain Masonic symbols as much as he was defending the system of symbolism as a whole as being the base of our fraternity and its method of instruction. But a contemporary scholar, Alex Horn, wrote of Calcott; "...the first of his kind he certainly was. His exposition of the design of the Masonic institution, and its social and moral basis; his defense of its principles and practices;

his justification of its habit of secrecy and its use of hieroglyphics and symbolism is for purposes of instruction, and its oaths to sanctify and reinforce our obligations—all this was in a style that was to be very soon followed, almost in a similar vein, by Preston. It succeeded in furnishing a sufficiently firm base upon which Preston was enabled to erect, expand, and develop his superstructure."[111] A century later, Oliver would say, "Calcott opened the mine of Freemasonry." This gentleman of the Ancient Craft has perhaps not received what is rightfully his due for the contributions he provided our noble and glorious fraternity. But Hutchinson and Preston both saw him as the pace-setter for their own work which would be published less than a decade later.

William Preston

It has been said that if you set the right example, you won't have to worry about the rules. To Freemasons, William Preston was one of those remarkable brothers who, by his own example and intellect, changed the culture of Freemasonry. But in the process of doing it, he was expelled by his Grand Lodge, and ostracized by members of his own lodge. His is a remarkable story indeed!

Of the three eighteenth century English luminaries who together gave us the formal structure of the Masonic craft ritual as is known today as the Preston-Webb form, by far the most has been written about Preston. He not only wrote extensively himself, but his biographer, friend, and admirer, Stephen Jones, kept a good diary of William's Masonic career. In addition, a two volume history was written about his lodge, enabling Masonic researchers access to a larger than normal amount of information about his life and times.

Preston was born in Edinburgh, Scotland on July 20, 1742, the second son and only survivor of a successful writer. His father was a Latin and Greek scholar, as well as a recognized poet. Needless to say, special care was devoted to his son's education. William learned Greek and Latin and could recite both by the time he was four. At age six, he had made enough progress in his education that he entered Edinburgh High School, where he excelled in Latin. He went on to College, where he was taught Greek, and so was able to read widely. While there, he caught the attention of Thomas Ruddiman, who was a Grammarian and scholar. Ruddiman was also blind and in need of an assistant. He apparently was impressed enough with Preston that he employed

WILLIAM PRESTON

him for that purpose. Their relationship would last for many years. Ruddiman became William's guardian upon the death of his father in 1751.[112]

After finishing school, Preston was apprenticed to Thomas's brother, Walter, who was a partner in their printing firm in Edinburgh. But he was also hired to read to the blind scholar, which undoubtedly greatly benefited his education. After Ruddiman's death, Preston gathered together much of Thomas's writings and published several of his works. He moved to London in 1760 at the age of eighteen, where, because of his education and credentials, he became employed by Mr. William Strahan, the King's printer. It was at this time that Preston was introduced to Freemasonry.[113]

Preston's natural impulse toward leadership and his independent nature as a Mason was evident from the beginning. He was initiated on April 20, 1763 into a lodge made up of Scottish brethren that had been given a dispensation to meet under the Ancients Grand Lodge (after being told that the Moderns would not permit a lodge to be constituted under the Grand Lodge of Scotland). He was not satisfied with the ways in which the Ancients operated and transferred his membership to another lodge that met in the Talbot Inn on the Strand. He then influenced the other members of his first lodge to do the same, and got the Grand Master to constitute the new lodge under the Grand Lodge of the Moderns. This was an extraordinary feat, considering he had only been a Mason eighteen months!

Once settled, he quickly became infatuated with the Masonic lectures. Brother Stephen Jones said William spared neither pain nor expense in learning about the science. In Preston's biography, Jones wrote:

> Wherever instruction could be acquired, thither he directed his course, and with the advantage of a retentive memory, and an extensive Masonic connection, added to a diligent literary research, he so far succeeded in his purpose as to become a competent Master of the subject. To increase the knowledge he had acquired, he solicited the company and conversation of the most experienced Masons from foreign countries, and in the course of a literary correspondence with the Fraternity at home and abroad, made such progress in the Mysteries of the Art, as to become very useful in the connections he had formed. He has frequently been heard to say that, in the ardour of his inquiries he

> has explored the abodes of poverty and wretchedness, and, when it might have been least expected, acquired very valuable scraps of information. The poor Brother in return, we are assured, had no cause to think his time or talents ill bestowed.[114]

One might say he had a passion for the Craft!

As can well be imagined, Preston did not take a liking to the Masonic lectures as these were communicated to the Brethren of his time. When he was Master of his lodge, he related that he was led:

> to inquire, with a more minute attention, into the contents of our various lectures. The rude and imperfect state in which I found some of them, the difficulties I encountered in my search after others, and the variety of modes established in our assemblies, rather discouraged me in my first attempt: persevering, however, in my design, I continued my pursuit; and with a few zealous friends to the cause, who had carefully preserved what ignorance and the degeneracy of a corrupt age had rejected as unintelligible and absurd, I diligently sought for the ancient and venerable Landmarks of the society.[115]

He managed to get employed by the Grand Secretary in 1769, and held the post of the Secretary's assistant for eight years. This position likely gave him access to much historical information, and perhaps motivated him to an in-depth study of symbolism and Masonic history. Whatever the reason, he determined to produce a much improved and better regulated version of the lectures within the restraints of the Landmarks.

By 1772, Preston completed his first such lecture, which proved to be a lengthy dissertation based on the initiation ceremony, the lodge layout, and the symbolism of the First Degree. His idea was to arrange the lecture in sections so that several people could deliver a portion of it in lodge. He then rehearsed his scheme before the Grand Lodge officers and other prominent brethren at a Gala he designed on May 21, 1772.

It was an occasion.

Preston spared no trouble to make the ceremony as impressive as he could. He styled it *"the "Grand Gala in honour of Free Masonry held at the Crown and Anchor Tavern."* A description of the lodge room is shown in figure 5 and was set out in the First Edition of the *Illustrations.*

Figure 5

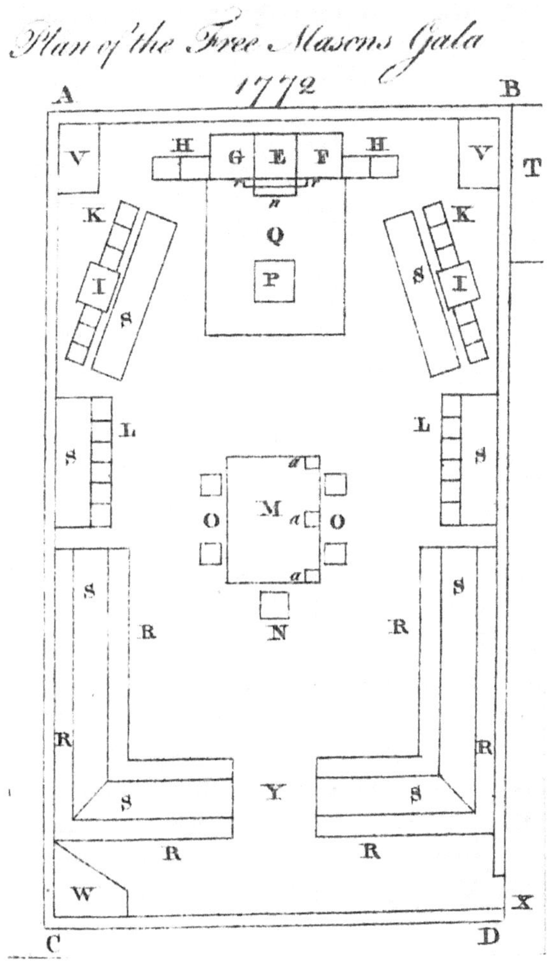

EXPLANATION of the PLAN.

A, B, C, D. The Extent of the Room.
E. The Grand Master on a Throne, elevated 1½ Foot.
F. The Deputy Grand Master.
G. The Past Grand Master.
H. The Past Grand Officers.
I. The Grand Wardens.
K. Respectable Personages.
L. Stewards for the Gala, with white Rods.
M. The Lodge.
N. The Master of the Lodge.
O. The Assistants to the Master of the Lodge.
P. The Pedestal, with the Furniture Regalia, &c. on a crimson Velvet Cushion with Gold Tassels.
Q. A rich Carpet.
r. Two Stands covered with green Baize.
R. Brethren seated in due form.
S. Tables covered with green Baize.
T. Gallery for the Music.
V. Two Side-tables properly furnished.
W. Repository for Wine.
X. Door of the Room.
Y. Grand Entrance for the Procession.
a,a,a. Three great Lights properly elevated.

The Gala plan as set out in Illustrations of Masonry

> Long tables were placed parallel to the north and south walls, with seats along both sides of the boards. An aisle for the grand procession was reserved in the middle of the room. The Grand Master was elevated in the East, with seats for the Deputy, the Past Grand Master, and other Grand Lodge officers to his left and right. Immediately in front of the Grand Master was a "rich carpet" on which stood "the pedestal (altar), with the Furniture, Regalia, Etc., on a crimson velvet cushion with Gold Tassels". Chairs lined both sides of the aisle for the seating of the Grand Wardens and Stewards. The lodge trestle board was placed in the center of the lodge, with the candles in a triangular form about it. The Master and his assistants sat in the West.[116]

To minister to creature comforts, tables were placed in front of the Wardens and principle officers. In the North West corner was placed a *"repository for wine."* A gallery for the musicians was placed at the South East of the room.

The lodge was opened by the Grand Master. The Ancient Charges were read by the Senior Warden, followed by a toast to "the King and the Craft," accompanied by a flourish of horns. Brother Preston then gave his oration, thus laying the foundation for his soon to be published *Illustrations of Masonry*. This was followed by another toast to the Grand Master, with a second flourish of horns. An Ode in three parts was sung, followed by another toast to the Deputy and Grand Wardens. The six sections of the first lecture were then given by Preston, accompanied with songs and duets and instrumental music, followed by another toast to "All Masons, both ancient and young, who govern their passions and bridle their tongue." Preston delivered the Charge on the Behavior of Masons, which was followed by perhaps the most famous of English toasts:

> May the cardinal virtues with the grand principles of Masonry always distinguish us; may we be happy to meet, sorry to part, and happy to meet again.

This was followed by the Entered Apprentice's Song, after which the Grand Master, Robert Edward, 9th Lord Petre, expressed his "great approbation of the regularity of the whole proceedings" and closed the lodge in due form. The party then adjourned for supper, with the evening being capped off with much joy and festivity!

The event and Oration was so well received that Brother Preston printed a summary of its proceedings, along with a brief account of the lecture given, in the First Edition of *Illustrations of Masonry* and published it the same year. He then proceeded to complete the lectures for all three degrees in 1774 under the title of *Private Lectures of Masonry in Twelve Courses* and presented these for a fee as public lectures to the craft at the Mitre Tavern, Fleet Street.[117] Elements of these were published in 1775 in the Second Edition of the *Illustrations* as remarks to the lectures, along with excerpts from them. A third edition was completed in 1781. But again, they were not the lectures themselves. He then issued a pamphlet compiled from his lectures at the Mitre Tavern entitled, *Private Lectures on Masonry by William Preston.* This material was offered from the set of instructions to the brethren who participated in the Lodge of Instruction which Preston organized as a part of the Lodge of Antiquity No. 1. This was the lodge that met at the Mitre Tavern and Preston became acquainted with a number of brethren of the lodge which led to an invitation to join. The workings of the Lodge of Instruction, along with his Chapter of Herodim, became the substance of the subsequent Editions of his *Illustrations.* Preston published *"The Pocket Manual or Freemason's Guide"* in two parts during 1790 and 1792. This work included more information than he had previously published. Still, it was not the lectures.

In fact, William Preston did not publish a complete treatise on his lectures in his lifetime.

Two Other Lecturers of Note

While Preston's first lecture received a kind of official approval from the Grand Lodge, the works of his contemporaries were less favorably treated. Before continuing with Preston's remarkable story, two of his contemporaries should be mentioned in any treatise dealing with the evolution of the craft ritual because their influence was considerable during the era leading up to, and after, the Union of 1813. As we shall see later, they also played a role in the work of the American ritual writer, Thomas Smith Webb, which would come to be known as the American Work. The two were John Browne and William Finch.

In 1798, John Browne published his *Masonic Master-Key through the Three Degrees* in cipher.[118] His work gave only the questions of the catechisms, with some explanation. He elaborated on the four cardinal virtues previously suggested by Preston. Brown's *Key* was successful enough to encourage him to publish a second edition in 1802, enlarging its contents to about four times the size of the first edition. In this edition he also included the answers as well as additional material. His text clearly indicates the globes on top of the pillars represented the terrestrial and celestial spheres. Preston had written of the same as early as 1771, also noting the globes as representing the system of the world as delineated in the lunar and solar nature of the spheres. Brown greatly expands Preston's explanation of the tracing boards or hieroglyphics. His lectures were generally much shorter than Preston's and represented exchanges between the RW Master and Senior Warden. In each, the first section included the ceremony; the later sections, the explanations. They follow the Modern's usage and they are definitely Christian.

Browne's key was much more disjointed than Preston and, since it was not presented in a literary style, it was more difficult to follow. Browne relied upon others for much of his material form. Notwithstanding, the key contained a fairly complete representation of Preston's lectures. Browne's work is noted here because it appeared to be widely used by lodges, and it formed the foundation for much of the English Emulation lectures.

The fuller 1802 edition consisted of one hundred pages, divided into sections, and it is interesting to indicate the number of pages devoted to each degree:

No. of pages		
First Degree Lecture......	pages 1-42...	42
Second Degree Lecture...	pages 43-64...	22
Third Degree Lecture...	pages 65-80...	16
Initiation of Candidate...	pages 81-82...	2
Passing	pages 83-84...	2
Raising	pages 85-86...	2
Origin of Hieroglyphics, etc....	pages 87-99...	12
Master's Charges to Officers......	pages 99-100...	2

It should be noted that the First Degree Lecture consisted of 42 pages;

the Second, 22; and the Third, only 16. This illustrates the great care taken in those days of imparting the fullest instruction to an Entered Apprentice before permitting him to advance to higher grades. Even though the ceremonies are brief compared to Preston's standards, still, there was an emphasis on the idea that Freemasonry was first, and foremost, an initiatory art, and the significant degree was the Entered Apprentice Degree; it being the only true degree of initiation.

There is some Preston in Emulation, but there is much more from Browne that is not found in Preston. However, his work is not as significant as Preston when tracing the lineage that resulted in the prevalent American workings; thus he is not a central originator of the American ritual tree.

A curious parallel exists between William Finch and William Preston. Finch was also a prolific author of lectures and, like Preston, made a trade out of Masonry. He published books, certificates, jewels, lodge paraphernalia, etc. He was not liked by the Grand lodge because his fundamental contention was that the "Lectures, Makings, Passings, Raisings, etc., according to the Ancient York System, is the only true method of working."[119] In 1801, he published *A Masonic Key* which appeared the next year under the name of *A Masonic Treatise.* Because of its mystical content, the Grand Lodge condemned it and he promised not to publish it again, choosing instead to issue it in manuscript form.

Like Brown's work, Finch's treatise was in cipher. The lectures are divided into sections. The first section of the First Lecture is very close to Browne's *Master-Key* with some Preston added which Finch acknowledged. The second section is also very much Brown and ends with the restoration to light. The third section, however, is very different from Browne. The EA's duties are as in Preston. Most of section five appears to be Finch's own composition, though 'Brotherly Love, Relief and Truth' are taken from Preston. The 'Two Great Pillars' are from Browne. With the exception of 'Temperance', the cardinal virtues are original. The Second Lecture includes a recapitulation of the opening and the ceremony of "passing."

The second section includes the steps and their explanation. In fact, Finch appears to be the first ritual writer to place the human senses, orders of architecture and liberal arts upon a fifteen step staircase. The winding stairs had been in the ritual working from the beginning, but, before Finch, the stairs seem to be confined to seven (or more) steps.

Finch has a staircase of three, five, and seven steps. It is thought Webb borrowed this part of the Middle Chamber lecture from Finch because Webb did not reference the steps with this specific division in his own editions of his Monitor until after Finch's work has been published.

Of the Five Orders of Architecture, only the Doric seems to be borrowed from Preston. The details of the 'five senses' are from Preston. Much of Finch's lecture of the liberal arts and sciences is unusual, that on geometry dealing with Newton and Herschel and having a long discussion on the sun. The account of Jephtha follows Preston and Browne, but the battle is fought "in a field of standing corn and by a falling cascade." The remaining sections refer to the traditional history, the tools, ornaments of the MM's lodge, and explanations of the building and furniture of KS's Temple, ark of the covenant, etc., and all come from workings in the north of England styled the 'Lodge of Lights.' Thomas Webb may have expanded on Finch's Third Section explanations of the covering of a lodge, the three pillars, the three theological virtues, the furniture, and the rough and perfect ashlars (which Finch expanded from Prichard's *Masonry Dissected.*)

Fifteen editions of the *Masonic Treatise* had been published by 1815, indicating that Finch's work was also much used by lodges. With the approach of the Union and the Modern's Grand Lodge action to revert from the Ancient Landmarks, he published, in 1806, his *Lectures on Freemasonry,* covering the three Degrees, one set for the Moderns, another for the Ancients. In 1810, he added *A New Set of lectures,* which were no longer in catechetical form, but were descriptions of the three degree ceremonies. Next, he published *Prestonian and Ancient York Lectures,* which he claimed included 'everything that is valuable to the whole system.' Lastly, in 1816, he published *The Origin of Free Masons* which included the new Union system under the Grand Mastership of the Duke of Sussex. Certain elements of this work, including the obligations, are exactly the same as those in the exposure, *Jachin and Boaz.*

There is not much original in any of Finch's lectures, although much of what is contained in them is found in modern English workings because of the pure volume of publications he produced. Never liked by the Grand Lodge, he primarily deserves praise for what might otherwise have been lost to the workings in the north and west regions of England. He died in 1816.

Preston's Credibility Takes a Hit

Resuming now with Preston's Masonic career, shortly after the publication of his First Edition, along with additional work on the lectures, Preston's fame and position of respect within the Masonic community greatly increased. He was known throughout all Masonic circles. He attended Lodges of Instruction regularly to promote his system of lectures. He was elected to the chair of Master in several lodges, and his popularity finally led him to the Lodge of Antiquity.

The Lodge of Antiquity was the oldest lodge under the English Constitutions. We do not know when it was organized, but it was working prior to 1700. It owns a copy of the Old Charges, dated 1686. It is believed to have been formed about 1680. It was the first of the four London Lodges to organize the Premier Grand Lodge in 1717 and therefore had no warrant or constitution. It was a *time immemorial* lodge. It was known by at least two other names before it settled on the seemingly appropriate title of the Lodge of Antiquity in 1768.

At that time the lodge was in bad shape. Few members were joining and many of the older members had resigned. When Preston came onto the scene, it had fewer than twenty members. The same Master held the position for three-and-a-half years, (1771 to 1774) and seldom were there more than seven in attendance at the meetings. It very much resembled many of our lodges of today. The old lodge simply had no energy left upon which to light a flame of renewal.

But a couple of enterprising fellows (namely one John Noorthouck, the Senior Warden; and John Bottomley, a Past Master) determined that if they could get brother Preston to join, he might just be able to get the lodge back on its feet. Preston had in fact visited the lodge on one occasion to deliver his lectures, but he was not present on June 1, 1774, when he was elected to membership. It was the following meeting of June 15th that Preston made his first appearance as a member of the Lodge of Antiquity. And he was elected Master that night![120]

Preston's authority and responsibility over the lodge achieved the desired effects. He threw himself into the work, using every advantage that he felt was in keeping with the regulations of a lodge that was 'immemorial' but under the English Constitutions. His efforts quickly paid off. He brought a number of new members into the lodge. He put young, enthusiastic brethren in officer positions, and, by 1776, the lodge had forty-eight members and the average attendance had grown to thirty. These new brethren became great admirers of Preston, and many of them regularly attended the Lodge of Instruction he directed in which the Craft degrees and their lectures were routinely rehearsed. This is not surprising since Preston made sure to sell to all new Masons made in the lodge copies of his *Illustrations* as part of their fee for initiation.

Unfortunately, this is not what Noorthouck and Bottomley had in mind. They and a few of the older members were content with the lodge in its old ways. They were proud of its history and traditions, wanted more members, but did not want to relinquish their influence over the lodge. They wanted more members and no change. When their discontent finally developed into an attack upon Brother Preston, Noorthouck filed a complaint with Grand Lodge, which read in part:

> Brother Preston after being not only admitted but honour'd with the Master's Chair crowded in such a Succession of young Masons, as totally transferred all the power of the Lodge to him and his new acquaintance, and enabled him to keep possession of the Master's Chair for three years and a half–During this time Bro. Preston kept up private Weekly meetings of these young Brethren, under the name of a Lodge of Instruction, in which meetings, he occasionally as you memorialists have been inform'd propagated notions of peculiar original powers residing in their Lodge, exempt from the authority of the Grand Lodge.[121]

Of course, Noorthouck failed to point out that Bottomley had served as Master for the three-and-a-half years immediately preceding Preston, at which time the lodge didn't do anything! Neither did he admit that during the entire time Preston presided over the Lodge of Instruction, he not once attended a session. His whole contention was based wholly on hearsay. It was evident that Preston's knowledge of Masonry and powers of memory caused more than a slight jealousy among Noothouck and his friends.

It wasn't long before there was a dissension within and without the lodge that was seeking a place for release. It occurred on St. John's Day, December 27, 1777. Preston and his lodge attended a church service that was being preached by the lodge Chaplain. They had put on their Masonic regalia in the Vestry and sat together in the same pew. It was only a few steps from the church to the lodge quarters at the Mitre

Tavern, so after the service the members decided to walk across the street to the lodge without removing their Masonic clothing. Preston reasoned that the lodge's business for the day was not yet ended since the lodge had not been closed, so he decided that the brethren could simply return as representatives of the lodge, without any formal procession as Masons.

While Noorthouck and Bottomly weren't present, their allies alleged that Preston's proceedings constituted a public procession of Masons in their clothing. Noorthouck filed a formal complaint with the Lodge, alleging that Preston was responsible for the irregularity.[122]

Preston then made an unfortunate political error. He argued that the Lodge of Antiquity was an immemorial lodge (having existed prior to Grand Lodge), and therefore the lodge had an inherent right to decide such matters for itself. It was empowered by inherent privileges vested in the fraternity at large. It was not subject to any edicts of a Grand Lodge!

Noorthouck and his friends immediately filed a complaint with Grand Lodge concerning the conduct and attitude of Preston.

PRESTON EXPELLED

Needless to say, Preston was dealt with harshly. After all, under Masonic Jurisprudence, one does not attempt to champion the cause of lodge rights. The only prerogatives a lodge has are those granted it by the Grand Lodge. In the eighteenth century, it didn't matter how old a lodge was--once it came under the English constitutions–it was under a higher set of rules. The Grand Lodge simply could not permit this kind of thinking in the ranks, and they demanded that Preston sign a formal document stating that he was sorry and that he would never in future promulgate or propagate a doctrine of inherent right, privilege, or pre-eminence in Lodge No. 1.

The Committee on Charity (the name given the Grand Lodge Board of General Purposes at that time) didn't stop there. They also ordered the lodge books be turned over to them so any inappropriate "records" could be expunged. Preston refused to give them the books, and then expelled the members of his lodge who were causing all his grief, including, of course, Brother Noorthouck!

That added insult to injury. Noorthouck filed another complaint, and now Preston was out of favor with not only some members of his own lodge, but with his Grand Lodge as well. As a show of authority by the Grand Lodge, Noorthouck was immediately reinstated to the Lodge of Antiquity. In response to that action, Preston called a meeting of the lodge on November 18, 1778, and caused a resolution to be passed removing the Lodge of Antiquity from membership in the Grand Lodge. He published the resolution as a manifesto, and mailed it to all the other lodges. That proved to be too serious an act of insubordination.

On January 29, 1779, he and his supporters were expelled from Masonry.[123]

Preston, not to be outdone, continued to meet with his lodge, refusing to give up the lodge's property, even at the demands of the Grand Lodge, and also refused to admit Noorthouck and his followers. Noorthouck was forced to organize another Lodge of Antiquity at another location, and Preston petitioned the Grand Lodge of all England, south of York, for recognition, which was granted![124] This caused an extraordinary situation. There were two Lodges of Antiquity, each recognized by a separate Grand Lodge.

The tension and divided sentiments that arose from the long and remarkable battle leading up to this point, and in events which followed, finally took its toll on both Preston and his rival, Noorthouck. In 1780, Preston had had enough. He quit attending his lodge, and finally resigned the following year. Noorthouck left his lodge in 1784, scarred with a reputation as a trouble-maker, a man hungry for power, and too driven by jealousy to truly serve the interests of his brethren. With both men removed, a reunion of both lodges ultimately became possible.

As for Preston, even at the most hopeless hour of his Masonic career, despite the harsh treatment given by his Grand Lodge, his devotion to the ideals of Masonry remained uncompromised. He wrote:

> To the institution of Masonry, I shall ever bear a warm and unfeigned attachment. I know its true value and I am convinced of its utility. To the Society of Free Masons I profess myself a true and steadfast friend.[125]

Fortunately, in 1786, Preston was invited to rejoin his old lodge. It had relocated to Freemason's Hall in London in 1782, and the "other" lodge he had created was finally abolished to resolve the problem of recognition.

Always a popular man among the craft, at the second meeting he attended after being reinstated there were seven petitions for new members. The lodge continued to grow, and his lectures were resumed. By 1789, all his past troubles had been forgotten. He was reinstated to membership in the Grand Lodge, and he even paid a visit to his old enemy, Brother Noorthouck, who, by then, had also returned to the rolls of membership. Both pledged to forever leave their differences behind them and work for the good of Masonry. Thus came to an end the long period of unrest in the Lodge of Antiquity.

Preston's Contribution to the Masonic Lectures

By the time Preston had been expelled by the Grand Lodge, his system of Masonic Lectures was too well known and popular to be discarded. No other lecturer had achieved such a high level of scholarship or perfection. His schools of instruction were well attended, and much of the memory work being used in the lodges was clearly the result of his system.

Consequently, even as an expelled Mason, Preston and his friends continued to meet and study. To avoid political trouble by working the lectures from without the fraternity, he devised a new scheme: the creation of an organization restricted to Masons and based on the working of his lecture system. This organization was named the Chapter of Harodim, and it met weekly from October to April. It had no authority to confer degrees, but it could work the ceremonies and lectures. By 1788, his system was developed to a point that he published another edition of the *Illustrations.* A number of influential members of regular lodges became interested in the new Order, which probably contributed to his reinstatement in 1789.

The numerous editions of the *Illustrations* have enabled researchers to trace the development of Preston's ideas regarding the three Degrees. He kept adding material as he printed subsequent editions, and his elucidations became so popular and useful in explaining the principles of Freemasonry that lodges came to believe his work to be as indispensable as the V.S.L. and the Book of Constitutions. The working of his lectures was so popular, in fact, that it created a need for an *aide-memoire,* which, as previously mentioned, he published as *"Pocket Manuals"* in 1790 and 1792, covering the First and Second degrees respectively. These were styled *Pocket Manual; or, Freemasons' Guide to the Science of Freemasonry.* They proved too difficult for the beginner to follow and were expanded and improved again in 1796 as *"Syllabus Books,"* or *"Books of the Courses."* Initially, these were catechetical and included only the questions, as he expected the lecturers to know the answers (although later printings had the answers). These were published in cipher, and were intended to be distributed privately only to members of the Lodge of Instruction or the Herodim. But after the Union of 1813, a *Syllabus* book for the Third Degree was produced and changes were made in all the lectures to accommodate the ritual workings adopted after the Union. By 1830 these had been published in a manner that was intended to reach the mainstream of Masonic ritual workers. Preston's *Syllabus* became the lectures that established the Masonic ritual system as we know it today.

Preston's contribution to our ritual practices is remarkable in that he did not seem to have derived much of his material from previous authors of catechisms. He did not use the same turn of phrase as a previous author; that is, he did not simply copy an older work. Of course, we must keep in mind that all lectures of this period were likenesses of older works since they were all based on the same traditional material of the ceremonies. It is true that he collected as well as wrote, but he molded the compositions to his own liking, and the results are clearly almost out of the main line of descent as we can trace them from the earlier exposures. He had a passion for systemizing these earlier works into a kind of logical and progressive sequence. His purpose seemed always to be an endeavor to correct, refine and amplify the old workings, combining the lectures, addresses, charges and eulogies into a complete system according to his method. He was in every sense an individualist–a pioneer in his own right.

His lectures in each degree are divided into sections representing the main divisions of the subject of each degree; six for the first degree, four for the second degree, and twelve for the third, together with an introduction and conclusion to each section. Each section was subdivided into clauses, and the brothers who learned these were called *Clause-holders.*[126] A Brother who had mastered all Sections of a lecture was known as a *Lecturer.*[127] C.W. Firebrace, editor of the *Records of the Lodge of Antiquity,* believed that Preston, as lecturer, asked the questions, with the officers and brethren of the lodge, as clause-holders, giving the answers.[128] As we have seen, this was the traditional form of ritual instruction in lodges from the operative days.

Some Examples from the Syllabus

There were a number of versions of the Preston *Syllabus* which were printed in manuscript form and privately owned. There is no set version because the lectures came from the actual Lodge of Instruction meetings. Preston intended it to be a course in Masonic Education, and he welcomed the knowledge of those who participated, and may have actually requested that they contribute to its development over time. He never claimed to be the sole author. In fact, it is almost certain that the leading lodge brethren of the Chapter of Harodim contributed significantly to the variations found in the different versions of the *Syllabus*. Preston himself stated that he had help from 'zealous friends.' Brother James suggested these included H.J. da Costa, Meyrick, Burckhardt, Laurence Thompson and Stephen Jones, all of whom took leading parts both the Chapter of Harodim and the Lodge of Antiquity's Lodge of Instruction.[129]

Unlike his early schools of instruction in which he charged a fee, there is no proof that Preston actually received any personal remuneration from the *Syllabus* lectures, so the usual incentive to 'claim' them did not exist. It can be said that Preston understood the ideal that Masonry is a progressive science which thrives upon its own dialogue, and he hoped that, by providing lodge brethren with a vehicle for instruction, it would continuously evolve in form and function.

To illustrate the catechetical form used in the lectures and the information presented in the various Sections to the degrees, several of the clauses are presented here from the First Degree. Again, there is no one version that is more accurate than any other. The lectures presented in the Syllabus versions covered a period from about 1795 to 1836.[130] This represents one of the most important periods in the development of the Masonic ritual (especially the English form, as this was the period of the union of the two English Grand Lodges and the era when the ritual was being formalized in the new United States). The clauses have been arbitrarily selected only to give the reader an idea of the content of each, and/or to show the close similarities to the degree workings of today. These are instructive not only for showing language links to our current ritual form, but in sharing with the reader some of Preston's remarkable philosophical insights in the symbols and themes introduced in the Craft degrees.

Preston included a general section in his *Syllabus* which explained the language for opening and closing the lodge, a short section (the first clause) describing the ground plan of Masonry, a discussion of the regularity of a lodge, salutations from the Master and Wardens, and an explanation of secrecy. These are not included here because they have either previously been outlined, or will be summarized in further sections.

He then outlined the Initiation ceremony, describing the questions asked of a candidate in his preparation to become a Mason, along with the reasons for the elements and peculiar arrangement of dress for the candidate. An explanation was given as to how the candidate is received, how he is managed about the lodge, the instruction on the steps, and the position of obligating. He explains the process of the ceremonies after the obligation, including the vesting of the words and grips, the apron presentation, the ceremony at the northeast corner, and the Apprentice charge. In addition, there are another twelve clauses in the First Degree lecture, all in catechetical form. Much of this information is found in the lecture sections practiced in most American lodges today.

We begin with a beautiful and profoundly symbolic opening instruction in the Entered Apprentice Degree:[131]

FIRST DEGREE
SECTION 1

> Masonry is an art useful and extensive. In every art there is a mystery, which requires a progress of study and application before we can arrive at any degree of perfection. Without much instruction and more exercise, no man can be skillful in any art; in like manner, without an assiduous application to the various subjects treated in the different lectures of Masonry, no person can be sufficiently acquainted with the true value of the instruction...

CLAUSE 1

What is the ground plan of Masonry?

Instruction.

Why is instruction the ground plan?

Because no man living is too wise to learn.

What will a wise man do?

He will diligently seek knowledge.

What will a Mason do?

He will do more, he will travel to find it.

Whence come you?

From the furthest extremity of the west.

Wither do you travel?

To the furthest extremity of the east.

What is the object of your travel?

To seek the Master that through him I may acquire knowledge.

Why may you not be disappointed?

There is always the stimulus that I never can be disappointed.

Why do you expect to find a Master in the east?

Because it ever has been, still continues to be and always shall be the situation of the Master when he acts in that capacity.

Why is instruction delivered from the east?

To commemorate three Grand Events:

First, that man, in the image of his Master compounded of matter and spirit was formed in the east.

Second, when spirit and matter had begun to act in unison and man gradually advanced to maturity, it was in the east that the first rudiments of knowledge and learning were impressed on the juvenile mind.

Third, when man had arrived at the state of virility and strength, to adorn the work of the Creator, it was in the east that arts and sciences embellished the Tree of Life.

Who are entitled to learn those instructions?

All men who have a desire to gain it and abilities to improve.

Who are better entitled?

Those who have been selected from the community at large and rank in the character of Masons.

Why are they better entitled?

Because other men may gain knowledge, it is true, by chance or accident, but Masons are let into the path to gain it and, if they fail, can never gain preferment in the Art.

Who are best entitled?

Free and Accepted Masons.

Why?

Because all the knowledge they have acquired they will cultivate and improve to the best advantage, and when they have so done they will not indiscriminately scatter it but prudently dispense it for the general good.

On this basis is the Ground Plan of our Masonic System established!

The First Section also contains a Clause II, which explains how a Mason is known and how he makes himself known to other Masons; and the signs, tokens and perfect points of entrance. Clause III discusses the regularity of a lodge; a Clause IV explains the friendly salutations from the three principle officers; and a Clause V describes the virtue of secrecy.

Section II of the Syllabus consists of six clauses, all relating to the initiation ceremony. Clause I describes the ceremony of preparation.

FIRST DEGREE
SECTION II
CLAUSE I

What preparation is necessary for Masonry?

A two-fold preparation, internal and external.

Where does the first preparation take place?

In the heart?

How is this exemplified?

In the assent given to the declaration before we were initiated.

What is that declaration?

That unbiased by friendly and uninfluenced by sinister motives we voluntarily offer ourselves as candidates for Masonry, that we were solely prompted to this measure by a favourable opinion conceived of the Institution; a desire of knowledge and a wish to become useful to mankind; that we were willing and ready to conform to all the ancient usages and customs which are established amongst Masons.

Where does the next preparation take place?

In a room adjoining the Lodge.

By whom are we prepared?

By a friend we afterwards know to be a Mason.

How are we prepared?

Deprived of all metal, h********d, s******d and otherwise properly prepared by having the r***** a** and l*** k*** bare.

Why so prepared?

For various reasons which we are ever ready to explain when

called for.

Why deprived of metal?

For three reasons; first reason, that no weapon be introduced into the Lodge to disturb the harmony; second reason, that metal, though of value, could have no influence in our initiation; third reason, that after our initiation metal could make no distinction amongst Masons, the Order being founded on peace, virtue and friendship.

Why h********d?

For three reasons; first reason, that in case of a refusal to pass through the forms and ceremonies of initiation we might not be able to discover the forms used amongst Masons; second reason, that the heart may be able to conceal before the eyes may be permitted to discover; third reason, that as we are first received into Masonry in darkness we may have the rest of the world in that state respecting our forms until they are legally gained.

Why s*******?

Because the ground we are about to tread is holy.

What rendered that ground holy?

The Name of God impressed on it, Who has declared--where my Name is there I am--and therefore it must be holy.

To what does this allude?

To a custom observed in the east of throwing off the sandals from the feet when they enter the Holy Temple.

To what does it farther allude?

To a circumstance mentioned in Holy Writing, that when the angel of the Lord appeared to Moses in the burning bush a voice was heard to utter this word--slip thy shoes from off thy feet for the ground upon which you tread is holy. What God commands must be obeyed.

Why otherwise properly prepared by having the r**** a** and l*** k*** bare?

To evince the naked truth and to show that in genuine Masonry there can be no deception.

Thus we define and illustrate the ceremony of preparation for admission into the lights of our venerable Institution.

The remaining Clauses of Section II relate to how the candidate is received, how he is managed about the lodge, the instruction on the steps, and the position of obligating. A few of these Clauses follow in order to give the reader a better understanding of the similarities and connections with our present work.

FIRST DEGREE
SECTION II
CLAUSE II

Having been prepared in the manner described where were you conducted?

To the entrance of the lodge.

How were you able to discover this?

By first meeting resistance and afterwards gaining admission.

By whom was your entrance opposed?

By the Outer Guard or Tyler of the Lodge.

What is his duty?

To keep off listeners and intruders and to see that the Candidates for the Order have been properly prepared.

How did you gain admission?

By three distinct knocks.

To what do they allude?

To an old adage inserted in the Scriptures--seek and you shall find, ask and you shall have, knock and it shall be opened to you.

How do you apply that adage?

You had sought in your mind; determined, you asked a friend; he, knowing in what manner to act, knocked and the door of Masonry was opened.

Who came to your assistance?

The Inner Guard or the representative of the J.W.

What is his duty?

To commune only with the Outer Guard.

What does he demand?

Who comes here?

What is the answer?

A poor blind Candidate for Masonry, worthy amongst men, well recommended to Masons, regularly approved in the Lodge, properly prepared, comes of his own free will, humbly to solicit, not to demand, the secrets and privileges of the First Degree of the Order.

What is then asked?

How he expected to obtain these secrets and privileges.

What is the answer?

Not from any vain merit he possessed but by the help of God and the tongue of good report.

What is then done?

He was then commanded to halt in his present situation till his intentions and approach should have been made known to the Master and his sanction obtained.

"Here we wait with patience the issue of the Master's decision."

FIRST DEGREE
SECTION II
CLAUSE III

How are you first received in a Mason's Lodge?

With a c******* around the neck and the point of a sharp instrument presented to the n**** l*** b*****.

Why so received?

Three reasons are assigned for this mode of reception: first reason, to show that we are exposed to double danger should our then present conduct deviate from our past declaration, for should we advance we might be in danger of being stabbed, or should we retreat we might have been strangled; second reason, to prove courage and fortitude of the heart; third reason, to impress on the mind we were about to enter on what was serious, solemn and awful.

How were you then disposed of?

Conducted to the J.W.

What does the J.W. demand?

Who comes here.

What was the reply?

A poor Candidate for Masonry who, having been duly proposed and approved in open Lodge, properly prepared by a Bro., now comes by his own free will accord to solicit, not to demand, the privileges of Masonry.

What ensues?

Conducted to the S.W.

What does the S.W. demand?

The same as the J.W.

What was the reply?

The same as to the J.W.

What was next done?

Conducted to the portals of the Lodge and there instructed to kneel.

Repeat the Invocation.

Vouchsafe Thine aid Almighty Father of the Universe, to this our present convention and grant that this Candidate for Masonry may dedicate and devote his life to Thy service and become a true and faithful Bro. amongst us. Endue him with a competence of Thy divine wisdom that by the secrets of this Art he may be better enabled to display the beauties of godliness to the honour of Thy Holy Name. Amen.

The Invocation being ended what question is asked?

In whom on the approach of danger can you most safely rely?

What is the answer?

In God.

What is then said?

If your confidence be in God, perilous as your situation may be with a c******* round your neck and the p*** of a s**** i****** at your breast, you may safely arise, follow your leader and fear no danger. Under the care of this kind Conductor we may safely rely for protection and defence.

Then we come to the fourth Clause of Section II which is repeated here because it provides a good example of how the lecture was used to inculcate Masonic education. Preston was adept at developing expanded descriptions of many of the individual, and more concise, phrases that the candidate encountered in the initiation ceremony.

FIRST DEGREE
SECTION II
CLAUSE IV

How were you then disposed of?

I was introduced into the body of the Lodge.

How did you appear?

Neither naked nor clothed, bare foot nor shod, but in a humble posture he moves and halts alternately.

Why so appear?

Three reasons are assigned for his appearance in this manner: first reason, that he may represent for a time a seeming scene of poverty and distress; second reason, that he may never forget the particular manner in which he was first received amongst Masons; third reason, that should he ever discover a Mason reduced by necessity to the same situation in which he appears from choice, the kindness which he then received may be extended to that Bro., pity flow from his breast and relief without prejudice accompany the feelings of his heart.

How was he then conducted?

He was led up to the north, traversed the east, passed the south and in the west was delivered over to the S.W. in due form as a fit object for Masonry.

Why so conducted?

That all the Brn. from the north, south, east and west may be invited to witness that he comes freely to be initiated into the Order, that he was properly prepared and is the real person who had been previously proposed as a fit object of Masonry.

Who are fit objects for Masonry?

Free men, upright in stature, without visible maim or defect, of mature age, sound judgment and strict morals.

Why are the privileges of Masonry restricted to free men?

That the vicious habits which are prevalent among slaves, may never taint the true principles of freedom on which Masonry is founded.

Why to men upright in stature and without maim?

That the rectitude of the person may agree with the integrity of the mind and the external figure add consequence to the Fraternity. That all may equally share the labour and no one encroach on the privileges of the Order.

Why to men of mature age?

That they may judge and determine with propriety in every measure which respects the general good.

Why to men of sound judgment and strict morals?

That they may discriminate the value of the Masonic Institution and enforce by example and precept a due observance of its rules.

"Thus we demonstrate the proprieties of our introduction within the body of the Lodge and point out the proper objects who are entitled to a participation of our privileges."

Section II, Clause VI gives an excellent description of the reasons why the candidate is arranged in a peculiar way when he is about to take the obligations of Masonry:

FIRST DEGREE
SECTION II
CLAUSE VI

Did the Master receive him in Masonry?

He did, in due form.

Describe that form.

K*** on the l. k. bare, the body erect within the square, the r. h. voluntarily laid on the holy law, the left either supporting the law or holding the cs. in the form of a sq. with one pt extended to the n l. b.

Why k****?

As a mark of humility and reverence to the great Author of his being, whose aid he was then about to invoke.

Why on the l. k?

Because the l. k. amongst Masons is deemed the weaker and less noble joint. In reference to the first degree of the order, into which we must first enter, and which ranks inferior to the most advanced degrees.

What moral do we draw from this part of the ceremony?

That though in weakness we begin, by perseverance we shall strengthen.

Why body erect with the sq?

To remind us that being obligated within the square, we are afterwards bound to act upon it.

What moral do we deduce from this part of the ceremony?

A strict observance of the golden rule: Do unto others as you would wish they should do unto you.

Why r h on the holy law?

That we may ratify our conformity to that law by the most sacred pledge the r. h.

Why the l h supporting that law?

Because it is our duty to uphold and maintain the law which is to be the guide of our conduct.

Why are the cs supported at our own n l. b?

Because the l b is nearest to the heart, which is the most valuable part of a man and ought to be properly guarded.

What moral do we derive from this part of the ceremony?

That what is then a seeming pain to the b, a violation of the law renders a lasting pain to the mind.

In this form what was he about to do?

He was about to enter into the solemn engagement of an

entered apprentice Mason.
Of how many parts does it consist?
Of three parts.
The first part?
That we shall not unlawfully disclose the secrets of Masonry by speech.
The second part?
That we shall not disclose the secrets of Masonry by writing?
The third part?
The penalty we shall incur by a violation of our engagement. Not less than the loss of life by having the t c, the t t up b t r, and b with the body in the s of the s.
Why so dreadful a penalty?
That the secrets of the order may be preserved inviolated.
Why should they be preserved inviolated?
Because we are to regard them as keys to our privileges, and estimating their value from their utility, prize them as sacred.(At this point the Obligation or Engagement would be repeated.)

Thus we exemplify the tenor of our engagements, with which we close the ceremony of initiation into our mysteries.

The third Section, Clauses I thru III explain the process of the ceremonies after the obligation; including the investment of the words and grips, and the apron presentation. Clause II is given here; again, for illustrative purposes.).

FIRST DEGREE
SECTION III
CLAUSE II

Being raised what information was conveyed to you?
That Masonry was a universal system.
What further information was given?
That it was formed on the purest principles of morality, founded on allegory and explained by Holy Symbols.
What were you ordered to do?
To advance one step.
Of what did the next information consist?
That there were three essential points in Masonry:
The first point?

That there are several Degrees in the Order and particular secrets restricted to each Degree.

The second point?

That these particular secrets are not indiscriminately given but regularly conferred according to merit and ability.

The third point?

That there are many mysteries amongst Masons which relate to their mode of government and these can only be acquired by a regular attendance on the duties of the Lodge.

What was then entrusted to your care?

The particular secrets of the First Degree or those marks by which Masons are known to each other and distinguished from the rest of the world.

What is the first secret?

The due guard of and E.A.M.

Give the sign--Done.

To what does it allude?

To the penalty of the obligation.

What does it imply?

That as a man of honour I would sooner have my t***** c** than betray my trust.

What is the second secret?

The token or grip of an E.A.M.

Give the grip--Done.

What is the use of this grip or token?

To distinguish Masons in the darkness as well as in the clearest day.

What is the third secret?

The word of an E.A.M.

Give the word--Done.

Give the word by letter and begin--by syllables--at length.

Done in a treble way and then a treble salute.

What advantages are derived from these secrets?

Courtesy and esteem from Masons wherever we meet them.

"Thus we illustrate the manner in which our invaluable secrets are communicated and the advantages to which possessions of them are entitled."

Clauses IV and V explain the ceremony of the N.E. corner, and describe what ultimately became the basis for the Entered Apprentice "Charge".

FIRST DEGREE
SECTION III
CLAUSE IV

Entrusted and invested in the manner described what is his proper situation in the Lodge?

At the north-east corner of the Lodge or at the right hand of the Master.

Why is he so placed?

That he may tread sure and obey the commands of the Master.

Why does he tread sure at the north-east corner rather than at any other part of the lodge?

Because there he treads on the foundation stone of the building.

To what does it allude?

To an established custom of laying the foundation stone of all capital buildings at the north-east corner.

What advantages are to be derived from this custom?

When the ravages of time or violence may have destroyed every vestige of the superstructure that stone, when it is discovered, will prove that such a building did exist, announce the names of the Founders and the purposes for which it had been erected.

How do we apply this in Masonry?

That when amidst the depravity of manners the influence of example may tend to subvert the principles of virtue which had been sown there might ward off the danger of infection, prevent the operation of the poison and preserve the mind uncontaminated amidst the general wreck of polished manners.

In what form does he appear?

With his feet formed into a square, body and eyes on the Master.

What recommendation does he then receive?

That as he then stood to all appearances before God and the Lodge a just and upright man and Mason so to maintain that character through life.

What next ensues?

The principle of charity, its beauties, excellencies, &c., are displayed.

What was your reply?

That I readily would assist whenever I had the power to do so.

What did the Master further observe?

That when from that spot I departed I should be resolved on and particular in maintaining through life my Masonic character.

"Here we close the ceremony of initiation with a lasting impression of our important tenet which alone dignities our character and conduct."

FIRST DEGREE
MASTER'S CLAUSE
SECTION III
CLAUSE V

What recommendations are given?

The recommendations given to support the character of an upright man and Mason are three particular recommendations and one general recommendation.

What is the first recommendation?

To study the Volume of the Sacred Law.

How should it be studied?

By considering it as the dictates of an unerring Being and the standard of truth and justice; and viewing it as the proper regulator of our conduct.

What is the second recommendation?

To practice the three moral duties; to God, our neighbor and to ourselves.

Explain the first duty.

That in the character of Masons we are taught to hold peculiar awe and veneration the Sacred Name of the Deity; to implore His aid in all our laudable pursuits; and to supplicate His protection in all our well-meant endeavours.

Explain the second duty?

In our acting on the square: to consider our neighbor equally entitled with ourselves to share the blessings of Heaven and to render unto him such friendly offices as we in similar situations should expect to receive.

Explain the third duty.

By it we are taught to use, but never to abuse, the bounties of Providence; not to impair the faculties by irregularities nor degrade the profession by intemperance.

What is the third recommendation?

That we should always conform to the government of the country in which we live; obey the laws which afford us protection; but never lose our attachment to the place of our nativity or the place we first drew breath in; nor the allegiance that is due to the patrons and protectors of that spot in our absence.

What is the general recommendation?

To practice benevolence and charity.

Why?

Because they have distinguished Masons in every age and country.

How is this exemplified?

In the power of sympathy which warms the heart with true philanthropy and inclines us to soothe affliction and alleviate pain.

What is the result?

That we listen to complaints with attention, bewail misfortunes and relieve the distressed.

"Thus we are instructed to support the dignity of our station as Masons and to maintain our real importance in life throughout the world."

There are six Clauses in Section IV and six Clauses in Section V of Preston's First Degree lecture. These discuss, in catechetical form, what is found in the third section lecture as practiced by most lodges today.

Another interesting feature of the Preston lectures is that he wrote GRAND MORALS at the end of several of the sections in his *Syllabus*. These applied to various elements of the lectures; such as the physical attributes of Solomon's Temple, the furnishings of the Lodge, the symbolism of the lodge building, and the four cardinal virtues. For example, in explaining the symbolism of the Lodge building, he compared it to the walls of Solomon's Temple. In the first degree, section IV, Clause IV, we find the following:

How were the walls constructed?

Of well-chosen material formed by nature, improved by arts and strengthened by everlasting cement.

Why were the walls so constructed?

That they may better resist the storm and tempest and alike ensure protection and defence.

What is the GRAND MORAL?

From the construction of our walls we deduce this moral: that men who are born free, improved by culture and strengthened by social union, will always be able to repel the hostile attacks of invasion, blunt arrow of affliction and stand the torrent of oppression.

"Thus we define the proper situation of the Masonic building and the protection we derive from the durability of its construction."

Then, in the same section, Clause V, he discussed the significance of the "covering of the lodge" in another moral.

What is the Grand Moral?

From the covering, then, we deduce the following moral: that when we fix our eyes on the celestial firmament and contemplate the beauties which are there displayed, we behold wisdom to contrive, strength to support and grace to adorn the handiwork of the Creator in the construction of this canopy.

"Thus we delineate the beauties of our splendid covering and confirm established truth in the Order, that neither from the eyes nor from the mind of the deserving Mason can the wonderful works of the Great Creator be obscured."

Preston also tied the Points of Entrance to the Four Cardinal Virtues in the sixth Section of the First Degree. This wonderful connection is worth repeating here because it is not found in most of the American workings.

FIRST DEGREE
SECTION VI
CLAUSE III

What impression does Masonry make on the mind?

Honour, fidelity and attachment to regulate his conduct in the general commerce of society.

How many principle points impress this on our memory?

Four.

Name them.

Gutteral, pectoral, manual and pedal.

Explain them.

The gutteral is intended to remind us of the dire effects of the breach of fidelity in reference to the penalty of the obligation. The pectoral is intended to shield the breast, which is the repository of our secrets, with the fence of honour against insidious attacks and refers to the compasses presented to the n**** b*****. The manual is intended to remind us of that truth and sincerity which are to guide our conduct in conformity to God's Law and refers to the right hand voluntarily laid on that Law as a pledge of our attachment. The pedal is intended to remind us of the path we are to pursue in the journey of life and refers to our position at the north-east corner of the Lodge and the recommendation which is there given.

To what do they allude?

To the four cardinal virtues.

Name them.

Temperance, Fortitude, Prudence and Justice.

Explain temperance.

By this virtue we govern our passions and check our unruly desires. The health of the body and dignity of the mind are equally concerned in its observance.

How is this applied to Masonry?

To the guttural point it applies for vicious habits and irregular indulgences might throw us off our guard and by a breach of fidelity subject us to the penalty of the obligation to which that point more immediately refers.

Explain fortitude.

By fortitude we are taught to resist temptation and encounter danger with spirit and resolution, alike distinct from rashness and cowardice. When possessed of this virtue we are seldom shaken and never overthrown by the storms which surround us.

How is this applied in Masonry?

To the pectoral point it alludes, for true courage can only centre in the breast where our treasure is lodged and from which cabinet our secrets can never be extorted without that lasting pain to the mind which the pectoral point so strongly inculcates.

Explain prudence.

By prudence we are taught to regulate our conduct by the rule of right reason, judge and determine with propriety in every measure which respects the general good. This virtue therefore, constitutes the best jewel that can adorn the human frame.

How is this applied in Masonry?

To the manual point it applies, for where can prudence be more properly exercised than when we pledge conformity to a solemn vow with the right hand which ought never to seal what the heart is not inclined to perform?

Explain justice.

By this virtue we render to every man his due without distinction. It is not only consistent with divine and moral law but it is the standard and cement of civil society. Without justice universal confusion would ensue, lawless force would overcome equity and social intercourse no longer exist.

How is this applied in Masonry?

To the pedal point it applies, for when placed at the north-east corner of the Lodge, resting secure on the foundation stone of the building, that virtue is warmly recommended in the prosecution of our journey through life to secure the esteem and merit the approbation of men.

"Thus we illustrate the means which the wise founders of the Art have adopted to inculcate a lasting impression of our tenets and enable them to maintain the character of true and faithful amongst Masons."

Then, in the next Clause, Preston gives a most significant explanation of the tenet of equality as was meant to be applied in a Masonic context.

FIRST DEGREE
SECTION VI
CLAUSE IV

What are the privileges of a Mason?

Free entrance into the Lodge and the benefit of fellowship there.

How do Masons rank?

As brothers to Kings, fellows to princes, regardless of situations or circumstances.

Why?

Because we are considered as members of the same family, children of the same Parent and brethren by the same tie.

What advantages are there?

In the Lodge a uniformity of opinion prevails and strengthens the ties of friendship and equally promotes regard and esteem.

ILLUSTRATE THEM.

Swayed by this principle a King when present is reminded that although the crown may adorn his head and the scepter the hand, the blood that circulates in the veins is derived from the common Parent of mankind and is no better than the blood that circulates in the veins of the meanest subject. The most polished statesman, the most distinguished orator and the most skilful artist are, in the Lodge, reminded that equally with others less favoured by Providence they are exposed to similar dangers and misfortunes; that an unforeseen accident or a disordered frame may impair their faculties and level them with the most abject of their species. This, therefore, checks pride and softens austerity of manners. Men in lower stations, feeling the advantages of this equality are encouraged in the Lodge to look up to their superiors and claim from them the benefits of confraternity. When they view before them the most exalted characters, divested of external pomp and blending their talents in the same school, bereft of partiality and prejudice, to accomplish the general good, veneration and esteem rivet the chain of attachment and the hearts of high and low are united in the bonds of true friendship. Virtue is true nobility and wisdom is the channel by which virtue is conveyed and directed. Virtue is, then, the prize at which we grasp; each rank vies to excel and he who is wisest and most virtuous in his station will ever by entitled to eminence and distinction amongst us.

"If these are the privileges which we enjoy as Masons how necessary it is to support the dignity of character from whence such benefits are derived."

It is easy to see there is much for the mind in Preston's *Syllabus* books. The GRAND MORALS remain among the most eloquent of all the statements penned for Masonry. Every Mason would gain if these were regularly included in the Lodge workings of today. Preston was first and foremost a teacher of the virtues of Masonry. He was an adept at developing expanded descriptions of many of the individual and more concise moral points the candidate encounters in the ritual ceremonies of the lodge.

Other Preston contributions include the origin of the Charge in the Fellowcraft degree, and the Charge after the Master Mason degree. While the First Degree Charge appears in his *Illustrations,*

Preston claims it to have been originally printed in 1769 independently (Calcott).[132] He also authored much of what is known today as the "Middle Chamber Lecture." He penned the lecture explaining the difference between operative and speculative Masonry. He authored the lecture on Architecture and the five Orders, which made its first appearance in the second, or 1775 edition of his *Illustrations;* and while almost certainly taking it from someone else's work of the classical system of the period, probably that of the Roman architect and philosopher, Vitruvius, he appears to have invented that part relating to the three oldest (Tuscan, Doric, an Ionic). It is likely his discussion of order in architecture (which appears in almost all Webb monitors) was borrowed from Isaac Ware's *A Complete Body of Architecture,* published in 1756. His explanation on Architecture was taken from a French architectural work entitled *Cours d'Architecture,* by Augustin Charles D'Aviler, which had a Paris edition in 1760.[133] He also devised the lecture on the five human senses, the seven liberal arts, as well as that on the globes, and the beautiful oration on Geometry.

His prayer at closing adds to the language penned by Calcott, and is now almost universally used in lodge ceremonies:

> "May the blessings of heaven rest upon us, and all regular Masons! May brotherly love prevail, and every moral and social virtue cement us! So mote it be."

Preston seems to be responsible for the questions asked every candidate previous to initiation, and he modified Calcott's work in the Entered Apprentice Charge. He also wrote much of the ritual used in lodge officer initiation, including the questions asked the Master, the explanation of the jewels attributed to the several offices, and the charges to the officers.

His 'Remarks on the First Lecture' concludes with a section familiar to all present day Masons—a dissertation on Brotherly Love, Relief, and Truth—which parallels our present monitorial language. "By the exercise of Brotherly Love," Preston said, "we are taught to regard the whole human species as one family, the high and low, the rich and poor; who, as children of the same parent, and inhabitants of the same planet, are to aid, support, and protect each other. On this principle Masonry unites men of every country, sect, and opinion; and conciliates true friendship among those who might otherwise have remained at a perpetual distance." His musing on 'Relief' reinforces Anderson's First Charge. Continuing with Preston; "Relief is the next tenet of the profession, and... a duty incumbent on all men, it is more particularly so on Masons, who are linked together by an indissoluble chain of sincere affection....Truth is a divine attribute, and the foundation of every virtue. To be good and true is the first lesson we are taught in Masonry. On this theme we contemplate, and by its dictates endeavor to regulate our conduct; influenced by this principle, hypocrisy and deceit are unknown in the lodge; sincerity and plain-dealing distinguish us; while the heart and tongue join in promoting the general welfare, and rejoicing in each other's prosperity."

His beautiful explanation of the globes or spheres that is often given in our stair lecture of the Second Degree, Preston penned as a footnote to his lecture on Geometry. Of the spheres, Preston wrote; "Their principle use, besides serving as maps to distinguish the outward parts of the earth and the situation of the fixed stars, is to illustrate and explain the phenomena arising from the annual revolution and the diurnal rotation of the earth around its own axis. They are the noblest instruments for giving us the most distinct ideas of any problem or proposition, as well as enabling us to solve it. Contemplating these bodies, we are inspired with a due diligence and attention to astronomy, geography, navigation, and all the arts dependent upon them, by which society has been so much benefited."

Finally, Brother Preston wrote much of the language that is used in the laying of cornerstones, dedication of Masonic Halls, and the burial service for a deceased brother. It is obvious that there is really little of what we know of the lectures today that were not in some way influenced by this pioneer of Masonic work.

Preston's later years were devoted almost entirely to the history of the Lodge of Antiquity of which he served for so many years. His last recorded attendance was on January 17, 1816. One of the great questions which perplex Masonic historians to this day is why he was not invited to participate in the Lodge of Promulgation (1809-1811) or the Lodge of Reconciliation (1813-16). These two Bodies were organized to resolve the ritual differences between the two Grand Lodges (Ancients and Moderns). Preston did not need to be present for his influence to be felt. While not appointed as a representative, his ritual system likely formed the basis of the changes made by the Lodge of Promulgation. First, the Duke of Sussex was Master of Preston's Lodge of Antiquity at the time. He and other members of this Lodge served as representatives for the premier Grand Lodge, which had an interest in bringing the practices of the Ancients into the Grand Lodge workings. It was an Antiquity Lodge member (Charles Bonnor) who was asked to articulate the ancient workings before the Promulgation. Those ancient workings were the craft system of William Preston.

Second, the compiler of the Preston workings in written form, H.J. da Costa, was asked by the Duke of Sussex to present the same at the Lodge of Promulgation. da Costa had earlier joined with Preston in compiling the *Syllabus Books*, and added the alterations made by the Lodge of Promulgation to later editions of the *Syllabus*. In fact, Preston made revisions in his own work as a result of the Promulgation. Thus, Preston was intimately involved with the 1809-1813 Union period.

However, his work was not sustained. Between 1813 and 1830, in spite of the Union of Grand Lodges and the work of the Lodge of Reconciliation to provide ritual forms for the new United Grand Lodge, the craft ultimately went a different direction (see Chapter 13), resulting in a ritual lineage that stayed in England; and another that journeyed to America.

In 1813, he made his Will, and left equal amounts of money to the Masonic Girl's School and the General Charity Fund of the Grand Lodge. He also created an endowment, founding the "Prestonian Lectureship" to perpetuate the Masonic education of the Craft.[134] A provision called for the delivery, once a year, of one of his original Lodge of Antiquity lectures. These were delivered in succession until 1862, when the lectures lapsed for a period of some sixty years. When the lecture series was re-instituted by Quatuor Coronati Lodge in 1924, it no longer called for one of Preston's lectures. Since then, the Prestonian Lecture has been given annually on a Masonic topic of the lecturer's choosing.

After an illness of nearly five years, he passed away at his residence on April 1, 1818.

There are few who left as rich a Masonic heritage. There are few who have displayed more zeal for our institution. And there are few indeed who have left a mark of scholarship on our noble fraternity equal to that of William Preston. He was, to a large degree, the *mind* of

Freemasonry. To him, the primary purpose of Masonry was to diffuse light and spread knowledge among men. To him, Freemasonry was an intellectual system, and its keyword was knowledge.

As the great American Masonic writer, Albert Pike, so eloquently said:

> that our influences shall survive us, and be living forces when we are in our graves; and not merely that our names shall be remembered; but rather that our works shall be read, our acts spoken of, our names recollected and mentioned, when we are dead, as evidences that those influences live and rule, sway and control some portion of mankind and of the world,–this is the aspiration of the human soul.[135]

9 The American Experience

When English, Scottish, and Irish Freemasons migrated to the American colonies, they carried their Masonry with them. Little did they realize the remarkable influence the fraternity would have on shaping the personal, social, and political relationships in their new environs. To appreciate just how Freemasonry earned this place of respect in eighteenth century America, it is necessary to understand something about the society which comprised the colonies during this period of rapid development and change.

The men and women came to America's shores during the seventeenth and early part of the eighteenth centuries for many reasons. Some came for gold; some for adventure, some for glory. Many came to chart a new course of religious freedom. Still others came to escape the degradation and hopelessness that had been their occupational lot in the mother country. Many others were farmers who came to acquire cheap or free land. In fact, most came for the very personal motive of carving out a new life and living for themselves and their families.

And with few exceptions, the emigrants to the new world were almost obsessed with a new ideal of freedom. This was especially true of the English. After all, they had already transformed their own monarchy in the last two centuries. They had executed one king and deposed another. The English Parliament had conclusively established its supremacy over the king. The English had written charters, penned bills of rights, regularized meetings of their parliaments, and even created a new line of hereditary succession. They had provided for citizen representation in the affairs of their government, and created a constitution especially dedicated to liberty.[136]

Everywhere in the colonies, people of every social rank, of every faith, and every political persuasion, could not celebrate their freedom enough. Of course, each group had different ideas about the kind of liberty that was proper for a "free English man", but the colonists collectively envisioned their life experience as a new opportunity for independence such as the world had never seen. Theirs would be a proper society, with allegiances more toward their own paternal and newly established family (rather than a Royal family), and driven by the common good.

A new breath of freedom was in the air. In fact, it had been a long time in coming. Things had not been good in England since the fifteenth century. At the same time the Puritans were settling in Jamestown, there were riots in the mother country, caused by forced and restricted farming policies. The farmer could not work his own land without allotments. It was even worse for the tenant who had no hereditary rights to ownership. Rents were high, and wages for farm laborers were kept very low. A worker earned no more in the reign of James I than he had a century earlier in the days of Henry VIII. Jobs were scarce and poverty ran high in the urban centers. The tales of an exotic land across the sea stirred the imagination of almost every adventurous spirit.

And the English government solidly promoted the idea. The scarcity of land and the spread of unemployment created the notion that England was overpopulated. It was also cleverly considered by the nobility that this new land across the Atlantic would provide a convenient dumping ground for the vagrant classes who had been a long standing burden to the English upper and middle class. Besides, there was much to be gained. If the working classes could be shipped to the colonies, they would in turn produce the raw materials needed at home, and, at the same time, reduce England's surplus of manufacturers. The merchant capitalists saw a new economic opportunity with emigration. Imagine building an empire of nation-states, controlled by private interests! It was enough to make the greedy mercantilist's mouth water.

Surely, it could be seen that his pursuit of profit in colonial projects was actually more of an investment in England's new territory; one that was serving the broader interests of the national welfare!

Of course, all this made little difference to the colonist. Up until the middle 1770s, it was typical for the emigrant to think of the mother country with great affection. He still thought of himself as a displaced Englishman. He was content to seize on whatever new opportunity would be his for making the perilous Atlantic crossing. He was satisfied to simply transplant the political institutions he had known so well at home, and use the old models to structure his new life. The typical colonist came from a rural area or small village. In his new home, he wanted to know his local officials on a first name basis. He expected to know the churchwardens who ran his parish, and who gave relief to the poor. He would be acquainted with the county justices and other local governmental authorities.

Sure, the American colonist brought with him certain concepts of constitutional government and civil liberties. But he wasn't looking for a new structure–he wanted one that would simply be an improvement over the faults of the older established system. He wanted to be "a free English man", who could raise a family, practice his faith, perhaps leave an inheritance, and participate in the overall good of the new society in which he lived.

His passion was with his God and his family. If the monarchy, the parliament, the church, and the English patronage system had not interfered with his life, it would have been a paradise on earth.

Indeed, until the turn of the century, the family was the basic model for both political and social relationships. To the colonists, much of their society was organized around the family. The family was the center of all rights and obligations. Almost everyone spent some time in his life living in an extended household. And everyone in the household was dependent on the will of the father.

The new world was ripe for the cultivation and growth of the fraternity.

The household, and hence, patriarchy, may even have been stronger in America than in England because of the weaknesses of other institutions, such as the guilds. The home was where most of the work was done, and where most of the education and training took place. The family became the primary vehicle for educating and training the young, disciplining the wayward, and caring for the old, the destitute, and the infirm. Family relationships determined the nature of most people's lives. Everywhere, families reached out and blended into the larger community.

Although the provinces were ultimately destined to become one interrelated complex of economic associations, during the century and a half of colonial birth and early growth, agriculture was the essential mark of the civilization. In 1760, ninety percent of colonial America's 1.7 million people relied on the land for their living. With the family, land was the other important basis of life during the early part of the eighteenth century. The economies of the colonies were very underdeveloped, with farming and the production of staples being the principal occupation of men. Two-thirds of the white colonial population owned land. There were no large banks, no trading companies, no centers for finance and business. The colonists imported far more than they exported. The colonial economic ties were still very much with England, but personal services between families residing within close proximity to each other was the glue that would bind them together in colonial unity. It became a significant factor in furthering the separation between the mother country and her child.

In reality, most economic exchanges in the colonies had to be personal, and were primarily between people who knew each other. By necessity, then, people depended on the honesty, integrity, and charity of their neighbors and business partners for their own livelihood. Farmers, merchants, craftsmen, and shopkeepers all relied on relationships with those they knew. And no relationship was exclusive. Each was relative, reciprocal, and complementary. For instance, it was not unusual for a merchant to have his ledger sheets listed with the names of those with whom he did business–a different sheet for each client. In many respects, even his business became an extension of his personal life. In some ways, the debts people owed each other became the social bond that linked them together. It was a remarkably domestic arrangement, where people paid little attention to how much profit they made at any given point in time. The relationship was the important factor governing the morals of the day.

In a word, the colonists valued, above all things, friendship. The idea of being a friend, making friends, and protecting one's reputation to the extent that it was always worthy of another's friendship, was central to how people behaved.

Privacy simply did not exist. The society was at a scale very similar to that of the very small rural communities of our own time. It was everybody's business to keep track of what his neighbor was up to. People simply interfered in other people's business, and accepted it as an inherent right.

And because people noticed everything, personal reputations meant a great deal. A man could go a long way just on what other people thought of him. One's good name was as precious as life itself. If you wanted to really get somewhere, you had to pay attention to the church you attended, the clothes you wore, the people you made contact with on the street, your behavior in dealing with those you had business connections with. Your good name was everything. And when it was brought in question, you were quick to seek legal remedy. The court records of the period are full of actions for slander and defamation of character. To call someone a liar, or to claim the products he made were inferior, was a serious criminal or civil offense.

Such concerns may seem trivial in our time, but the protection of one's personal and family reputation was serious business to the colonist. The actions of people were of much greater significance than the events of the day. People were not so much interested in what happened, or how it happened, as they were in who did it. All actions were taken by individuals who were known, or could be identified. And they were to be held personally accountable for what they did.[137]

This personal accountability was significant in both business and government. If prices on goods changed, specific persons were blamed. If one had a transaction involving the local courts, a customs collector, or a legislator, that magistrate was known by name. The relationship was always an intimate one. It was likely you had already wined and dined with him, attended church with him, played cards with him, and socialized with him on a personal level. No activity of government was significant enough that it could not be dealt with by some leading individual.

Likewise, there was no particular separation between public and private matters. People used public funds for private business, and private funds were regularly used to take care of public concerns. Governments existed primarily for the purpose of enlisting private persons to carry out public ends. If streets needed cleaned or paved, public works departments were not created to take care of the need; instead an ordinance was drawn to require each person or business abutting the street to clean or repair it. If a community wanted a college, it did not build it and run it; it enlisted private individuals to build and run it themselves, and granted them legal rights to do so. Almost every public action depended on private energy and funds.[138] Even criminal defendants who were acquitted were required to pay the costs of their trials![139]

Government was viewed as a process of delegating responsibility to the individual, rather than taking care of the needs of its constituency in everyone's behalf. In fact, in the 1700s, everyone in the society had an obligation to help govern the colony in accordance with his own social rank. Important offices were only to be held by the most worthy; those who had already achieved economic success. Only the gentlemen of leisure were expected to provide leadership. This is why Brother Benjamin Franklin retired at age forty-one. He wanted to become a gentleman, and he knew he could not do it as one employed in a daily occupation![140]

Of course, the fact that only men of wealth were expected to be engaged in the leadership of the colonies meant that families with names and influence controlled much of the focus of progress. In actuality, this created too much of a threat that another aristocracy would be created in America, simply replacing that which existed in Europe. Ultimately, this concern over inequality in leadership became one of the principle issues over which the Revolution was fought.

But, nonetheless, the early social structure of the colonies, being one based largely on patriarchy and patronage, enabled men and their sons to be connected together in a mutually dependent and beneficial way. The awesome burden of preserving one's personal reputation and his social ties to the colony created an environment in which Freemasonry could thrive.

Republicanism and Enlightenment Values

There were other value systems at work that contributed to the popularity of Freemasonry. By the middle of the eighteenth century, the old patriarchy and patronage systems began to erode. Anything suggesting hierarchy and the old ties to monarchy became very suspect. Republicanism evolved as the ideology of the Enlightenment. And

America seemed ready for it. There was no ironhanded established church forcing its will on the people. If England had thirty churches, the colonies had hundreds. There was no titled nobility. No bishops, no earls, no dukes, no priests, no deacons, no kings. No great distinction of wealth, and no large segment of the population sunk in poverty.

Everywhere, men looked to the classical virtues for their concept of how they should live, what their relationship should be to the family, the state, and to other individuals.

And to find it, they sought out the models offered by the ancient republic of Rome. Every educated man had read the writings of Cicero. Tacitus, Virgil, Plutarch, and Cato. The ancient ideas of leadership and public morality and values became the archetype of the Western culture. Men were expected to participate in government, to be disinterested toward their private wants, and to demand more of themselves morally for their country. The best men were to be selected to lead–men with spotless character and integrity. The hope of the country rested on virtuous men. By placing the most disinterested in public office would minimize the threat of tyranny. Only when rulers were virtuous could common people place their trust in them. Only then could a society openly establish a bill of rights, execute contracts, write charters, develop public institutions, and protect the rights of individuals.[141]

By the middle of the century, yet another phenomena had created an impact that contributed largely to a declaration of independence, and that was the rapid movement of people. In the forty year period from 1750 to 1790, the colonies grew from one million people to four million.[142] Emigrants poured in by the thousands, uprooting long established families and creating crowded urban centers. The surging population forced men and families inland from the seaboard communities. New towns were established overnight. Sons left their homes because they were too young for an inheritance, and began to look westward in pursuit of their own opportunities. The growth and movement of people broke apart families, churches, and entire communities. Continual migration eroded the connection to family, and scattered them everywhere. Each move made the next one easier.[143]

But, the population explosion, coupled with its equal impact on trade, resulted in a country literally liberated from itself. If there were any ties to England and the old monarchy during the mid 1700s, these were surely gone by 1780.

Established religion also felt the burdens of growth. The rapid change in population broke down the traditional hierarchies and the old, established church authorities. The old patterns, the high style, and the luxury of the Anglican Church became suspect as the religious model of a free people. Protestantism began to flourish. Methodists, Baptists, and Presbyterians attracted more and more new converts. Religion was in upheaval. No single religious denomination was ever able to control all thirteen Colonies. Although predominantly protestant, the religious groups were fragmented. In 1776, only twenty percent were Church of England; at least double that number belonged to the various Calvinistic denominations (the Congregationalists, Puritans, Presbyterians, and Dutch and German Reformed Groups). The other colonists were Quakers, Lutherans, Baptists, and Methodists. There were also about 55,000 Catholics and 2,000 Jews.

It is interesting to note that, although the Protestant sects had come to America to seek religious independence for themselves, it never occurred to them to be tolerant of others. The Puritans, for instance, wanted to purify the Church of England by scraping its prayer book, changing its ritual, and strictly observing the Sabbath. They wanted a national Church. The state should pay the preacher's salaries. There would be no separation of church and state. The ministers would interpret the scriptures, and the judges would apply these opinions as divine law. If a dissenter, such as a Baptist or Quaker, didn't conform, he could either move on, or be hanged! The Congregationalists, on the other hand, wanted each church to be self-governing, with the congregation selecting its own minister. Rhode Island disfranchised Catholics and denied Jews the right of naturalization. Maryland was established to be a refuge only for Catholics. In Massachusetts, voting was confined only to members of the Puritan Church, and freedom of speech was denied to opponents. In many respects, religious liberty was only that liberty to think or act within the covenant between God and man–as interpreted by the Puritans.

It would take another century before the ideal of religious toleration would come to fruition. The Great Awakening, as it was called, also swept the colonies at this time. This evangelical movement was the result of people trying to adjust to too rapid social, economic, and demographic change. Their lives were unsettled, and the long established practices of religion were no longer able to meet their emotional needs. The "stump" preacher, with a gift of oratory, could attract a sizeable crowd with a hellfire-and-brimstone revolt against rationalism. While many were enraptured with the squeals, the swoons, and the appeal of the revivalist, just as many others were repelled, creating an even greater division among the faithful.

There was yet another movement that came to America in the form of the scientific, intellectual and philosophical community. It was termed the Enlightenment. The enlightenment population looked for a different means of explaining the world. The revivalists promoting rationalism became a major force, moving people even farther away from established church authority. People were taught to trust only in their "self-examination" as to the nature of Deity, and to think for themselves in matters of faith, as if "there was not another human creature on earth." Contrary to the Puritan view that God was the stern God of the Old Testament, in the enlightened age, God could not be absolute and arbitrary. It was no longer accepted that the church could entreat men to believe anything without being convinced that what they believed was right. The New Testament ideal of brotherly love replaced the absolutism of the Old Testament Jehovah.

Brotherhood and fraternity were mutually agreeable ends. And Freemasonry suddenly became important.

Freemasonry offered enlightenment ideals. Its teachings were optimistic, forward-looking, and convincing. Virtue could be taught, and the enlightenment leaders saw the fraternity as a school for good-reasoned men. Moral education could be provided through its various rituals. To the enlightened mind, republican attitudes meant changing the culture of society.

And changing the culture meant spreading light and knowledge. What better arena existed for achieving this end than the local lodge?

Could it be possible that "pushing back the darkness" could be successfully managed through this global association of men? Freemasonry offered a vehicle for the free exchange of ideas. If enlightenment was to be found in understanding nature, then discussions in the natural sciences would be on the agenda. If others saw enlightenment in religion, then Freemasonry taught religious toleration, and the elimination of superstition. If still others thought it occurred in politics, then Freemasonry could be the driving force in pronouncing against tyranny and creating free governments.

Of course, Freemasonry blended so well with the time because it was itself an enlightenment institution–and always had been. To Freemasons and republicans, enlightenment was, above all else, a matter of personal and social morality. It was the way that men and women treated each other, their children, their dependents, even their property.

The eighteenth century revolutionary ideal was that people were here to be benevolent toward each other. A gentle society required that its component parts be gentle. Conversations were polite, manners were gracious, and courtesies toward one's fellow man added up to human happiness. To be a gentleman was to think and act like a gentleman. It implied being reasonable, controlling one's passions, being tolerant in all things, and, above all, being virtuous, honest, and sincere in one's dealings with others. It meant being free of prejudices and parochialism–having a larger view of humanity and human affairs–standing on elevated ground.

It meant having a liberal arts education. To have a liberal arts education was to display the marks of an eighteenth century gentleman, and to yearn to become a classical hero in every sense. No generation in American history has ever been so self-conscious about moral and social values.

Is it no wonder that Freemasonry was at the center of the universe? One acquainted with the rituals and lectures of Freemasonry cannot help but see the enlightenment influence in almost every breath and turn. In fact, even our Masonic obligations are satiated with enlightenment tenets.

To the republican spirit, a man's values needed a seal. And oath-taking became the adopted practice of sealing one's vows of fidelity and loyalty to man and country. Late eighteenth century artists were always painting oath-taking scenes. Everybody in the public sector was administering oaths. It was a solemn business, indeed.

But it had a more profound purpose. The oath was a social bond that a man made with the larger society. It was the mechanism whereby people could attach themselves to one another and to the state. It was effective, emotional, and natural. It represented the love and benevolence that men felt toward each other. Again, it was a republican classical virtue, modified to reflect the new era of tying virtue to a person's relationship with his society.

The Masonic lodge became a focal point of demonstrating this new form of social politeness; men of good morals mingling together and sharing experiences, creating affection and fellow feelings; one to the other. Through its connectedness with men, Freemasonry formed a chain of confidence and friendship that transcended all social and economic differences between them, and their states, and the world.

Its success then, and now, depends on this ability to relate to strangers, to see in them their humanity, and to strive to establish an extended brotherhood in the world.

Gordon S. Wood, in his Pulitzer Prize winning, "The Radicalism of the American Revolution", stated it boldly and openly:

> It would be difficult to exaggerate the importance of Masonry for the American Revolution. It not only created national icons that are still with us; it brought people together in new ways and helped fulfill the republican dream of reorganizing social relationships. For thousands of Americans, it was a major means by which they participated directly in the Enlightenment....it transformed the social landscape of the early Republic.[144]

> Masonry was looking for the lowest common denominator of unity and harmony in a society increasingly diverse and fragmented. It became the 'Center of Union and the means of conciliating friendship among men that might otherwise have remained at perpetual distance.' That strangers, removed from their families and neighbors, could come together in such brotherly love seemed a vindication of the enlightened hope that the force of love might indeed be made to flow outward from the self. A Mason found himself 'belonging, not to one particular place only, but to places without number, and in almost every quarter of the globe; to whom, by a kind of universal language, he can make himself known--and from whom he can, if in distress, be sure to receive relief and protection.' This was the enlightened cosmopolitan dream.[145]

10 The Provincial Grand Lodge System in America

As stated earlier, Freemasonry came to America's shores with the migration of Masons seeking settlement in the Colonies. There is no way of knowing exactly when lodges were first organized, or where; although it is generally recognized that a fellow named John Skene, who was made a Mason in Aberdeen, Scotland in 1682 and migrated to Burlington, New Jersey the following year, is the first known Mason in America.[146] A fellow named Jonathan Belcher is given the distinction of being the first native-born Freemason in what is now the United States. Born in Boston in 1681, he graduated from Harvard in 1699 and is believed to have been made a Mason around 1704 on a visit to London.[147]

Skene, and other sojourning Masons, established lodges wherever "two or three were gathered", without authority, warrant, or sanction from a Grand Lodge--because there was no Grand Lodge in the late seventeenth Century period. They simply formed "occasional lodges" under immemorial rights, met together as Masonic brothers, and "made" Masons using the simple ceremonies they knew at that time.

Like their English brothers, the Colonial Masons usually met at their favorite drinking establishment–the tavern. As can well be imagined, it was among the earliest of colonial institutions, following close upon the settlement of most places. Again, taverns served a recognized need which provided food and drink for the traveler, and in many instances, sleeping quarters for the night or week (it was illegal for strangers to be brought into homes in many villages). Licenses were required, and were immediately granted. In fact, by 1647 the number of applicants for license to keep taverns was so great that the General Court (District Court) required that this function be handled at the county level so as "this court may not be thereby hindered in their more weighty affairs."

Names like the White Horse, Green Dragon, Bunch of Grapes, the Royal Exchange; all figured as prominent landmarks of Masonry in Boston, which became the birthplace of "Regular" Freemasonry in America.

It happened with all the formality required of the premier Grand Lodge, but it was really just a formality. The fact is there were several lodges in Boston before any formal warrant was issued, the earliest indirect record being a lodge that met at King's Chapel in the early 1720s. The record is cloudy on this particular lodge, but there's an interesting story that it met in the King's Chapel, which was an Episcopal Church (Church of England) in Boston. The newly established Church of New England (Puritan) was in a fight with the older denomination because the Puritans did not want the Church of England in the colonies. They also protested the introduction and establishment of Freemasonry because they thought it was being sponsored by the Episcopal clergy to attract more men to that faith. The lodge ceased to exist, but the Episcopal Church managed to erect three churches in Boston in spite of the public opposition.

The formal method of becoming regularly chartered was by the sanction of an English Provincial Grand Master. Provincial Grand Lodges had been in existence in England since 1726.[148] These were created to give the lodges in the English Provinces a Grand Lodge officer who could help organize and coordinate the Masonic festival days. However, with the extraordinary increase in the Craft during the 1720's, and with so many Masons migrating to other countries and forming irregular lodges of their own, the premier Grand Lodge found it was necessary to create the office of Provincial Grand Master so there would be a 'Head' to whom the sojourning Masons might apply for the purpose of organizing their lodges in a proper manner.

The Provincial Grand Master was in reality merely the Grand Master's Deputy. He derived all his authority from the Grand Master himself, and not from the lodges that might comprise his Provincial Grand Lodge.[149] He was appointed for the convenience of administering the affairs of the Grand Lodge of England in much the same manner that District Deputy Grand Masters are appointed today.

The Provincial Grand Lodge had no authority other than that which was vested in the Provincial Grand Master. It was a Deputy Grand Lodge, convened by a brother who was the Deputy of the Grand Master. It possessed no sovereign power. The lodges under the jurisdiction of the Provincial Grand Master were not necessarily registered under his Grand Lodge. They were simply returned to England, registered in the Grand Lodge there, and were classified as belonging to a certain Province of England. The allegiance of the lodges and of the Craft was to the Grand Lodge of England, and to the Provincial Grand Master, whose power was less than the Grand Master, and whose authority was temporary, being derived (and taken back) from the English Grand Master. The Provincial Grand Lodge was not permitted to meet except when the Provincial Grand Master sanctioned it, and it ceased to exist upon his death, resignation, or removal.

It became a useful tool to the premier Grand Lodge because it gave its officers at least an implied authority over the spread of Masonry in foreign countries. The only duty of the Provincial Grand Master in the colonies was to warrant lodges and submit a list of those so constituted to the premier Grand Lodge annually.

In 1730, the Duke of Norfolk, then Grand Master, issued a deputation dated June 5, 1730 to Danial Coxe of New Jersey to serve two years as Provincial Grand Master of New York, New Jersey, and Pennsylvania. There is no evidence that Coxe exercised his deputation as he was known to be in America only four months during this period. Three years later, a new Grand Master, Anthony Lord Viscount Montague, issued a similar deputation appointing Brother Henry Price as Provincial Grand Master of "New England and the Dominions and Territories thereunto belonging."[150] Price was born in London about the year 1697 and moved to Boston in 1723. He travelled back and forth between Boston and London for a decade, but once he received his deputation he returned to Boston and remained in America the rest of his life. He was an active Freemason during the colonial era and has

Henry Price

been called "the founder of duly constituted Masonry in America" by more than one Masonic writer.

On July 30, 1733, Price called an Assembly of Masons together and formed the Provincial Grand Lodge of Massachusetts in Boston. He named Andrew Belcher his Deputy Grand Master (Belcher was the son of the then Governor Jonathon Belcher, noted earlier as the first recognized native-born American to become a Freemason). The first business was the presentation of a charter to eighteen Masons to form Lodge No. 126. It was the first lodge in America to be "duly constituted" and appear on the registry of the premier Grand Lodge in London. And, of course, the Assembly was held at the sign of the Bunch of Grapes Tavern, located at the corner of State (then known as King) and Kilby streets.[151]

Thus, "Regular" Freemasonry had made its first appearance in this country–at the "best punch house in Boston." The tavern had its beginnings in the seventeenth century and was open as a public inn until after the revolution. When the lines became drawn between national loyalties, the Bunch of Grapes became the resort of the High Whigs, (those supporting independence from Great Britian) who made it a sort of political headquarters and it became known as the Whig tavern. As military occupation further intensified public sentiment, lines between Whig and Tory (those supporting the British crown) houses were drawn at the threshold of the inns. Gentlemen formed cliques of their own within the houses. One of the groups that regularly met at the Bunch of Grapes described themselves as "belonging to the Society of Free and Accepted Masons now residing there." As with most lodges meeting in taverns, the lodge had not received any prior warrant or charter. The first recognized lodge in America was a 'time-immemorial lodge."[152]

It is also interesting to note that the number assigned to the new lodge was '126.' This may give an indication of the number of lodges that had been officially recognized in the colonies at that time (although it is more likely that this was the total number of lodges constituted under the Provincial Grand Lodge system, operating in all countries to that date). Also, nine of the eighteen petitioners of the lodge had already been "made" there at an earlier date. The lodge had probably been meeting for several years prior to its being made regular. There is no record of how long it had been in existence. But the Bunch of

Grapes tavern was in operation before 1658, the year one William Davis sold it to William Ingram.[153] The lodge only conferred the first two degrees, since the third degree was still a few years away from coming into practice in the colonies. The lodge is now known as St. John's Lodge of Boston.

The second lodge in Boston was organized on December 22, 1738, and had the exclusive right to confer the Master Mason degree (although the record is not clear whether this lodge actually conferred the third degree, or installed the Master into the chair as Master of his lodge. This was often referred to as the *chair degree.*) A third lodge was founded in February, 1750. It met at the Royal Exchange tavern, and Henry Price served as its first Master. The Royal Exchange tavern was a two story brick structure that operated as early as 1711. The Boston Massacre took place in front of this house, and the first stagecoach ever run on the road from Boston to New York was started from this tavern. It went every fourteen days.

The fourth lodge was constituted in March of the same year. It met at the White Horse tavern, and Henry Price was also its first Master. This lodge removed to the Bunch of Grapes tavern in 1752.

Henry Price was also a contemporary of Brother Benjamin Franklin, who was made a Mason in Philadelphia in 1730. Price met Franklin in Boston in 1733, and gave him a copy of the Anderson's Constitutions. Franklin published it the following year in the *Pennsylvania Gazette,* which is probably the reason it became the law for Freemasonry in America. It gave the colonies a Masonic system which closely resembled that of the English Moderns.

The second lodge to be constituted elsewhere in the colonies was the lodge at Savanna, Georgia (now known as Solomon's Lodge). It was chartered by Provincial Grand Master of Georgia, Lord Weymouth, in 1735. Other Provincial Grand Lodges named between 1736 and 1737 included North and South Carolina and New York.

In the meantime, Benjamin Franklin wrote Henry Price a letter in June, 1734 seeking to have Price named as the Provincial Grand Master of all of North America because the brethren in Philadelphia wanted to confirm their privilege of having previously organized their own Grand Lodge under Danial Coxe as Provincial Grand Master in 1731. The brethren wanted to continue to meet in annual Assembly and elect their own officers. Apparently, Franklin and his other American brothers were not very certain that their Grand Lodge had been created under a legal Masonic authority, or what was expected of them in the eyes of the premier Grand Lodge. Coxe had failed to formally exercise his authority of deputizing the Grand Lodge. It is noted that Benjamin Franklin was elected Grand Master of Pennsylvania by his own brethren on June 24, 1734 without the sanction of the Provincial Grand Master. He requested and was named by Price as the Provincial Grand Master of Pennsylvania in February, 1735. In reality, then, we have the Grand Lodge of Pennsylvania first asking for the deputizing of a Provincial Grand Master, and then turning to Henry Price, at Boston, to ask him to extend his authority over Pennsylvania.

The Provincial Grand Lodge system was in a state of flux during almost the entire time of its existence. Communication was neither regular nor convenient between the mother Grand Lodge and her colonies. The Provincial Grand Masters were never certain of their role as Deputies. They primarily wanted to be the vehicle for promoting their system of Masonry, and spreading the same as far and wide as possible. They rarely assumed any degree of management over their lodges.

In addition to this passive form of administration from within, the Grand Lodge of England was not very careful in regard to its own rules and practices among the several Provincial Grand Masters. For instance, the Grand Lodge of Massachusetts, of which Price was Grand Master, was a Provincial Grand Lodge, properly instituted by him. His authority was then subsequently extended over the whole of North America. Did this give the Grand Lodge of Massachusetts authority over all of North America? Apparently so, in the eyes of the Grand Lodge of England, except where it chose to constitute other Provincial Grand Lodges on its own--which was regularly done. Again, the rule must have been that a Provincial Grand Master of North America was deemed necessary for the presumption of control, and the authority vested in such a person was broad enough to provide for the establishment of provincial authority wherever it was convenient and necessary. But his authority was always indirect, being derived from the mother Grand Lodge. The result was that a Provincial Grand Master of all North America had full authority to constitute lodges in any territory, except in such places as had been cut out of that authority by a direct appointment from England.

Another complexity that caused much confusion was the fact that local lodges in the colonies were warranted by Provincial Grand Masters of either the Moderns or the Ancients, or the Grand Lodge of Scotland, or Ireland, or in some instances, established by their own assembly. It is necessary to point this fact out because the Masonic ritual which followed usually bore a relationship with the workings of the mother Grand Lodge to the colony. Whenever there existed more than one "working" in the same colony, ritual diversity became an issue within the same geographic area or village. The local brethren became very territorial and protective of the system they had learned, or had brought with them from their original homeland.

A good example is the Grand Lodge of Pennsylvania. The Ancients appointed its first Provincial Grand Master for Pennsylvania in 1751 two decades after the colony had established its own Grand Lodge, which operated under the Moderns system of working. Pennsylvania then had two complete and separate systems of Masonry until it organized its own independent Grand Lodge in 1786. It turns out that the Ancients influence prevailed, which has resulted in the Pennsylvania ritual being unique among the American Grand Lodges, being distinctly Ancient in its ritual, laws, and ceremonies. However, those who believed in the Moderns system soundly denounced the Grand Lodge of Pennsylvania as "a bastard offspring of a bastard Grand Lodge."

South Carolina, Maryland, and New York each had Ancient Provincial Grand Masters. While the Ancients did not create as many lodges in America primarily due to its rather late beginning in 1751, it was a much more aggressive group of men than its Moderns cousin. The more humble social rank among the Ancients encouraged their interest in creating military lodges, and was an active supporter of this practice in the colonies. The result was that many of the early lodges converted to the 'Ancients' way of practicing Masonic ritual by the time their independent Grand Lodges formally organized. Of course, the Grand Lodge of Scotland appointed a number of Provincial Grand Masters in North America before the war. This added to the divisive character of Masonic practice which prevailed throughout eighteenth century American Masonry.

This working in the same colony among several Grand Jurisdictions created a schism that lasted for years, particularly in Massachusetts. A lodge which met in the Green Dragon tavern received its charter from the Grand Lodge of Scotland in 1756. This upset the English Provincial Grand Master, and he issued an order forbidding Masons from his Grand Lodge from visiting the Green Dragon Lodge. This action didn't seem to have much of an effect, so he took a stronger and bolder action by declaring all the charter members of the lodge irregular, or clandestine. Of course, this reaction brought on the wrath of the Grand Lodge of Scotland, which revoked the Provincial Grand Lodge's order. It was a dispute that would not be settled for forty years.

The antagonism that existed between these two Massachusetts Grand Lodges was, at times, just as pointed between the English Ancients and the Moderns. In the old country, theirs had been primarily a problem of class, with the premier Grand Lodge excluding men whom it felt were of the inferior classes. They even made changes in their ritual, partly because of the Prichard exposure, but the result was to keep Masons who belonged to the Ancients from being recognized in the Moderns lodges, thus adding to the fusion.

In some instances, this same attitude carried over to the colonies, and lodges became the real victims of a "Grand" political shortsightedness. Some were forced to accept charters from whichever Grand Lodge would have them at a particular point in time. Of course, this not only created ritual work that was not uniform within the same colony, but welded local brethren to their particular brand of Masonry on political grounds. Unless something was done to resolve these differences, the future of Masonry, as an institution that could thrive in America, was literally in jeopardy. In the case of Boston, a Grand Lodge was even created in 1769 (by the Grand Lodge of Scotland) for only the Boston area. This created three Grand Lodges in Massachusetts at the same time. It also made the Scottish lodge (St. Andrew Lodge) and the Boston Grand Lodge one and the same. Joseph Warren, who would later fall at Bunker Hill while fighting along side another Mason, a brother named Prince Hall, was named the Grand Master. Four years later, Scotland made Warren the Grand Master of Masons for the continent of North America. Now there were two, and in some instances three, Grand Masters serving the same territorial jurisdiction.

The tide of fate changed forever for Massachusetts when General Warren died, leaving the Boston Grand Lodge without a head. As stated earlier, a Provincial Grand Lodge ceases to exist without a Provincial Grand Master. But the Boston brethren, fueled by the death of their

Grand Master, disregarded this fact and continued to meet as a Grand Lodge without any authority. On March 8, 1777 they elected their own Grand Master, without seeking anybody's permission, and after five more years of operating as a technically illegitimate Grand Lodge, they voted their own Grand Lodge into existence as an independent Grand Lodge. And then claimed it had exclusive jurisdiction over the other two Grand Lodges! Needless to say, the brethren of St. Andrews lodge did not agree with the new Grand Lodge, and took their fate into their own hands. On a split vote of twenty-nine (for Scotland) to twenty-two (for Massachusetts), they declared themselves a local lodge once again, and voted to stay with the Grand Lodge of Scotland. This created a division within the lodge that could not be overcome. The minority group broke off and organized its own lodge. Now, Boston not only had three Grand Lodges, but two lodges of the same name operating within the city. To minimize the confusion, the second St. Andrew lodge was renamed Rising Sun Lodge, and another well-known Mason, Brother Paul Revere, was named its first Master.

It would be another six years before the question of Grand Lodge authority and union would get resolved. The end came rather quickly when, in 1787, both the Grand Masters of the Ancients and Moderns Grand Lodges died within two months of each other. This resulted in the union of the two. Once this was accomplished, a committee of union representing both the Ancients and the Moderns was appointed, and on March 5, 1792, the Grand Lodge of Massachusetts was born–by dissolving the one not tied to the Provincial Grand Lodge, and by closing the other, thereby creating a legal succession from the premier Grand Lodge.

All in all, the Ancients Grand Lodge proved the most popular in America. A majority of the lodges constituted by Provincial Grand Lodges in the colonies held their warrants from the Ancients, and not from the original Grand Lodge of England of 1717. In fact, when the British troops came to the colonies, the Ancients lodges rapidly increased. But between the two English systems a fierce battle waged, each claiming to be legitimate and the other spurious, or clandestine. The contest was not settled until the two Grand Lodges in England united by forming the United Grand Lodge of England in 1813. The two English Grand Lodges worked side by side in the same territory. The Ancients, believing they had been in the right from the beginning, required the Moderns, when a union was affected, to be reinstated in lodges of the Ancients. On our own soil, the last of the controversy was settled in South Carolina, by the two Grand Lodges (Ancients and Moderns) joining hands in 1817.

The Sanctioning of Masonry in the Colonies

To summarize the evolution of legitimate Masonry in the thirteen colonies, and the mix of jurisdictional authority in each, the following brief outline is presented. The chartering Grand Lodges are listed, along with the first lodges to be chartered. It should be noted that, in many instances, these Grand Bodies chartered a number of lodges in each colony, thereby adding to the diversity of ritual workings. This information was derived from the publications of the Missouri Lodge of Research and the seminal work of Hugo Tatsch.[154]

Connecticut–Freemasonry was brought to Connecticut from three chartering authorities. St. Johns Provincial Grand Lodge at Boston (Moderns) chartered the lodge at New Haven in 1750; the pre-Revolution Provincial Grand Master at New York (Moderns) chartered St. Johns lodge in the county of Fairfield in 1762; St. John's Lodge in Hartford was chartered by a Provincial Grand Master in Boston in 1763. The next three lodges were chartered by the Provincial Grand Lodge of New York; Union Lodge in 1764, St. John's Lodge in Norwalk in 1765, and Stratford Lodge in 1766. One of the most famous lodges of the American Revolution, American Union Lodge, was chartered by the Grand Lodge at Boston in 1776. It was a military lodge. The Massachusetts Grand Lodge chartered several more Connecticut lodges during the 1780s, including the lodge at Norwich in 1785. The Grand Lodge of Connecticut was first formed in 1784, and a Grand Master selected. This Grand Lodge apparently did not survive. Finally, at a convention held in Hartford in 1789, the Grand Lodge of Connecticut was formed.

Delaware–the Provincial Grand Lodge of Pennsylvania (Ancients) issued a warrant for Lodge No. 5 at Cantwell's Bridge in Dover on June 24, 1765. This was a time-immemorial lodge as its minute books reflect activity before 1760. Four other lodges would be established during the Revolution, all of which aided in organizing the Grand Lodge of Pennsylvania in 1786. The Grand Lodge of Maryland added another, and the Provincial Grand Lodge of New York (Moderns) chartered a lodge at Dower in 1775. The Grand Lodge of Delaware was formally organized at Wilmington in 1806.

Georgia–in 1735 the lodge at Savannah, which had been in existence since 1734 as an unwarranted lodge created by James Oglethorpe, was chartered by the Grand Lodge of England (Moderns) during a visit Oglethorpe made there while serving as Master of the Lodge. No record exists of when Oglethorpe himself became a Mason. The Grand Lodge of Pennsylvania (Ancients) chartered a second lodge in Savannah in 1784. These two lodges met together in 1786 and created the Grand Lodge of Georgia.

Maryland–In 1750, the Provincial Grand Master of North America under the Moderns system may have chartered a "time immemorial" lodge at Annapolis, but no records exist of the lodge after 1764. The Provincial Grand Lodge at Boston warranted a lodge at Port Tobacco some time prior to 1759 and another at Leonardtown the same year. In 1765, a lodge was chartered by the Moderns, but it secured another charter from the Provincial Grand Lodge of Pennsylvania (Ancients) in 1782. This Grand Lodge chartered ten lodges in Maryland between 1766 and 1782. In 1783, it granted a warrant to form the Grand Lodge of Maryland, but the local Masons did not consider the matter formally until four years later. The Grand Lodge of Maryland was formally organized by convention April 17, 1787.

Massachusetts–First lodge chartered in Boston in 1733 by the first Provincial Grand Master of New England (Moderns), Henry Price. The Provincial Grand Lodge of Massachusetts was chartered the same day, with Price as the Grand Master of the new Provincial Grand Lodge. A second lodge was organized in 1738 as a 'Master's Lodge'. This Grand Lodge would issue charters in eight of the colonies as well as three Canadian Provinces between 1738 and 1775. Then, in 1752 a group of Masons met in the Green Dragon Tavern and formed a lodge under 'ancient usage'. They soon realized their situation and requested the Grand Lodge of Scotland to issue a charter, which it did on 1756, but it did not reach Boston until 1760. Thus, this lodge was officially chartered at Boston by the Grand Lodge of Scotland in 1760. It was known as St. Andrew's Lodge. Thus, there was a St. John's Grand Lodge and a St. Andrew's Grand Lodge in Massachusetts at the same time. Nine years later, a Provincial Grand Lodge was established in Boston by Scotland and a Provincial Grand Master named. His name was

Joseph Warren.[155] Then, in 1771 another lodge in Boston was granted a charter by the Atholl Grand Lodge of England (Ancients). After the dissolution of the St. Andrews Grand Lodge in 1782, and the union of the other two Grand Lodges, the Grand Lodge of Massachusetts was formed on March 5, 1792 by joint assemblies of both bodies.

New Hampshire–the first lodge was warranted as St John's lodge at Portsmouth in 1737 by the Provincial Grand Master of England (Moderns). It was the only lodge in New Hampshire chartered by the Grand Lodge of England. The lodge only conferred two degrees until 1749, providing evidence that the third degree was considered optional in the early lodges of the colonies, as well. In fact, the Master Mason degree was conferred separately in a Master's Lodge until 1790, when a vote of the members provided for only one set of officers. A second lodge was formed in Windham by a warrant from the Grand Lodge of Ireland. The third lodge was chartered in Portsmouth by the Grand Lodge of Massachusetts. In 1789, the Grand Lodge of New Hampshire was created by a convention of lodges.

New Jersey—the first lodge on record to be warranted in New Jersey was St. John's lodge in Newark, warranted by the Provincial Grand Master of New York (Moderns) in 1761. A lodge in Elizabethtown was chartered by the Provincial Grand Master of New England (Moderns) in 1762. A lodge at Princeton was chartered by the Grand Lodge of Boston in 1765. In 1767, a lodge at Baskingridge was chartered by the Provincial Grand Master of Pennsylvania (Ancients). The Grand Lodge of New Jersey was formed in 1786 by a group of Masons rather than by an assembly of delegates from lodges, the reason being that the Grand Lodge of Pennsylvania declared itself independent from New Jersey, which forced the Masons to form their own Grand Lodge.

New York–the first lodge in New York was probably chartered by the first Provincial Grand Master of England, Danial Coxe, but he left no records. It is known that several lodges were meeting in New York during the 1730s because they advertised their meetings in the New York *Gazette.* St. John's Lodge No. 1 was warranted on December 7, 1757 as Lodge No 2, which implies there was an earlier chartered lodge. A Scottish lodge record indicates that Royal Arch Lodge No. 2 existed in 1759 and could have been warranted as early as 1738. Another lodge may have been chartered in Albany by the Provincial Grand Lodge of England in 1755. The records are not adequate to confirm the actual chartering date. After 1753, the Provincial Grand Master of New York began actively chartering lodges, having chartered eighteen before 1765. By 1782, there were eight lodges still in existence under the jurisdiction of the Modern Grand Lodge; another nine lodges of Ancient, Scottish, or Irish origin. The lodges came together and organized the Grand Lodge of the State of New York in 1781. It became a sovereign American body on June 6, 1787.

North Carolina–the first lodge, known as St. John's which had been in existence since 1735 in Wilmington, was chartered by the Moderns Provincial Grand Lodge of England in 1754. With the exception of a few English lodges which met independently of any sanctioned authority because they were too clannish to apply for one, the English Moderns was the only Grand Lodge involved with the development of Masonry in North Carolina. First Lodge Crown Point in Pitt County was chartered in 1766; Royal White Hart lodge in Fairfax was chartered in 1767. The Grand Lodge of North Carolina was finally organized by an assembly of lodges on December 9, 1787, declaring itself independent from England.

Pennsylvania–There is some evidence that Freemasonry may have existed in Pennsylvania as early as 1727, again through newspaper articles announcing meetings, but the first lodge to be warranted was St. John's lodge which met at the Tun Tavern in Philadelphia. It was warranted in 1731 by the Grand Lodge of England (Moderns), and a Grand Lodge of Pennsylvania was born that same year. Benjamin Franklin served as its Grand Master in 1734. But it was not a Grand Lodge in the sense of being organized by an assembly of lodges. Rather, it was St. John's Lodge of Philadelphia choosing to function as a Grand Lodge. It never had more than four lodges under its jurisdiction. It became a Provincial Grand Lodge of England ('Moderns') in 1749. All the early lodges were Moderns lodges. The first Ancients lodge was warranted by the Atholl Grand Lodge in 1758 as Modern Lodge No. 4. Its charter was revoked when it was discovered to be using Antient practices so it petitioned the Grand Lodge of the Antients in London (consisting of the Irish lodges that formed the 1751 English Grand Lodge) for a warrant in 1758 as Lodge No 1. All connections with the Grand Lodge of the Moderns were severed. It applied for a charter as a Provincial Grand Lodge which was granted in 1761. The new Grand Lodge declared itself independent from England in 1786 and the Grand

Lodge of Pennsylvania was chartered by the Ancients Provincial Grand Lodge that same year.

Rhode Island–the first lodge was warranted in Newport by the Massachusetts Provincial Grand Master of the Moderns in 1749. St. John's Lodge was alleged to have been in operation since 1658. It was one of only three lodges to be granted a Master's Lodge charter prior to 1768. A second lodge at Providence was chartered in 1757. These two lodges were the only two formed in Rhode Island during British rule. The two met and organized the Grand Lodge of Rhode Island on June 27, 1791.

South Carolina–first lodge was warranted by the Provincial Grand Master of England (Moderns) at Charles Town in 1735. Solomon's Lodge No 1 was formed in 1736. The Master of that lodge was also the Provincial English Grand Master of the Colony. A Provincial Grand Lodge of South Carolina was organized sometime in 1737, although the exact date is not known. In 1787, another Grand Lodge appeared in South Carolina under the name of the "Grand Lodge of Ancient York Masons." It was organized by five lodges that did not accept allegiance to the English Grand Lodge. This Grand Lodge took its allegiance from a third English Grand Lodge that organized in 1738, but which did not long survive. The Provincial Grand Lodge of South Carolina was reorganized in 1754. These two Grand Lodges served South Carolina for thirty years. In 1818 the two groups met in Charleston and organized the Grand Lodge of Ancient Freemasons of South Carolina.

Virginia–the lodges in this state held their charters from five different authorities, including England, Scotland, Ireland, Pennsylvania and America. The first lodge working in Virginia was the Royal Exchange lodge at Norfolk, organized either in 1733 or 1753. The correct date has never been proven, but the 1733 date is thought to have been a Scottish printer's error. The Grand Lodge of Scotland warranted the same lodge in 1763. Fredericksburg lodge was warranted by the Moderns Grand Lodge sometime between 1743 and 1752. However, the Grand Lodge of Scotland issued the same lodge a charter in 1758. In 1768, a charter was issued by the Provincial Grand Lodge of Pennsylvania to Winchester Lodge at Winchester. In 1783, the Provincial Grand Lodge of Pennsylvania issued a warrant to Alexandria lodge. This lodge received a charter from the Grand Lodge of Virginia in 1788 with the number 22. George Washington was named its first Worshipful

General William Augustus Bowles

Master. Finally, representatives of the Virginia lodges began meeting and on October 30, 1717, the Grand Lodge of Virginia was formed.

A Unique Provincial Grand Master

One other special mention is made that is extraordinary and perhaps the least known of all appointments given among those who were to be the Provincial Grand Masters in the Provincial Grand Lodge system. The minute book of the Prince of Wales Lodge No. 259, England, recorded that on January 20, 1791, one General William Augustus Bowles was elected an honorary member the same evening.[156] It is noteworthy to point out that this action was taken by the lodge of which the head was later to become the King of England! The lodge was instituted to consist only of those who were honored with appointments under King George. Bowles had taken a group of Cherokee and Creek tribal leaders to England and, during that visit he was made a member. He was introduced as the Chief of the Creek nation.[157] It was not widely known at the time that the Creek nation had six treaties of alliance between the King of England and their nation. This placed Bowles in an influential position of alliance himself.

As a result of his reception by the Prince of Wales, he was "appointed Provincial Grand Master of Creek, Cherokee, Chickasaw and Choctaw Indians" under the Grand Lodge of England, and his name appears in the calendar of that period.

General Bowles was then the chief of the Creek Nation and an ardent and loyal Mason. He was born in Maryland in 1763, and joined the British army in Philadelphia when he was thirteen years of age. He was a staunch English loyalist who brought Masonry to the leaders of the southeast tribes. He was properly positioned to do so. On a sojourn to Florida, Bowles joined up with a party of Creek Indians. This would later lead him to a position as chief, and he was appointed to lead the Civilized Tribes in the war against the Colonies. He married a Creek woman and eventually became totally integrated into the Creek tribal culture. He led the Creeks on several attacks against the Spaniards, and was the commander of the tribe when the Creeks were engaged on the side of the British at Pensacola in 1780. After the war, he became the Commander in Chief of the tribe, but ran afoul when he was taken prisoner by the Spaniards for what they charged as his disturbing the peace in several states. He escaped once, but was recaptured, and died in prison in Havana in 1804.

Military Lodges

In addition to lodges created or warranted by Provincial Grand Lodges or newly chartered Grand bodies, there were a number of military lodges that functioned throughout the colonies. Prior to the Revolutionary War, fraternal bonds were often forged between regular British troops and their colonial colleagues. These lodges carried different names, often styled military, army, regimental, foot, traveling, or ambulatory lodges, and, by their nature, were intended to be mobile. The officers carried their regalia in trunks along with the regimental colors and other military paraphernalia. The lodge minutes were carried in the saddle bag.

In England the system of military lodges was regulated by special provision of the Grand Lodge constitution and was strictly limited to the purposes for which the warrants were granted. No new lodge could be established without the concurrence of the commanding officer, and no individual lower than the rank of corporal could be admitted. When the lodge was disbanded, the warrant was given up or exchanged for one authorizing the establishment of a regular lodge.

There is no question that the travelling craftsmen aided in the spread of Freemasonry in the colonies. Not only were the armies exposed to the tenets of the craft, the men who were initiated into Masonry within the military lodges ultimately returned to civilian life qualified to join local lodges. Masonry's values built a close connection between the army and the fraternity.[158] Of course, these mobile lodges also contributed to ritual diversity and confusion regarding the ceremonial forms of Masonry.

The earliest known warrant creating a military lodge was issued in 1732 by the Grand Lodge of Ireland to the First Foot, now the Royal Scots. The Grand Lodge of Scotland followed nine years later and both of the English Provincial Grand Lodges issued charters to these travelling Mason companies. The military lodges were considered to be a fruitful source of maintaining Masonic unity with military groups and promoted Masonry throughout the new world.

On May 13, 1756, the Provincial Grand Master of North America under the Moderns at Boston granted a charter to an army lodge headed by Richard Gridley. In November of that year the same authority chartered Abraham Savage to "congregate all Free and Accepted Masons in the expedition against Canada in one or more lodges."[159] At least seven additional military lodges were chartered within the British army by 1762. By 1780, at least twelve military lodges were warranted by the Provincial Grand Lodge of Pennsylvania, Massachusetts, and New York. During the war itself, every regiment serving the British army except one had a Masonic lodge attached to it.[160] Perhaps the most famous of all military lodges in the Revolution era was American Union Lodge, organized in Roxbury in February 1776 just outside Boston by Provincial Grand Master John Rowe of St. John's Grand Lodge while engaged in the siege of Boston. It was the first military lodge organized during the Revolution itself. It did not survive the conflict and was re-organized in 1779. It met as a military lodge until April, 1783. The second was Washington Lodge No. 10, chartered in October, 1779 by the Massachusetts Grand Lodge. The Master of American Union Lodge constituted the lodge, acting as a proxy of the Grand Master. The purpose given this lodge in the constituting address by Brother Jonothan Heart perhaps best articulates the real purpose military lodges were established during the revolutionary era. The dispensation was given "under the title of 'Washington Lodge' to make Masons, pass Fellow Crafts, and raise Masters in this state or in any of the United States, where there is no Grand Lodge..."[161]

It was American Union Lodge, however, that promoted a singular and unique accolade in the annals of Masonic history. In a meeting held at Morristown, New Jersey on St. John's Day in the winter of 1779, it proposed that a General Grand Lodge in the United States be formed and a Grand Master be appointed over the said Thirteen United States of America. At a subsequent meeting held on March 6, 1780, among delegates of the military lodges in Connecticut, New York, New Jersey, Pennsylvania, Delaware, and Maryland, along with the delegates of Regimental Lodge, the staff of the American army and the Corps of the artillery, a resolution was drafted to the Grand Masters of the lodges in the United States for "establishing one Grand Lodge in America, to preside over and govern all other Lodges of whatsoever degree or denomination...upon the Continent; that the ancient principles and discipline of Masonry being restored, we may mutually and universally enjoy the advantages arising from frequent communion and social intercourse."[162] George Washington was to be nominated as the first national Grand Master. But opposition from the Provincial Grand Lodges effectively killed the effort and thus the first of many attempts to form a General Grand Lodge of the United States, establishing a unified Charter, and adopting a standard ritual format for the preservation of the work of symbolic Masonry, failed.

The Diversity of the Ritual

The great Masonic orator, Roscoe Pounds, summarized very clearly and succinctly the reasons for the vast differences in the workings of the Masonic degrees during the last two centuries in an address given to the Grand Lodge of Massachusetts in 1915 and reprinted in the December, 1922 issue of the *Duluth Masonic Calendar*.[163] Brother Pounds suggested that there were six major causes of the diversity.

1) "Masonry was transplanted to this country while the ritual was still in a very formative state in England.

2) There were several primary centers of ritual influence, along with several other smaller cores of Masonry in the United States, "from each of which was transmitted its own version of what it received."

3) The schism between the Ancients and Moderns which initiated in England in the last half of the eighteenth century, led to two rituals in this country during the formative period of American Masonry, and "later these were fused in varying degrees in different jurisdictions."

4) It was not until the end of the eighteenth century in England, and not until the first quarter of the nineteenth century in this country, that literal knowledge of the work was regarded as of paramount importance.

5) New Grand Lodges were formed in this country by the union of lodges chartered from different states, and these unions "gave rise to all sorts of combinations."

6) Each jurisdiction, when it established a Grand Lodge, became independent and preserved its ritual as it had received it, or "made it over by way of compromise or worked it out, as a possession of its own."

The historical overview of the early established lodges and Grand Lodges presented in this Chapter has confirmed the accuracy of Brother

Pounds' observations. Some received their Masonry in the period of the Premier Grand Lodge, which was itself just developing the form of the Masonic ritual during its formative years from 1723 to 1738. It was also the formative period of the development of the "esoteric," or what we now consider the "first section" parts of the work–the old seventeenth century Masonry.

Others took their work from the period of the great schism between the two English Grand Lodges. This was the period during which the lengthy and elaborate lectures and philosophic elements of the ritual came into being. It was also the time when a system of working the three degrees came into regular practice.

Still others received their work under the ritual systems of the Grand Lodges of Scotland which was established in 1736; others, from the Grand Lodge of Ireland, instituted about 1725. Both of which adopted the form of the English ritual but with their own adaptations. Then we have the influence of the Lodge at Kilwinning in Scotland, which withdrew from the Grand Lodge of Scotland in 1743 and acted as an independent warranting body for more than sixty years. It chartered lodges in Virginia. And, as has been shown, in many of the colonial lodges established before the Grand Lodge of England and which worked without charter, the rituals that came into being were no doubt a combination of what the men brought with them who organized those first "time immemorial" lodges.

In addition to the original thirteen colonies which we have covered at some length in this chapter, there was a second group of jurisdictions which represented the first movement of Masonry from the original colonies. These are the Grand Lodges organized during and immediately following the Union of the Ancients and Moderns, up to 1840. These are Maine, which derived its work from Massachusetts; Vermont, which came from the Ancients; Ohio, which derives from Massachusetts, Connecticut, and Pennsylvania; Indiana, which derives from Ohio; Michigan, from the Ancient Grand Lodge of Canada and from New York. There's Kentucky, which received its work from Virginia; Tennessee, which came from North Carolina; Alabama, which received its work from North Carolina, South Carolina, Tennessee, and Georgia; Mississippi, which came from Kentucky and Tennessee; Louisiana, which derived from South Carolina, Pennsylvania, and France; Florida, deriving from Georgia, Alabama, and South Carolina;

Missouri, which came from Pennsylvania and Tennessee; Illinois, which derived from Kentucky; and the District of Columbia, which received its work from Maryland and Virginia.[164]

With the rapid expansion of Masonry paralleling that of the United States population migrating westward, it is no wonder that the ritual took on a diverse variety of forms and workings. Efforts to establish any kind of ritual uniformity were, at best, local or regional in nature, if they were considered at all. Uniformity of Masonic ritual was simply not seen as something which was important during this period of population and economic expansion.

It can be argued that William Preston would have accomplished more to standardize the form of Masonic ceremony and degree workings in America by his profound influence on the English ritual, except for the fact that the colonies became engaged in a war with England, which resulted (after the Declaration of Independence) in essentially every State and Provincial Grand Lodge declaring its independence from all the Grand Lodges of the "Old World."

For the first time in the history of the Craft, they became sovereign Grand Lodges in their own jurisdictions. As will be seen, perhaps no single action by a collection of jurisdictions has had a more profound impact on the practice and mores' of Freemasonry in this country than this declaration of independent authority over things Masonic.

The time leading up to and during the Revolutionary War brought much confusion among the Craft. And it wasn't that the lodges were organized around political agendas, although some historians have assumed that the Ancients and the Moderns were nothing more than different political points of view and sympathies.

For the most part, the Masons of the colonies were too conservative to become involved with revolutionary partisan issues. Masonry generally discouraged overt partisanship, preferring to play a role in more fundamental political questions about the ordering of power and authority. Bullock suggests that "Masonic prohibition on direct political involvement within the lodge actually helped delay the development of full-scale political parties until the 1820s and 1830s."[165] Masonry's stubborn resistance toward partisan political discussions in lodge hindered any sustained attempts to use the fraternity to serve a particular group or party. Furthermore, during the post-Revolution era, the fraternity identified itself with the ideals of the nation as a whole. By celebrating morality and individual merit, Masonry seemed to exemplify the ideals necessary to build a society based on virtue and liberty.

Even during the conflict, fraternal leaders tended to recognize that there were many Masons who were loyal to the Crown–and perhaps as many others who opposed it. In many cases, rather than cause hostilities within the lodge, those who were loyalists simply went into exile during the conflict. It was a difficult time for men who believed in and held true to their Masonic obligations. In reality, an understanding developed among the brethren that there were divided political loyalties, that many could not subdue their passions; so they solved the problem of enmity by simply avoiding each other.

As can be imagined, this caused a cessation of Masonic activities in many colonies during the war. For those who actually participated in the conflict, many met in military lodges, where they experienced a diversity of ritual they had not before seen.

This added yet another element to overall ritual diversity. And when the conflict was over, many lodges simply had to start from scratch in reviving their Masonic ritual workings–adopting a combination of practices which had been learned in a variety of ways and places by their members. Not long after, the infamous Morgan Affair added yet another debilitating blow to ritual stability. The period between 1826 and 1835 was one of Masonic chaos in this country. With the political excitement that ensued after the purported murder of William Morgan in New York by his Masonic comrades, many lodges dissolved or ceased to work. By the time the storm had passed in 1840, there was confusion among the workmen, and the work itself was unsatisfactory.

It was a time when Freemasonry desperately needed some stabilizing influence that would bring it back to its roots as a fraternity with a single identity of purpose. It needed to find that one common thread that would lace the fabric back together, and mold it into one united and universal brotherhood, creating a single source of identity for all who would pass through it. That common thread had to be the ritual. It was the only constant that would preserve Masonry as a source of brotherhood, education, and personal fulfillment that was unique to the old institution.

But if an established and uniform work was ever to become molded into a cohesive and united system, it would now require a man of commanding talents and influence; a man who had an extensive knowledge of the rituals, and a zeal which no difficulties could repress. It would require an individual who could establish a system of work which would become universal among American Masons; a man who could grasp the various discordant systems which prevailed among the lodges. And then, from all these conflicting forms, arrange and perfect one complete system that would be in harmony with the landmarks, a legitimate exponent of Masonic principles, and commend itself to the approval of Masons everywhere.

Such a man was born in Boston on October 30, 1771. He would become known as the father of the American Masonic ritual. His name was Thomas Smith Webb.

THOMAS SMITH WEBB

11 Thomas Smith Webb; The American Ritualist

See how the great mass of men worry themselves into nameless graves, while here and there an unselfish soul forgets himself into immortality. –Emerson

And thus Brother Herbert Leyland begins his biography of the man who would have a greater influence on the American Ritual of Freemasonry than any other man of his time.[166]

Thomas Smith Webb was born in Boston the same year that William Preston was preparing his first series of lectures for the English degrees. His father, Samuel, was a bookbinder by profession, and Thomas was the sixth of eight children to be born of Samuel and Margaret Webb. He was named after his grandmother's brother, Thomas Smith, who had received a Master's degree from Harvard College in 1720, and was ordained a Congregational minister; a profession he would hold for sixty-eight years.

Young Thomas attended the Boston public schools and the Latin school, where he learned the Greek classics, which may have been the basis for his extensive treatment of what is considered a liberal education in the Middle Chamber Lecture of the Fellowcraft degree.

Young men who attended the Latin schools were prepared for college with a well-disciplined curriculum. School lasted all year, and classes were held from seven in the morning to five in the evening, six days each week. Spelling and reading were taught from the bible and from the New England Primer. In the classics, Cicero, Virgil, Sallust and Caesar's Commentaries were read. Gloucester's Greek Grammar was used for the study of that language, and the Greek Testament and Homer were read. The classical studies would occupy the last 4 of 7 years of a student's schooling. Webb became proficient in these studies, as well as French and Music.

After completing his schooling, he was apprenticed to his father in the bookbinding trade. In the spring or summer of 1790 (after serving 4 years as an apprentice) young Thomas completed his apprenticeship. He then decided to leave Boston and ply his trade for himself at another locale.

In July of that year, Webb stuffed his saddlebags with the tools of the bookbinding trade and traveled by horse to the rural community of Keene, New Hampshire. There, he set up shop as a bookbinder, and began to advertise weekly that he not only bound books, but also had a nice quantity of books and stationary of various types for sale.

Freemasonry had come to Keene seven years earlier, when Rising Sun Lodge was issued a Charter by the Grand Lodge of Massachusetts (there being no Grand Lodge in New Hampshire at the time). The Charter bore the signatures of John Warren as Grand Master, and Paul Revere, as Deputy Grand Master. The lodge met in the hall of Ralston's Tavern. In 1792, a Grand Lodge was established for New Hampshire, and Rising Sun Lodge became Lodge No. 3 on the New Hampshire rolls.[167]

Less than six months after his arrival in Keene, Webb was proposed as a candidate. He was only nineteen at the time. He and William Blake were balloted on, admitted, and initiated on December 24, 1790. The two new Masons were passed and raised to the degree of Master Mason the following week on Monday, December 27th. The day was the occasion of the Festival of St. John the Evangelist. And although the brethren of Rising Sun lodge couldn't have known it at the time, since Webb was a candidate, this would be the most important meeting ever to be held in their lodge.

Webb was a regular attendee at the lodge during his brief sojourn in Keene, but upon his father's death early in 1792 he returned to Boston to help his mother earn a living. He again set up a bookstore and stationary shop, and worked at his business until early the following year, when he moved his family to Hartford, Connecticut. It was here that Webb became a partner with Zachariah Mills, and learned how to manufacture wallpaper. While residing in Hartford, Webb attended the lodge of St. John's, which met at the Bunch of Grapes Tavern. He carried his dimit from the lodge at Keene, but he apparently showed no interest in joining St. John's. During the brief time Webb was in Hartford, he joined the Connecticut Militia, and was also very active in the social affairs of the city. But his business was his most pressing responsibility, and having earned enough money to send his mother and two sisters back to Boston within a year, he set off for Albany, New York in hopes of finding there an economic reward adequate enough to regularly send money home to his mother. Webb arrived in Albany in November, 1793.

Union Lodge No. 1 was one of two lodges in Albany at the time, and Webb immediately joined upon his arrival. A big lodge by eighteenth century standards, his was the two hundred and sixty-eighth signature to appear on the rolls. At the annual meeting in December, Webb was appointed lodge secretary.[168] The next year, he entered into a partnership with a prominent Albany merchant named Thomas Spencer. Together, they established a combined bookstore, circulating library, wallpaper business, and department store. Having finally settled into an enterprise that provided some financial stability, Webb found time to once again give Masonry his attention.

Then in June, 1795, Webb had an encounter with another Mason who would have a profound influence on Webb's Masonic career.

The event was St. John the Baptist Day. It was celebrated in a two story tavern called the City Hotel, which served as the Village Inn of Lansingburgh, a borough situated outside of Albany. A year before, a man named John Hanmer came to America and settled in Lansingburgh. He was said to have been a member of the Lodge of Antiquity and had received the Preston Lectures in one of Preston's Lodges of Instruction. On his arrival at Albany, Hanmer exhibited a document from the Grand Master of England, setting forth that "he was well skilled in the ancient lectures and mode of work as approved and practiced in England, and recommending him to the favorable notice of the Masons of the United States." After listening to Hanmer's lectures and mode of instruction, Webb and a brother named Ezra Ames, along with Gideon Fairman, Phillip S. Van Rensselaer, and several others, put themselves under Hanmer's instruction (including the work and lectures of the Chapter degrees).[169]

Hanmer owned the City Hotel. The assembly room was on the second floor, and also served as the meeting place of Hiram Lodge No.35. Hanmer joined the lodge while he was the proprietor of the Inn, and was present at the St. John's Day celebration, along with several other brethren who had congregated from three of the area lodges. It is at this meeting that Webb and Hanmer met. The following year, the new friends, along with Ezra Ames, would become the moving force in organizing a new lodge in Albany, named Temple Lodge. A petition was drawn up in the summer of 1796, asking for a warrant for the new lodge. Hanmer was named the first Master and Webb the Senior Warden.

Hanmer and Webb apparently established this new lodge so they could work the Royal Arch Degree, which was unique to the Ancients Grand Lodge workings. The lodges in New York had all received their charters from the Provincial Grand Master of the Moderns Grand Lodge at London before the Revolutionary war. During the war, most of the Moderns lodges suspended their activities because they were loyalist in their sympathies. The lodges established after the Revolution were Ancients lodges, having received their Charters from an Ancients Provincial Grand Lodge established in New York in 1782. But, the lodges to which Hanmer and Webb belonged had stayed with their original charters, and thus had no sanction to perform the Royal Arch Degree. Both Hammer and Webb had previously received the degree; Webb, while on a visit to Philadelphia in May of the same year. It is not known where Hammer received the Royal Arch degree, although he was a Royal Arch Mason before 1796. There is some evidence he brought the Royal Arch ritual work from England. But nonetheless, the two brethren wanted to have a lodge where the Chapter degrees could be worked.

It was during this time that Webb learned the Preston lectures.

It is generally believed that Hanmer taught these to him while they were both actively engaged in the work of Temple lodge. Webb was elected Master in December of 1796, and conferred the degrees on a number of candidates during the next few years. There is at least one thread of evidence that Webb learned the lectures before he was Master because there is a surviving note in the minutes of the period that the candidates were given instruction beyond the ritualistic work, and Webb was given the task of instructing them.

Soon after the Albany Lodge was created, Webb married a young belle named Martha Hopkins. He then purchased a home in Albany and settled in to enjoy married life and organize Masonic bodies wherever the opportunity arose. It seems Webb had an intuitive notion that the stability of the fraternity would depend on the organization of strong national and state Masonic bodies. He went to work to create such bodies, primarily to preserve the traditional methods and integrity of their ceremonies. He apparently had a personality which was conducive to persuasion, and decided to first establish the Capitular and Templar Orders in New York. He and Hanmer would be partners in these ventures, with Webb generally elected to the east and Hanmer assisting in the west.

Notwithstanding what would become a major legacy in and of itself for Webb, that of organizing the Grand Encampment and the Grand Capitular Bodies of the York Rite in the United States; still, the most significant thing he did was his third achievement of 1797. He published his first *Monitor*.

It was to become the most widely purchased and used Masonic text in the world. It would clearly establish Webb as the Father of Freemasonry in America.

Webb was searching for development of consistency in the mode of work carried on by lodges and he felt this work had to be uniform throughout the country if Masonry was to survive. Since the time of the pre-revolutionary war period, the influence of the British military lodges, the time immemorial workings, the differences in the workings of the new, young Grand Lodges–all these things contributed to radical differences of one lodge's work over another. Webb needed an instrument that would bring a permanent stability to the fraternity. The answer came in the form of a *Monitor*–a book intended to explain and help the reader remember the wording of the non-esoteric work of the lodge.

Actually, the birth of the Masonic Monitor occurred in London in 1772 with William Preston's Gala, which has been discussed previously.

His lectures of that evening were published the same year. It is likely that Webb conceived of the need to produce an American work as a result of Preston's publication of his *Illustrations* in 1796. It had been advertised for sale in the Albany bookstore, and Webb purchased a copy as soon as it was available. He immediately saw that a similar book would be of great benefit to American Masons, and he set out to create such a text by revising and re-arranging Preston's work. His purpose was not to create a new and improved ritual for Masonry, but to arrange Preston's work in a way that he thought would be simpler and more convenient for the lodge ritualists. In fact, Webb pointed out in the Foreword of his First Edition that:

"The observations on the first three degrees are principally taken from 'Preston's Illustration of Masonry' with some necessary alterations. Mr. Preston's distribution of the first lecture into six, the second into four, and the third into twelve sections, not being agreeable to the present mode of working, they are arranged in this work according to the general practice."[170]

It is clear that Webb intended to follow Preston closely, and a comparison of the two reveals very little was changed by him. In fact, 64 pages out of a total of about 350 published with the first edition were a faithful copy of the corresponding portions of Preston's 1792 edition of the *Illustrations.* Webb wrote the complete monitor of lectures in the Symbolic Degrees, and also decided to add the monitorial material for the York Rite Degrees. The first edition included a system of seven degrees which were being worked in New England, New York, and Pennsylvania. Webb's intention was to create an aide to the memory work and he probably did not realize it at the time, but by adding the York Rite work to his Monitor, he literally promulgated this Rite in America. One other interesting fact about the first edition of the Monitor is that Webb published it anonymously, as "...a Royal Arch Mason, K.T., of M..." This author has not been able to find if a reason was ever given by Webb for not claiming authorship to his first edition.

Brother Leyland informs us that the material for Webb's book came from several sources. He obviously drew the data for the Symbolic Degrees from Preston. He obtained the material for the Mark Mason Degree from the St. Andrew's Chapter in Boston. The sources for the Most Excellent Degree came from Newburyport Chapter, also in Boston. Hanmer gave him the Order of Priesthood work, and a

Dr. Thaddeus Harris provided the Masonic Charges, Songs, History and Constitutions from his own 'Harris Constitutions.'[171] From these sources and other Masons Webb was associated with along the Atlantic Seaboard, he compiled the Orders of Knighthood, the History of Freemasonry in America, and the Masonic Directories which were included in his Monitor.

For financing the first edition of his Monitor, Webb entered into a partnership with Henry Spencer, with whom he was a partner in the Wallpaper and Bookselling business (he would later buy Spencer out when they parted company as business partners). Other booksellers offered the volume for sale, and Webb carried copies to Boston and Providence for distribution there. Sales were also augmented by advanced advertising. The *Albany Chronicle* featured an announcement of Webb's forthcoming text in its August 28th issue, in which appeared an ad listing it as "The Freemason's Monitor, or Illustrations of Masonry."[172] Upon publication, Webb had the Monitor copyrighted.

His subsequent work in organizing the Grand Chapters of the northeastern states and later, the constitutions for that body and the United States Grand Encampment of the Knights Templar; insisting on the uniformity of work in all of the Masonic Orders, along with the distribution of his own Monitor through his travels to Massachusetts, Ohio, Kentucky, and most of the other New England and Atlantic seaboard states, certainly placed Webb in the position to become the foremost ritual instructor in the United States.

And that's precisely what happened.

Of course, Webb's own lodge required many evenings of his time, instructing in both the Work of the Lodge and the Royal Arch Chapter, while serving as the lodge Master. Temple lodge moved to a new location during the year, and Webb developed a dedication ceremony for the new lodge building. In addition, over thirty meetings were held that year, with much ritual worked on new candidates. Webb was elected Master the following year, as well.

During the winter of 1798-99, he moved to Providence, Rhode Island. He set up his wallpaper and printing business, and purchased a two story home for his growing family (which would ultimately include nine children). In January, 1800, Webb attended his first lodge meeting of the new lodge in Providence, called Mt. Vernon Lodge #4. In October, he entertained the brethren after an Apprentice's lecture in which the lodge minutes reflected he "sang a most excellent song to the manifest satisfaction of the Brethren." In the meantime, the older lodge in Providence, St. John's #1 decided they wanted to acquire Webb as a member and literally invited him to become one by mailing him a formal invitation. Webb cordially accepted.

By spring, Webb had been invited to instruct the officers and brethren of both lodges in his mode of lecturing. Later that same year, he set up a Saturday lecture/instruction night for the benefit of any brother who wanted to learn the work. The brethren met each Saturday evening from November through February. This may have been the first school of instruction for the teaching of Masonic ritual organized in the United States. Webb insisted on the work being taught by the "mouth-to-ear" process, and he certified the proficiency of each brother in a report to his lodge. The school proved so popular that the lodge voted to conduct it for another three months, and to pay for the candles and wood required to heat and light the lodge room.

By 1802, Webb determined to print a second edition of the Monitor. This time he listed himself as the author of the work. As soon as the book was published, he requested the Grand Chapter of Rhode Island to adopt it as the guide for the Chapter work in that state. A committee was appointed to review it, and at their next annual convocation, the Monitor was adopted. The Grand Encampment and Grand Lodge of Rhode Island subsequently did the same, thus giving the Webb work an official sanction which other Grand Bodies would later recognize.

There is no question that Webb's active involvement with Royal Arch and Templar Masonry beyond the confines of his own state contributed much to his reputation as a credible ritualist. Almost from the time he published his first edition of the Monitor, he was regarded as an authority on Masonic jurisprudence. He served on the committees to write the constitutions and by-laws for several Grand Chapters and Grand Encampments. His insistence on ritual uniformity in all his Masonic endeavors, and his love for teaching the ritual wherever he traveled had a great influence on the acceptance and formal adoption of the Webb work in his young and expanding America. His command of the Craft work was such that the phrase "Preston-Webb Work" came to mean to the typical lodge ritualist the rightful characterization of the Blue Lodge ritual practiced in the United States.

Webb always saw Freemasonry as a national organization, not so much in the form of a national Grand Lodge, but as a nation-wide system having local degree-conferring bodies as its subsidiaries. While he was unable to accomplish a legally constituted national organization of Grand Lodges, the York Rite system of Masonry today is clearly the result of Webb's untiring work toward national oversight and unity in that Masonic system.

Yet it's interesting to note that he never personally saw the Templar Orders to be Masonic. He made the statement which was recorded in the minutes of St. John's Commandery, December 5, 1808, that "they are, in comparison to it (Masonry) societies of but yesterday; and all of them fall short of the excellence, harmony, universality and utility of that noble institution."

On June 24, 1813, Webb was given a well-deserved reward for his overall service to Masonry when he was elected Grand Master of Masons in Rhode Island.

Webb's Monitor

In total, there would be seven editions of the Monitor printed during Webb's lifetime, selling more than sixteen thousand copies in ten years. It would become the model and source of Masonic instruction for many American Freemasons. The first edition (1797) was a compilation of the Eighth Edition of William Preston's *Illustrations,* which had been arranged into four books. As mentioned earlier, Webb's Monitor carried the same name, and was printed in two parts. The first part consisted of three books, and was basically a reproduction of Preston's first book, with a few omissions. The text and chapters of Part One were taken almost exclusively from Preston's *Illustrations.* Only a small portion of this first "Preston-Webb" material is in our present Monitors. However, the monitorial introduction to the lecture of the Third Degree relating to King David's death, Solomon's elevation to power and his request of King Hiram to send him someone skilled in the arts and sciences; all appear to be taken directly from the several pertinent passages of the Book of I Kings, and may be a composition of Webb himself. Preston included the same lecture in his *Syllabus,* but it is not known if this text was available to Webb before he published this edition of the Monitor.

The second book of the Monitor (1802) was entitled, "General

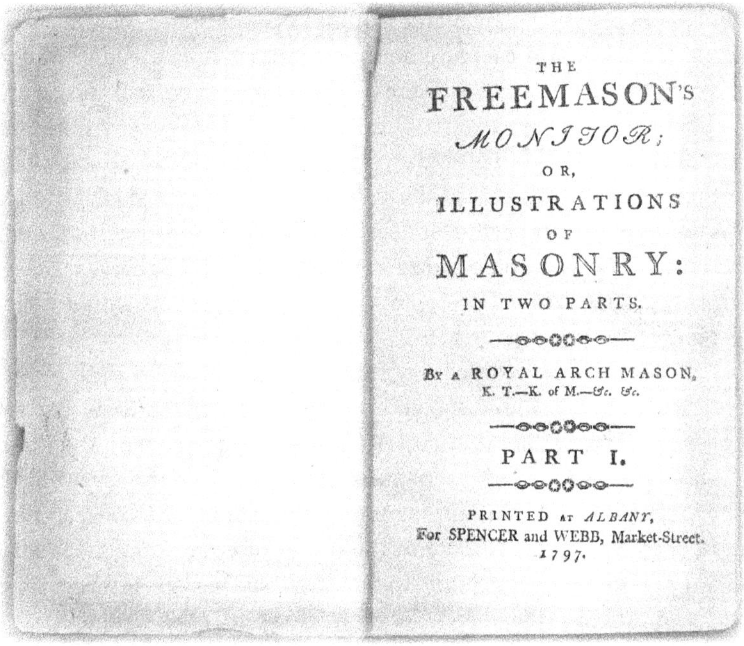

WEBB'S MONITOR, FIRST EDITION

Remarks: including an Illustration of the Lectures; a particular description of the Ancient Ceremonies; and the Charges of all the Degrees." Webb substantially re-arranged Preston's monitorial work in this section and altered the chapter titles. The new information appears to be original to Webb. For example, we find the "Charge at Opening a Lodge" which we still see in print in our Grand Lodge Monitors, citing quotations from *Psalm 133*. There is the lecture on the Working Tools—the 24 Inch Gauge and Common Gavel of the First Degree; along with the familiar lecture on the 'Lambskin Apron as the "Badge of a Mason." These lectures were all new in the sense that they were Webb's words, but he was also following the English ritual traditions of "moralizing" the work. This is the reason it is often difficult to state with certainty that ritual language derives from a single individual. Often it was the result of a collective of ideas. For instance, the moralization of the common gavel can be found in non-Masonic literature, as in *The Pilgrimage of Perfection,"* 1526, in a section that Masons would easily recognize.[173]

Webb obtained the ceremonies of a consecration of a lodge, dedication of Masonic Halls, and the Masonic Funeral Service from Thaddeus Harris's *Constitutions*. After Webb had dealt with the three symbolic degrees, he wrote a chapter on the Mark Master Degree (York Rite). Next came the ancient ceremonies; including the consecration and dedication ceremonies, and the laying of cornerstones. He also added monitorial work relating to the Ineffable Degrees, the York Rite Orders of Knighthood, the Order of the Red Cross, the Order of High Priesthood (of Irish origin), and the History and Constitution of the General Grand Chapter.

Also of note is that the prayer now given in the second section of the Master Mason Degree (at the grave) and found to be composed of parts of the Book of Job, Chapter 14, was first introduced in the 1802 edition of the Monitor. It was apparently written by Webb.

And there is at least one element of ritual that Webb took from a source different than Preston, Browne, Finch, or Prichard. He gives a detailed moralization on the working tools of a Master Mason, but notes these to be "all the implements of masonry indiscriminately, but more especially the trowel." This particular designation is taken from *Bristol* working on the west coast of England, where it is said the trowel is used by operative masons for spreading the cement that unites the structure into one common mass. The *Bristol* lecture continues "as we are not all Operative Masons, but rather Free and Accepted, or Speculative Masons,...we are taught to use the Trowel for the noble and glorious purpose of spreading the cement of Brotherhood amongst whom no contention should ever exist, but only that worthy emulation as to who best can work and best agree." Browne's work (of which we have already seen was familiar to Webb), describes the trowel but the wording is so different there is no comparison. Finch makes no mention of it at all; neither does Preston. And it is not found in any present day *Emulation* working, which is said to be the most popular English working. Bristol working is also claimed to be the oldest in England. The Bristol language regarding the trowel is the precise language found in most American rituals. [174] The closeness of Webb's working to the Bristol may speak for itself.

It is interesting that Webb at this point determined to remove all previous (Preston) allusions to the Monarchy. In Preston's Charge at Initiation into the first degree, for example, we find the phrase "monarchs in all ages have been encouragers and promoters of this art..." is changed in the 1802 Webb to "the great and best of men..." The reference to Monarchs may have been hard to digest that soon after independence had been won, and a new constitution set for the young country. Finally, an explanation of the Royal Arch degree (York Rite) finished the second book of the Monitor.[175]

The third book was styled, "Sketch of the History of Masonry in America," wherein Webb gives an account of the Provincial Grand Lodge system, along with the general history of Masonry in the colonies.

Part Two of the Monitor consisted of the work of the eleven "Ineffable degrees of Masonry" (Scottish Rite), and nine Masonic songs that were used in the degrees of the period, most of which Webb composed himself.

The third edition of the Monitor came out in 1805. The most substantive change introduced in this edition was the third section of the Master Mason Degree, including a description of the form, supports, furniture, ornaments, and jewels of a lodge; and its dedication to the two Saints John. In this edition, we also find the lectures on the universality of Freemasonry and an explanation of the three pillars of Wisdom, Strength and Beauty. Again, some of the emblems and concepts such as the forms of a lodge, how a lodge is situated, its supports, furniture, mosaic pavement, blazing star, the moveable and immoveable jewels, and the 'indented tarsel' can all be traced back to Prichard's *Masonry Dissected,* 1730; but Webb elaborated on these, and transposed them to suit his taste. It should be noted that Webb's explanation of the Temple… "this famous fabric being supported by fourteen hundred and fifty-three columns, and two thousand nine hundred and six pilasters; all hewn from the finest Parian marble" is taken from Anderson's 1723 Constitutions.

Webb may also have taken some of the third section elements from Finch's *Treatise,* because, for instance, he deleted the Christian reference to the Saints Johns and made them the 'patron saints of Masonry.' Finch's work, on the other hand, preceded the Union of 1813, when the rival Grand Lodges de-Christianized much of the eighteenth century craft ritual. In his *Treatise* (1802), we find in the catechism: Question; "…. To whom do we, as Christians, dedicate them [Lodges]? Ans: "To St. John the Baptist, and St. John the Evangelist."

In the fourth edition (1808), the general histories of the Grand Lodges and Grand Chapters were brought up to date. For this edition, Webb may also have borrowed from Finch and Brown. He followed Brown's elucidation of the four cardinal virtues, published in 1802, as these were much more elaborate explanations compared with Preston. Setting Browne and Webb's words side by side, it is clear that Webb made some further observations on the virtues. The same holds true when comparing language of Finch and Webb regarding the supports of a lodge, ornaments, furniture, and the point within the circle. One can almost trace the development and expansion of these lecture elements from Preston to Brown to Finch to Webb.

The fifth edition (1812) was a reprint of the 1808 edition. The sixth edition was published in 1816 and added the installation ceremonies for the officers of a chapter of Royal Arch Masons. Webb had previously written and used this for the installation of the Newport officers in 1811.

The seventh edition of the Monitor (1818), and the last to appear during Webb's lifetime, deleted previously printed historical work on the Pennsylvania Grand Encampment, and added an interesting text entitled, "Rules for the Guidance of Christian Masons." Also, the history of Freemasonry in America was rewritten.

Webb died a year later at Cleveland, Ohio, while on a trip to the West. He expired in the Mansion House Hotel on the evening of July 6, 1819, after suffering a cerebral hemorrhage that same morning while waiting for a rented horse and buggy to make a hundred mile trip to Worthington. He was buried in Cleveland the next day with Masonic honors conducted by Concord Lodge, with forty-three members attending the services.

It was soon learned that, earlier in his life, Webb had requested, should he die away from home that his body be buried in his family plot in Providence where he had erected a vault of brick for that purpose. The Grand Lodge investigated the matter, and, by September had raised adequate funds for a committee to journey to Cleveland, pay for the exhumation, transport Webb's body, and reinter it in the plot with his first wife and three children. Webb's funeral in Providence turned out to be a Masonic occasion.

On Monday, November 8, the Grand Master of Masons of Rhode Island opened a special session of Grand Lodge at St. John's Hall. The Governor of Rhode Island, together with Past Grand Masters from Rhode Island and Massachusetts, were in attendance. When the Grand Master and his following descended to the street, a processional was formed. Led by a band, columns of Masons followed; first, all visiting Master Masons, then members of Mt. Vernon Lodge and St. John's Lodge; next came the Royal Arch Masons and Knights Templar; then the Grand Master and his officers. These were followed by the clergy, the hearse, the mourners and relatives. The funeral services were held at the beautiful new Meeting House, with 350 friends and brothers present. Afterward, the processional proceeded across the river to the cemetery, where the six Past Grand Masters serving as pallbearers, deposited the remains into the vault.[176] The Masonic graveside ritual which Webb himself wrote was read by Carlile. The brethren deposited their sprigs of evergreen and the tomb was closed. The Providence *Gazette* reported the Masonic part of the procession which attended the solemn event was believed to be the largest ever seen in the town.

As an interesting epilogue to this section on Webb, It was the intention of Webb's son, Thomas Hopkins Webb, to publish another version of his father's Monitor, but it didn't happen because another man beat him to it; which caused quite a stir in his own heart. In a letter written by Thomas on August 2, 1858, not revealed until a splendid series of monthly articles were published about his father in the *Freemason's Repository* from 1871 to 1874, Thomas describes his belated sentiments. From the June, 1874 issue, we read, in part:

> Boston, August 2, 1858
> Dear Sir:–When I saw you, during my June visit to Providence, you will recollect that I stated in the course of a conversation respecting my father, that I had for a long time contemplated having issued a new edition of the "Freemason's Monitor," both out of a filial regard to the memory of its departed author, and because (though not of the Fraternity) I felt qualified to decide that the work was one of too great value to be allowed to pass into oblivion either by getting out of print, or by being supplanted by others constructed of its fragments, or raised on its ruins.
>
> I subsequently learned that an edition, with sundry additions, has this very year been printed in Cincinnati; and during the past week, I have had an opportunity to partially examine a copy of it. In the Preface to the supplementary part the Editor, E.T. Carson, P.R.G., 32°, says in relation to certain "grades" he "upon examination" found my father's "work so and inaccurate, that it meager became necessary to re-write every part of it." This volume contains what is offered as a likeness of my father, but is in reality a miserable caricature; attributable not to design, but probably to the employment of an inferior artist or lithographer. Be the true cause what it may, the publishing of such a thing, is nonetheless objectionable to myself and other relatives.
>
> I feel now more desirous than ever of having an edition issued in this section of the country, and am ready, and urgent to do whatever is necessary or advisable, to qualify myself the better to superintend the task. I suppose that one of the most important movements for this will be to join the Fraternity; and I am prepared to take the requisite steps for this, so soon as I can ascertain what they are, and where they had better be taken, provided the expense that will thereby be necessarily incurred is within the limits of the means at my disposal. I should prefer being admitted through the Lodge over which my father once presided, if there be no impropriety in it, from the fact of my residence being elsewhere.
>
> I am aware that the western editor and publishers had a legal, but certainly not an equitable right to pursue the course they have, without consulting the author's family; for justice certainly is a

> cardinal virtue with Masons.
> Even the legal right they would not have acquired, had not certain individuals misled me years ago, and thereby induced me to suffer the copyright to run out. I know not in what lodge they sat, or by what Master they were taught the work, but certainly they were not regulated by the plumb of rectitude, nor did they square their conduct by the precepts of the "Monitor."....etc.[177]
> Yours truly, Thomas H. Webb

Fortunately, Thomas, the father, did not leave the matter of carrying on his work in the hands of his son. It is obvious that, had he done so, the time which elapsed from his death until the above referenced communication, would have been too great to insure the maintenance of his life's work among the craft.

And this brings us to the period between the 1818 edition of Webb's Monitor and the 1843 Baltimore Convention. What happened to the Masonic Ritual after Webb died? How was the work conveyed to the lodges after the father of the American ritual was no longer around to influence its growth and development? The answer is found partly in the legacy which Webb left in the hands of a few faithful and devoted students.

Direct Students of Thomas Smith Webb and Other Noted Ritualists

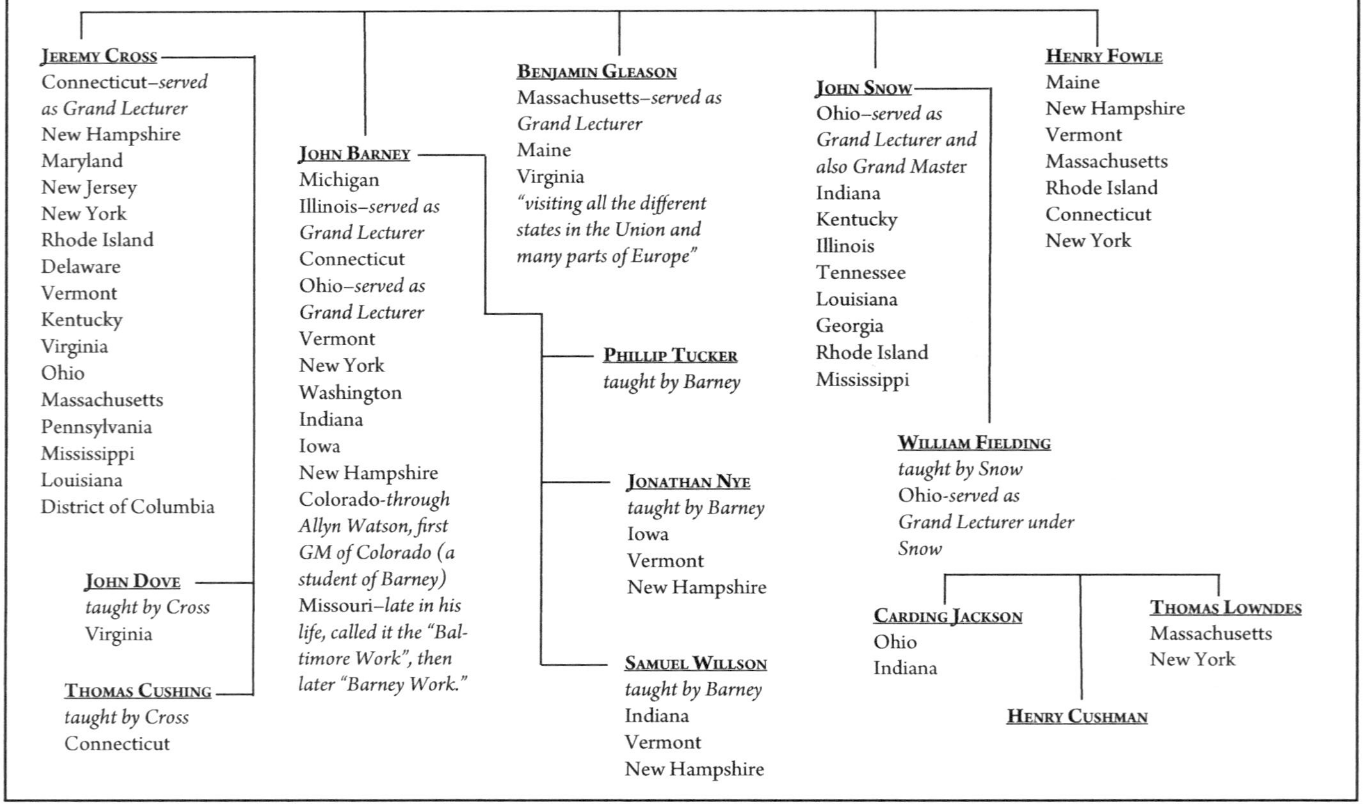

12 The Roving Ritualists

To spread his doctrine on Freemasonry, Webb needed to recruit a few disciples who would learn his mode of work and the lectures, and spread the same far and wide across the land. His labor was rewarded by a small group of trusted men who learned and loved the work of their mentor. Their names were John Snow, John Barney, Jeremy Cross, Henry Fowle, and Benjamin Gleason. Their stories are worth telling because, while it was the Preston-Webb work that ultimately found its way to almost every Grand Lodge in America, it was this group of transient lecturists who carried the word to the Craft; literally one lodge at a time. We owe much to their dedication to Webb, and their zeal for the ritualistic work of our fraternity.

John Snow

A young goldsmith named John Snow opened his store in Providence the same year (1803) that Thomas Webb was serving as Commander of St. John's Commandery, Deputy Grand High Priest of the Grand Chapter, and Senior Grand Warden of the Rhode Island Grand Lodge. While the young businessman would not become a Mason for another five years, in January, 1807, he opened an Inn which the local Masons patronized. The Golden Ball Inn, as it was called, was an enormous house which set across the street from the State House. It had a large assembly room which the local Masons used for dinners. In June of 1808, the Grand Lodge held its annual meeting in Providence, and afterwards retired by a grand procession to the Inn for a formal dinner. Snow had become a Mason the month before and was a Fellowcraft when the gala at his Inn took place. He was made a Master Mason in Mt. Vernon Lodge #4, Providence on June 13th.[178] It was there that he and Webb would forge a close friendship–perhaps the closest of any that Webb made. It was a friendship which would last a lifetime. In fact, Snow would serve as the administrator of Webb's estate in death,[179] and as an avid adherent of the Masonic heritage his mentor left him.

After joining Webb's lodge, Snow immediately became an active Mason of Providence. He was designated member No. 124 of the lodge. Webb instructed him in the ritual work, and was very impressed with Snow's ability. Snow's Masonic career gained momentum when he was exalted a Royal Arch Mason in April, 1810. He received the Knight Red Cross a year later, and continued to absorb himself in Masonry and so impressed the Masters and members of Mt. Vernon Lodge with his proficiency of the work that he was elected Master in 1814, installed by Webb himself. He would later be elected as Grand Secretary of the Grand Lodge of Rhode Island for the year 1816-17.

Webb was obviously impressed and proud of Snow and wanted to show him off as often as he could before his own circle of influential Masons. When Webb's dream of forming a General Grand Encampment of Knights Templar of the United States took shape at the Grand Commandery Conclave of Massachusetts and Rhode Island in Boston on May 15, 1816, he appointed a committee to draft a constitution and appointed Sir Knights John Snow and Henry Fowle to serve with him on it. The recommendations of this committee were unanimously adopted. The following June, the General Grand Encampment was born. Webb was elected Deputy Grand Master; with Snow as General Grand Standard Bearer. It is to this day the only sovereign Masonic Body in the United States.

In 1816 Webb visited Worthington, Ohio, and, while there, became impressed with a manufacturing business that had been established in Worthington, and in which he purchased stock. He returned to Providence to commence selling his business interests there and to entice his close friend and star pupil, Snow, to take up the new business venture with him. Always the faithful friend and brother, Snow immediately set out to sell his own business interests, and in June, 1817, he and Webb both began moving their belongings to Ohio.

Although the two invested heavily in the new business, the change in location did not suit Snow. The business thrived and Snow planted deep roots in its success, but he visited the shores of Providence as often as he could.

It didn't take Snow long to pursue his Masonic interests in Worthington. He and Webb formed an Encampment of Knights Templar the same year, and organized another Encampment of the Northwest Territories the following year. They named it the Mount Vernon Encampment. Snow would be its Commander for the next 23 years. He also concurrently served as Master of New England Lodge and as High Priest of Horeb Chapter during the years 1818 to 1822 and again from 1827 to 1832. At the annual Grand Lodge Communication held in Columbus in December of 1823, Snow was elected Grand Senior Warden. The following year, he was elected Grand Master of Ohio, and served again in 1829.

Until Webb's death, John Snow and he were almost inseparable. The closeness these two men seemed to have for each other was rare indeed. In the early years they were constantly traveling together in forming Grand Chapters and integrating them with the General Grand Chapter, as well as pursuing Webb's dream, the Grand Encampment of the United States. Snow was devastated by Webb's death and proclaimed in a letter written to several Masonic bodies in the area of Worthington that "Webb, who was a star of the first magnitude in the Masonic Temple, by this afflicting dispensation of Divine Providence, Masonry has sustained an irreparable loss."[180] It was Snow who organized Webb's funeral and carried it out.

After Webb's death, Snow felt a new drive to carry on the work of his fallen friend. He traveled extensively and taught the Webb form of working to Masons in Ohio, Kentucky, Indiana, Tennessee, Mississippi, Louisiana, Georgia, and Illinois. He was well disciplined in the work of all the Bodies and saw to it that others would also conform. He almost single-handedly taught the Blue Lodge workings to the twenty three lodges in northeastern Ohio during the year he was Grand Master. He found most of them in need of Masonic information and proficiency and stayed in the field working with them for four months. His abilities as a lecturer in the symbolic degrees were carried over to the Chapter and Templar Orders, where he was constantly requested to give lectures instructing the work through the same areas he visited with the lodges. He was appointed the Grand lecturer of the Grand Chapter of Royal Arch Masons at the Ohio Grand Convocation in 1827. His ability in giving lectures was very demanding on him. He was constantly requested to give and teach the lectures throughout the areas he visited. He was elected Grand Lecturer of Ohio in 1827 and continued in that office for many years.

In 1838, at the age of 58, Snow was still promoting his influence in all the degrees of the Masonic fraternity. He would carry Webb's torch until he was summoned himself by the Supreme Architect on May 16, 1852. In fact, to some, he was revered as much as Webb. As the years passed beyond Webb's death, it was not unusual for Webb's students to be revered with as much enthusiasm as those who were first taught by Webb. One bit of corroborating evidence we have that Snow's instruction in the symbolic degrees was highly regarded was a letter he received from William Fielding, the Grand Lecturer in 1848, inquiring what year the Grand Lodge had adapted Snow's model of work. Apparently, some lodges had gone astray and the man intended to reconfirm the Snow work was the official work.[181] Fielding wrote the letter to Snow because he was preparing a report to Grand Lodge at the next annual communication. Fielding felt sure that the Grand Lodge of Ohio had adopted Snow's mode of working, but there is no record in the Grand Lodge proceedings to verify this.

John Snow lived a well-rounded life and served the fraternity with distinction for fifty years. His old friend, mentor, teacher, and partner–the father of Freemasonry in America–would have indeed been proud.

John Barney

Brother John Spargo, Grand Historian of the Grand Lodge of Vermont said, "John Barney, of Friendship Lodge No. 20, Charlotte, Vt., made the greatest contribution to Freemasonry ever made by any individual."[182] He further claimed that Barney personally influenced more Masons in Vermont, through his work, than any other brother in the history of that Grand Jurisdiction.

That's the legacy Barney left as another of the several important students of Webb; he was an itinerant teacher of the Masonic Ritual.

Brother John Barney was indeed made a Mason in Friendship Lodge No. 28. The lodge didn't last very long, having been formed about the turn of the century; it was out of existence by 1852. But, if

Masonry wanted to point to a man with the humblest of beginnings, and boast of what a difference one man can make, John Barney would be the example to raise from the archives of the dust.

He was a tailor by trade, and worked in farming when he could not otherwise find work. He and his wife, Lucy Ann, moved to Charlotte sometime around 1807 and lived there in what has been described as "the honorable humble poverty of the honest poor." But the fifteen years they would live in Charlotte was a period of active involvement of Friendship Lodge. Barney joined in 1810. He was thirty years old.

His zeal for the fraternity was unbridled. It would even be said that his zeal was greater than his prudence; that it may have actually interfered with his bread-winning. Considering his accomplishments for the craft, there may well have been some truth to that.

Barney was a cripple from boyhood, and was unable to walk without a cane. He was an unassuming man in every sense. He had a remarkable memory, and was therefore deeply impressed that rote memorization was the path for communicating the Masonic ritual and its purposes. He achieved great proficiency as a ritualist in his lodge, and it wasn't long until he was much admired and appreciated by his brethren.

A friend informed him that Thomas Smith Webb had learned the English Masonic system from William Preston and was considered by most Masonic scholars to be the greatest ritualist American Freemasonry had produced. That was all he needed to hear. He resolved in August, 1817 to go directly to Boston for the expressed purpose of receiving instruction directly from Webb. He convinced his lodge that if he could learn the Preston-Webb form directly from the Master himself, he would be able to impart it to the Masons in Vermont who desired to learn it.

He also determined that he could partly support himself and his family by becoming an itinerant teacher of Masonic ritual. He felt he could in this manner augment the too meager income he derived from tailoring, and do an important service to his fraternity at the same time. His efforts might have the effect of making the ritual uniform throughout the state of Vermont. His vision was apparently convincing because the members of Friendship lodge residing in Charlotte and Hinesburg collected the funds to enable him to make the trip to Boston. They even committed to sustain his family until he returned home.

So, off he went to receive the course of instruction under Brother

JOHN BARNEY

Webb. There was one problem, however. He didn't bother to make arrangements with Webb to give him the work. When he arrived in Boston he found that Webb was too busy to teach him. Webb simply had more requests for instruction than he could take care of. It was quite an embarrassment for Webb. He made a special arrangement to meet Barney's situation and save him from disappointment. Webb called on another of his favorite graduate students, a fellow named Benjamin Gleason, to assist Barney in the work. Gleason agreed to teach him.

At first, Barney protested, arguing that he had come a long distance, and at a considerable expense to his lodge, to learn the work so that the Masons of Vermont might benefit from it. He also insisted that the Vermont brethren wanted the Webb work, and none other. The trio worked out an agreement. Webb considered Benjamin Gleason his best graduate pupil. Webb would have Gleason teach Barney considerably more than half the work, and he would give him the remaining portion himself. And he would occasionally listen to Barney "recite" and promised that he would personally examine Barney, listen to him rehearse the work, and, if he found him proficient, give him a signed certificate of proficiency as one of his pupils. This he did, and John Barney went back to Vermont prepared to teach the Preston-Webb system.

Actually, he made his credentials official in his own state by attending the annual session of the Vermont Grand Lodge, held in October. Brother Barney was admitted and registered as a Visiting Brother. It is not known why he registered as a visitor. It could have been because he had not been a Master, or Past Master of any lodge. Also, there were five or six lodges from his area that were opposed to Barney because they had been using an unofficial, mutilated work, and they did not want any Grand Lodge authority to visit them, or inspect their work. Perhaps Barney determined not to let his presence be known to prevent these few Masons from organizing an effort against him. Whatever the reason, during the session Barney got a brother he knew named Jonathan Smiley to present, on his behalf, a petition for recognition and approbation as a "Lecturing Master." With that, Barney got an audience and presented the certificate signed by Webb, along with other credentials. He was examined and gave a recital of a large part of the Preston-Webb work. Having been thoroughly tested as to his qualifications, the Grand Lodge voted to give Brother Barney a letter of recommendation to all lodges and brothers in the Grand Jurisdiction of Vermont "wherever he might travel."

Having found a competent teacher, the Grand Lodge immediately voted to adopt the Preston-Webb work.

The result is that the Vermont ritual has remained unchanged for 178 years. So proud are they of John Barney that the Vermont "old timers" to this day can be heard bragging about the fact that between William Preston and Thomas Smith Webb, there was only one intermediary, and that was a Preston-certified and vouched for friend and student (the Englishman John Hanmer); and, therefore between William Preston and John Barney; only two intermediaries. To a Vermont Mason, that's worth bragging about. They will tell you that if you think of the Webb version of Preston's work as the Webb work, then their Grand Lodge received it through a brother who received it directly from Webb himself, with a certificate attesting the accuracy of his rendition of it!

Anyway, John Barney was launched upon his career as an itinerant teacher of the Masonic ritual with the authority of the Grand Lodge of Vermont. He taught the brethren in his own lodge, and then traveled about the state giving instruction to Master Masons who desired to be taught by him. His approach was probably typical of most of the itinerant lecturers. He would accept an invitation from a key lodge in an area, and then would remain there in a private home, sometimes for weeks. He would often take his wife with him, and would teach ten or twelve of the lodge members at a time. And, in addition, Barney would instruct individual Masons.

In 1822, after thoroughly traversing his own state teaching the work, he left Charlotte and lived for a while in New York. He taught there for three years and his fame spread to the point that he was invited by the Grand Lodge of Connecticut to work the Masonic lectures there. Before he moved to that state, however, he decided to pay a visit to his old friends in Vermont. It was then that Brother Samuel Willson (whom Barney had taught earlier) had the happy inspiration to persuade Barney to remain long enough for the two to get all the lectures written down in a master copy, with their certification of its complete accuracy. Barney carefully dictated every word of the work, while Willson wrote in down in longhand. Then each sentence, when completed, was read back by Willson to Barney, who checked it for accuracy.[183] This would later become known as the Barney-Willson work, as Willson also went to work as a traveling ritualist. Willson would become a major figure in the restoration of the work after the anti-Masonic fervor of the mid-1800s and became affectionately known as Vermont's greatest Grand Lecturer.

In 1825, after a year of correspondence with that Grand Lodge, Barney moved to Connecticut to begin his work there. From that time forward, one state after another would follow Connecticut in inviting him to become their Grand Lecturer. From Connecticut, he went to Ohio (1834) and was elected its Grand Lecturer. He served in that position from 1836 until 1843. While in Ohio, Barney affiliated with New England Lodge No. 4 in Worthington. The remarkable thing about that was that John Snow (Webb's earlier student) had been its Worshipful Master, and Thomas Webb himself was also associated with it while living in Worthington. In fact, Snow had deeded his own property to the lodge to use as a lodge room. With Barney as a member, that little lodge (it had less than fifty members) could look upon its sidelines and consider that at one time or another there had sat–Webb, Barney, and Snow!

After serving nine years in Ohio, Barney moved to Chicago. He remained there, working in both Illinois and Michigan. He then moved to Michigan, partly to teach the work and partly to revive Masonry in that state. While Michigan had a Grand Lodge, it had not conferred the work in even one lodge from 1829 to 1841, a period of eleven years. This was during the height of the Morgan affair and the Cerneau controversy[184] and Masonry was literally shut down in many states because of the political furor the anti-Masons had managed to create over these disruptions. So in 1844 we find him in Detroit, teaching the Masonic ritual and taking an active part in settling difficulties which go along with any Masonic renewal program. Acting under proxy from the Grand Master of New York (New York had originally chartered the Grand Lodge of Michigan); Barney reconstituted the lodge in Detroit, and, in so doing, reorganized the second Grand Lodge of Michigan. He stayed in Michigan a little more than a year, and then moved to Illinois. In 1845, he was elected the Grand Lecturer of the Grand Lodge of Illinois. He taught the Webb work to the lodges in Illinois, and journeyed to Indiana and taught there. His influence in that state was so great that the Webb form was adopted there, and is claimed still to be in use today. Barney was appointed Grand Lecturer of the Grand Lodge of Illinois in 1845. With his legacy of being a direct student of Webb and his reputation in ritual instruction in at least seven states, Barney earned a modest income, both as a Grand Lecturer and as a private instructor of the ritual for those brethren who would employ him.

Then in 1847, Barney went to Missouri to resolve a division in that Grand Lodge over the ritual work. Missouri at that time was divided over adopting the work of the Baltimore Convention (which I will outline in a later chapter), and desired Barney to offer an alternative. Having remained there for some weeks providing instruction to some brothers in St. Louis, he succeeded in bringing harmony to the work of that state.

He set out for his home in Chicago, and became suddenly ill. Worn out and ill, he stopped at Peoria and there he died in a hotel room on June 22, 1847 at the age of sixty-seven. His death was unnoticed in the news of the day.

Brother John Barney, itinerant Masonic ritualist; a humble man, poor and obscure by the standards of his day, made an indelible mark on the history of Masonry in Vermont, Ohio, Connecticut, Illinois, New York, Indiana, Michigan, and Missouri. He was a living testimony that one man with enough passion can make a great difference.

Benjamin Gleason

In an account of the installation of the officers of Mount Lebanon Lodge (one of the oldest in Boston) on the 29th of December, 1858, Brother Charles W. Moore made the following remarks:

> Among the Past Masters of this lodge we notice the name of the late Benjamin Gleason, Esq., who was the associate and co-laborer of the late Thomas Smith Webb, in introducing into the Lodges of New England, and subsequently into other sections of the country, what is known as the Prestonian system of work and lectures. The labor of promulgating the work mainly devolved on Brother Gleason, and it is not too much to say, that as an accurate, consistent and intelligent teacher, he had no superior, if an equal, in this country.[185]

And thus we see that yet another American ritualist had made his mark on the advancement of the Masonic ritual in his time.

Actually, not much is known about Brother Benjamin Gleason's personal life. But he is noted in the annals of American Masonic history for the impact he left on the spread of the Preston-Webb form. He was born in Boston in 1777.

He was also the first known student of Thomas Webb.

One of Webb's first acts after joining St. John's Lodge No. 1 in Providence was to propose Gleason for membership in that lodge. Gleason was a student at Brown University and was then in his junior year of college. Webb made his recommendation to the lodge and it was approved by the Master. A $7 fee was paid, and Gleason was elected in March of 1802. One month later, it was then discovered that, because he had previously made his home in Boston, Gleason had already joined the Lodge of Saint Andrew in that City on January 22, 1802! The lodge refunded the joining fee.[186]

It is not known how Webb and Gleason became acquainted. He was six years younger than Webb, and he only resided in Providence a short time. He graduated from the University in 1802 and returned to Boston.

But between April, 1802 and his graduation, Gleason visited St. John's lodge and learned the Masonic lectures from Webb. In fact, he became Webb's favorite pupil.

It was during this time that Webb instituted his Saturday night school of instruction in Providence, and it is likely that Gleason was a regular attendee. There is no doubt that Webb was his teacher. Years later, Gleason would write a letter to Brother Moore which said, in part;

> It was my privilege, while at Brown University, Providence, Rhode Island (1801-02), to acquire a complete knowledge of the lectures in the first three degrees of Masonry, directly from our much esteemed Brother T.S. Webb, author of the Free Mason's Monitor; and, in consequence, was appointed and commissioned by the Grand Lodge of Massachusetts and Maine, Grand Lecturer, devoting the whole time to the instruction of the Lodges under the jurisdiction—and for many years subsequently (as Professor of Astronomy and Geography), visiting all the different States in the Union, and (1820-30), many parts of Europe—successfully communicating to numerous Lodges and Associations of Brethren, these same valuable "lectures of the Craft," according to the Ancient Landmarks.[187]

Gleason's career as a lecturer began in Massachusetts. He had affiliated with Mount Lebanon and King Solomon's Lodges, serving as Master of Mount Lebanon Lodge immediately following his tutorage under Webb, then again in 1809 for King Solomon's lodge. In 1804, the Grand Lodge adopted the Preston-Webb ritual as its standard of work. In March, 1805, the Grand Lodge issued a *Circular Letter* to all Freemasons in Massachusetts, with the prefatory remark that "Great and serious inconveniences have arisen and continue to arise, to our Most Ancient and Honorable Fraternity, from the rude, imperfect, and in many instances, erroneous Lectures and Modes of Work in many of our lodges; and the respectability and credit of every lodge demand that those inconveniences should be removed as speedily as may be." The Circular goes on to aver that "Many officers of Grand Lodge and other respectable brethren in various parts of the Commonwealth, have earnestly requested the Grand Lodge to establish a regular and uniform mode of Masonic labor in all the several Degrees; and that the most excellent and highly-valued lectures belonging to those Degrees, and which diffuse true Masonic light and information to the Craft, may be taught invariably in all the lodges and agreeably to the Ancient Forms and venerated Landmarks of the Fraternity."[188]

These 'excellent and highly-valued lectures' were those which Thomas Smith Webb had received some eight years before at Albany NY and already published in two editions of his *Monitor*, and, in which he had already instructed Benjamin Gleason.

At its Quarterly Communication held in March, 1805, by a unanimous vote, the delegates empowered Isaiah Thomas, Grand Master, to "use such ways and means as he should judge would best accomplish this important object." Thomas met with a number of present and past Grand Officers, examined Benjamin Gleason and found him "an excellent workman in Ancient Manner and Form, and well-skilled in the several Degrees of Masonry." Thomas informed the Grand Lodge that "he had appointed Brother Benjamin Gleason, P.M., Grand Lecturer and Instructor, and that he had contracted with him to visit all the lodges in the Commonwealth under the Jurisdiction (which also included what is now the state of Maine), and to instruct them in the ancient mode of work." Gleason was twenty five years of age at that time. During his performance of duty as its ritualist, he was exclusively employed by the Grand Lodge during the next year, and probably two or three years after that, visiting the lodges in Massachusetts and instructing the brethren in the work.

It was an arduous assignment. The Grand Master directed Gleason to visit all the Masonic Districts in the Commonwealth and notify all the Right Worshipful Masters and Worshipful Wardens of the lodges in said Districts to meet with him in their respective lodge rooms so that he could communicate and instruct all the officers and members in the lessons and instructions of the Degrees of Entered Apprentices, Fellow Crafts, and Master Masons; with the regular mode of Opening and Closing the lodge in those Degrees; including the illustrations, lectures and ancient principles and usages of the order, as well as the mode of installing officers. Gleason was to spend at least six consecutive days, and no more than twelve days, in each lodge. He was to make an accurate list of who attended, the time spent and the amount of money contributed to him by the members. Gleason's compensation was to average about fifteen dollars in each lodge, which, by today's standards, was a fair remuneration.

This was the onset of Gleason's career. He would serve as Grand Lecturer of Massachusetts for the next thirty-seven years. From that time forward, the Webb working has been the only recognized Masonic work claimed in that grand jurisdiction.

When Gleason's appointment of direct employment under the Grand Lodge expired, he then launched a career on his own to travel across the country teaching the Webb mode of ritual working, and pursuing the fruits of his own occupation.

He was perhaps uniquely qualified for this role, as his profession was that of a teacher. As a result of his classroom experience, Gleason developed a series of thirteen lectures in geography. In 1815 he told a diarist friend, one William Bentley of Salem, Massachusetts, that he intended to travel and lecture on his system. Mr. Bentley stated in a diary entry of January 10, 1815 that, "Mr. Gleason tells me that he intends the tour of the United States. He intends to travel with his system of teaching Geography. He is afraid of no man. And at times a Universalist preacher and schoolmaster besides his character in Geography he intends the world shall pay his passage."[189]

Bentley also makes reference to Gleason's interest in things Masonic. Obviously a Mason himself, Bentley goes on to write; "Besides he (Gleason) is a noted Free Mason and has rendered himself a great name in our most celebrated lodges by his lectures, and his intimate acquaintance with the usual modes of Initiation in all the common degrees. He tells me he shall write History."

Gleason apparently made his mark toward that end, and, in fact, had launched his career several years before. He managed to do pretty well for himself, while helping others. He was an incredibly popular speaker, and a dozen or so of his "addresses" are in print. He also published a geography textbook titled "Remembrance."

His relationship with Bentley covered a period of several years, for Gleason's extensive travels as a lecturer in geography is evidenced by a pair of earlier diary entries of Bentley's:

"October 22, 1813.... This evening, Mr. Gleason gave his public introduction to his 13 lectures on Geography which he has been to Canada and through the United States to exhibit."

"November 21, 1813.... ...Mr. Gleason has finished his classes to whom he gives his 13 lectures in Geography. He says that he has had 60 scholars since he paid this visit at $5 each and now leaves for southward."

Having set out to lecture and teach; Gleason left the employ of Massachusetts and traveled extensively across the United States, lecturing in astronomy as well as geography, and instructing brother Masons in the work in nearly every town that he visited. For his "gratuitous communication of the lectures" to one George Richards, then Master of St. John's Lodge at Portsmouth, New Hampshire, he was presented a Past Master's jewel and collar. Richards then disseminated the work throughout that state.

He even managed to make a tour of Europe in 1829-30, where he lectured before large assemblies in England, Ireland and Scotland. Moore claimed Gleason exemplified the Preston-Webb work before the Grand Lodge of England, whose authorities pronounced them correct. He not only demonstrated the craft degrees, but also taught in those of the Chapter and Encampment, and received several tokens of fraternal regards from the officers of those Grand Bodies. Brother Moore notes that "the Provincial Grand Lodge of Lancester especially manifested its appreciation of his skill as an accomplished lecturer; and he (Gleason) rarely failed when conversing upon the subject to express the great satisfaction he derived from the circumstance that his own work and lectures corresponded so nearly with the old, or Preston work and lectures as then practiced in many of the provincial towns of England." Gleason therefore became America's lone ambassador in taking the lectures he received from Webb to many parts of Europe for the education and enjoyment of the brethren in those countries and provinces.

Gleason continued his travels and lecturing for years. He is on record in Virginia as early as 1819 and as late as 1837. In 1838 he was elected Master of King Solomon's Lodge twenty years after he served his first term as Master. In 1839-40 he was District Deputy Grand Master of Boston and the surrounding area. He is reported to have taught the Preston-Webb form in Maine, New Hampshire, Rhode Island, Vermont, and New York.

On September 18, 1847, death swallowed up the life of Brother Benjamin Gleason after a span of seventy years. He died without a will in Concord, Massachusetts. He was survived by his wife, Rebecca, and one daughter, Juliet-Rebecca. Juliet had married William Wheildon, who drew up a petition and was appointed as the administrator of Gleason's estate. Brother Charles Moore, another Mason who would earn his own place in the annals of American Masonry, would serve as trustee.

Masonry had thus lost another roving ritualist and favorite son of Thomas Smith Webb.

Henry Fowle

Charles Moore, Grand Secretary of Massachusetts and editor of the *Freemason's Monthly Magazine*, wrote as a preface to an autobiography Henry Fowle submitted to the magazine, published in 1865, that he was "one of the most active and distinguished Masons of his time, and in connection with the late Brothers Thomas S. Webb and Benj. Gleason, may be regarded as the author and founder of the present Masonic system and organization of this country. It was our good fortune to be intimately associated with him and Brother Gleason in our early Masonic labors, and to have received the benefit of their experience and instruction.... "[190]

Regrettably, the author of this present text has not been able to find much additional information about the man who was supposedly "the founder of our present system of working." Brother Fowle, who had been a block and pump maker by profession, considered himself an old man (he was sixty-seven) when he wrote his autobiography for the Grand Lodge of Massachusetts and unfortunately there is little information contained in it of Masonic interest. For this publication, he chose to delight his audience with a series of personal anecdotal, and oft times, humorous tales about his life. It is a fun read, and highly recommended as a good poultice to any heavy heart!

One cute little story which simply can't go without telling relates to his apparent "rebirth" at age two. Brother Fowle wrote that he "made his appearance on the stage of human existence" the 19th of September, 1766. He added, "But for some time I was a weak, puny thing, and when two years old I appeared to die, was laid out, and a coffin prepared; when an old lady, who had been very fond of me, saying she would see the poor little thing once more, came into the room were I lay, and thinking my clothes were not well adjusted, attempted to put them in order, when perceiving a little warmth at my back, she called for a blanket, and placing me in it brought me again to life!"

Fowle was indeed a man who would be subject to a lot of illness throughout his life, primarily brought on by rheumatism, but still he survived three wives, and managed to sire nineteen children!

Concerning politics, he admonished that "I am, and always have been since I could distinguish good from evil, a republican of the Washington school, and detest the demagogue of any party, whatever may be his professions." On religion, he stated "do unto others as you wish them to do unto you, is the sum and substance of religion. I shall never puzzle my head in conversing the merits of Infallibility, Transubstantiation, Total Depravity, Eternal Torments, or any such dogmas, which from time immemorial have divided Christians,– consigned thousands to the stake, and driven many to self-destruction!"

Fowle was a member of the Massachusetts artillery company for a brief time until his health prevented him from continuing in service. He also was active in the Humane Society, the Massachusetts Mechanic Association, and the Fire Club.

In fact, in his young adulthood, he appears to have been a joiner. David Kilmer, a recent compiler of Fowle's autobiography, surmised that his preference toward a Masonic career had to do with the Craft's grounding in enlightenment ideas, its ideal of brotherhood, and the mysteries of the ritual. These would have had a natural appeal to Fowle's religious and philosophical sentiments. But Kilmer suspects the first and foremost reason Fowle became a Mason was because there, more than any other aspect of his life, he was able to realize the promise he first displayed in his childhood; he could rub shoulders on terms of equality with the most prominent men on the Boston waterfront and still remain a mechanic. Fowle believed in the equality of humankind above all else.[191]

In addition to being a freemason, he also joined the "Lodge of the Odd-Fellows" because he had some friends who belonged who frequently solicited him to join, and he was curious if it was "an encroachment on Masonry." The Order was vindicated upon his initiation and he thought highly of its benevolent aims. He resigned on amiable terms with the members a short time after joining primarily because the men in it were not among his particular peer group.

On the evening of April 10, 1793, Fowle was initiated an Entered Apprentice in St. Andrew's Lodge in Boston. The lodge met at the Green Dragon. In fact, St. Andrew's Lodge had owned the tavern since the year before Fowle was born. During the 1770s it had been a hotbed of Revolutionary sentiments. The members continued to meet there until 1817. Fowle was passed in May and raised a Master Mason in November that same year. Three years later, he joined the Chapter of Royal Arch Masons. It was through that Body that he met Thomas Smith Webb. The two met, probably the first time at Boston in August, 1797 when Webb visited St. Andrew's Chapter. Fowle was then serving as the Scribe of the Chapter. Their relationship grew as Webb continued to attend the Chapter meetings. By 1797, the York Rite had determined that, for want of regularity and uniformity in the work, lectures and government, a convention was needed for the purpose of establishing proper rules to bring about stability of the York Rite system. In January, 1798, that convention group met in Hartford, Connecticut. Fowle was a delegate from the Boston Chapter and Webb was elected the General Grand Scribe of the newly organized General Grand Royal Arch Chapter of the United States. It is believed that Fowle studied with Webb at some time following the convention because he became proficient enough in the work to be asked to organize and head a new lodge.

In 1800, Fowle's name appeared at the head of a petition to charter Mount Lebanon Lodge. He became its first Master. Being discouraged by the improprieties and errors that had long crept into the work and lectures, one of his objectives was to set out to find a few zealous brothers who could assist him in teaching the proper method of ritual to his lodge without the fear of being denounced as an innovator of the work. He was apparently successful because he mentioned with some pride in his autobiography that the brethren were so delighted with his work that it soon became the standard working in Massachusetts. The Grand Lodge offered to pay Fowle $1,200 ($100 each month) to spend a year in teaching his method to the lodges under their jurisdiction. He refused to do so because he felt he could not leave his business, but convinced the Grand Master to hire Benjamin Gleason, who he said was equally well qualified. Gleason was employed and paid by the Grand Master.

Fowle later returned to St. Andrew lodge and served as its Master for six years in succession. In 1801 he was appointed Junior Grand Deacon of the Massachusetts Grand Lodge and was subsequently elected Senior Grand Warden. He was also commissioned a District Deputy Grand Master, and in visiting all the lodges in his District, he regularly corrected errors he found in the work. He was paid all his expenses plus $4 per day. His ability as a ritualist would get him appointed Grand Lecturer of the Grand Chapter of Royal Arch Masons, an office he held for a number of successive years. He was elected the first Grand Commander of the Templars in 1805 and would serve in that capacity for twenty years. He also served as Grand Master of the Grand Encampment of Massachusetts and Rhode Island.

During all these years, he regularly traveled with Webb, whom we have seen was equally zealous in promoting the York Rite system throughout the northeast. They became close friends, and it was not unusual for Fowle, Webb and Snow to be seen together as delegates to the Grand meetings of the York Rite Bodies. It was very likely the three took every opportunity on their travels to impart the craft work in the lodges they visited. Fowle is known to have personally taught the work in Maine, New Hampshire, Vermont, Massachusetts, Rhode Island, Connecticut and New York.

A man who loved Masonry, he was one of its strongest proponents during the dark days after the Morgan tragedy. Perhaps it is appropriate that we leave our essay on Henry Fowle by quoting from his biography a wonderful sentiment he left concerning the fraternity and the church:

"I have been censured, by some severely, for my attachment to Masonry. I know it has taken a good deal of time and some money,

Henry Fowle

but I have never repented it. The Institution has suffered, and is still suffering, under a cloud of calumny and misrepresentation, but if the Christian Religion is worth preserving, (and no honest man will deny it,) Masonry is worthy of our support. There is not a sentiment or principle in real Masonry which is not recommended and enjoined in the New Testament. If love to God and love to man be inculcated in the Christian Religion, it is no less so in Masonry."

Jeremy Cross

"Brother Jeremy Cross was an unlettered man. His knowledge, even of the English tongue, was extremely limited. His orthography was bad; his grammar execrable. He knew nothing of the history of Masonry, and cared nothing for it. To all questions outside of the mere 'Work' and 'Lectures,' his honest answer was–and he had learned it from his Master (Webb) who was much wiser than he–"When you memorize what I am teaching you, you will know as much about Masonry as I do!"[192]

And thus begins an article about Cross published in the *Voice of Freemasonry* in 1862. It could easily be judged that Jeremy Cross was another of the fathers of American Freemasonry who practiced his Masonry in the same way that most lodge ritualists do today. What he knew of the ritual is what he knew of Masonry. His success was wholly based on his literal accuracy of repetition. He always did the same thing in the same way, and repeated the same instruction in the same words. He varied neither gesture, nor step; neither word and syllable; nor letter. He had that remarkably drone qualification of doing a part as it was set down. And that is precisely why his pupils liked him. They could depend on the accuracy of his words.

Indeed, many a brother's knowledge of things Masonic extends no farther than how adept he is in the art of memorization. It can well be argued that the last sixty years has seen such an emphasis on the language of the Masonic ritual that it is today the single most significant detriment to our fraternity. Of course, the emphasis was the same in Cross's time. But at that time, it was a necessary thing because there was no single adopted prescribed form for the making of Masons. The uniformity of the ritual was an important challenge not only to Cross, but the other members of this small team of Webb students. As we have seen, Masonry needed a glue that would make it a national and unified

Jeremy Cross

organization. A ritual language that could be universally practiced in all lodges and across all jurisdictional boundaries was just such an elixir that would ensure a national identity.

And Jeremy Cross was as faithful an adherent to Webb's model as any man of his period. In fact, it has been said that no man since the death of Thomas Webb has exercised so widespread an influence upon the practical workings of Masonry in this country than did Cross.

He was born in Havervill, New Hampshire on June 27, 1783 and was made a Mason in St. John's Lodge at Portsmouth in 1807. A hat maker by profession, Cross traveled in New Hampshire and Vermont to apply his trade. It has not been determined when Cross and Webb first became acquainted, but it is almost certain he learned the work from Webb shortly after he became a Freemason. He was certified by the Grand Lecturer of the Grand Lodge of New Hampshire in November, 1813 to be well acquainted with the Lectures on the first Degrees of Masonry, "according to the 'Prestonian arrangement' as received, sanctioned, and directed to be taught" by that Grand Lodge. Benjamin Gleason was honored that same year for his work in teaching the Webb form in New Hampshire. However, it is not likely that Gleason initially instructed Cross in the Work because Cross noted in his diary he did not meet Gleason before 1820. Barney did not receive the work from Webb until 1817. Cross must have received the work directly from Webb sometime between 1808 and 1812.

Cross went to Providence, Rhode Island early in 1816 to meet with Webb. He was teaching under Webb's influence as early as March. He was with Webb at the time a Templar Convention took place in Philadelphia in June, 1816. Cross was apparently travelling widely giving instruction on the ritual by the end of that summer. A letter from one Henry Timberlake, written in Paris, Kentucky on September 26, 1816 suggests that "Cross visits this country for the purpose of ascertaining the difference of the Work in the East and West, to deliver the lectures to the different lodges he may visit and with the ultimate and laudable purpose of aiding the establishment of a General Grand Lodge at Washington City..."[193]

But it is clear that Cross had knowledge of the lectures for some time prior to the autumn of 1816. We have at least one published record that he was made a Royal Arch Mason in Champlain Chapter No. 2, at St. Albans, Vermont on July 11, 1815, while engaged in "Lecturing the Lodges" in that State.[194] There is little question as to whether he learned Webb's mode of instruction; or travelled from lodge to lodge teaching the work during and after 1816. While his letters mention lecturing in lodges as early as March, 1815, he clearly was reporting his activities directly to Webb after 1816. He kept a detailed diary of his activities covering the period August, 1817 through March, 1820. In it, he notes lecturing with Webb, and mentions frequent visits to lodges in his diary. Soon after, he would begin writing Webb with some frequency, reporting on his activities in the lodges which he visited. If he did not consider himself a disciple of Webb, it is unlikely he would have taken the trouble to report to Webb on the status of the work in the lodges he visited.

Cross was an exceptional pupil, having an amazingly retentive memory. He embraced the teachings of Freemasonry as an art to be practiced as well as learned. In a diary entry on June 1, 1818, in response to a request of a friend to know what the circumstance was for his changing his religious views, Cross wrote, "Soon after I was 21, I joined the Society of Free and Accepted Masons, and finding the Institution was founded upon Christian morals and not interfering with any sect or denomination any farther than morality and good work are concerned, I became very attached to the society and strove hard to become a proficient in the mysteries, and, in so doing I had frequently to consult the Bible, and while in my Masonic researches I found my universal fabric on a tottering foundation and concluded to abandon it. About 4 years since I commenced the occupation of a Masonic Lecturer and as it became my duty to teach and persuade others to be strictly moral, I conceived it all important that I should be so myself or else my theory and practice would not agree–I therefore set about correcting my own morals, broke myself of profane language, which I was occasionally in the habit of, and many other foolish practices that would abase the man. "[195]

Cross launched his lecturing career as soon as he had learned the lectures. And he traveled for Webb. He would visit cities and lodges teaching the work, even while on probation as a lecturer. In 1817, he received a commission from the General Grand Chapter (which Webb had created) as General Grand Lecturer. In August, he journeyed to Boston and exemplified the work before the officers of the Grand Lodge of Massachusetts, and received their hearty approval. He then received the same acclamation from the Grand Lodge of Rhode Island, and was able to secure the written certification of his ability as an Instructor in both the Symbolic and Capitular Degrees. The certificates were signed by Webb himself.

In 1818, Cross moved to New Haven, Connecticut and entered into a business partnership with brother Amos Doolittle to engrave aprons. He affiliated with Hiram Lodge No. 1 in New Haven, but continued his travels throughout the country. He almost single-handedly disseminated the Select Master's Degree of the York Rite system to the brethren of the period. It is estimated he established nearly thirty-three Councils of Select Masters in various parts of the United States. His travels in teaching the Masonic lectures would take him to Pennsylvania, Ohio, Kentucky, Mississippi, Louisiana, Virginia, Delaware, New Jersey, New York, New Hampshire and Vermont.

It was also during this time that he corroborated with Doolittle to prepare illustrations of the several Masonic emblems. Doolittle was one of the earliest American copperplate engravers. He spent his life around New Haven and apprenticed as a jeweler and silversmith. He taught himself engraving and became a prolific producer of historical and satirical engravings, bookplates, portraits and biblical illustrations.[196] He was already well known when Cross met him, having produced a popular series of engravings portraying the Battles of Lexington and Concord. As early as August of 1818, Cross would spend days drafting the emblems with Doolittle for a Masonic Chart, which he intended to publish. Over the next twelve months he would spend his idle time drafting the liturgy for his 'Chart.' It would become his singular contribution to the ceremonial form of Masonry as it was to be practiced from that day forward.

Jeremy Cross published his manual shortly after Webb's death in 1819, which he entitled, *The True Masonic Chart or Hieroglyphic Monitor*. Doolittle penned some forty emblems as an adornment to the overall work. These beautifully penned drawings became an integral reason for the success of the Monitor, as brethren found them to be wonderful aides to memorizing the text. In fact, it appears that Doolittle was the actual author of the "Weeping Virgin over the Broken Column" emblem that is now almost universally used in the lecture of the Third Degree. In the first edition of Cross's Monitor, a credit line is given to Doolittle for designing the emblem. But it does not appear in any later edition. Cross bought the copyright to the emblems from Doolittle soon after the first edition was published. The Monitor ran through sixteen editions during Cross's lifetime.

Cross marketed his Monitor as being a compilation of the works of Preston and Webb, along with other recognized authorities. He claimed to embellish it only to the extent that it strictly conformed with the 'ancient system.'

We can conclude that Cross personally authored nothing in the way of text (although, being a man strong in his personal faith, he reinforced a few of the Christian references found in Webb's work). It is even generally agreed that Doolittle's pictorial emblems originally came from Preston's work sometime during the mid-1700s; and some were copies of those found in Webb's published works. Cross published his Monitor primarily to correct what he felt were differences in the various modes of working and what he considered "improper classifications of the emblems."

Cross also stayed away from most of the previously popular references to history, doctrine, general purposes, origin, and government of the fraternity, as he knew very little about these matters, and was generally not concerned with Masonic education outside the recitation of the language of the work. Throughout his life, in guiding subsequent publications of his Monitor and in teaching the work in more states than any other Webb student, Cross was driven only by the goal of ceremonial uniformity. He carried copies of his Monitor with him in his travels, he routinely sold them to students whom he personally taught, and he included them with sales of Masonic aprons and other paraphernalia requested by lodges.

The emblems published in Cross's Monitor proved so popular that they became the standard forms for lodge use in almost every State of the Union.

Cross lectured in lodges, and instructed brethren in his 'uniform' work throughout the northeast. He, and several other personal students of Webb, namely John Snow and Henry Fowle, lectured together as a team whenever the opportunity presented itself for any two of them to be together. Cross was given permission to teach the work of Symbolic Masonry, as well as the Chapter, Council, and Commandery work in New Hampshire, Massachusetts, Rhode Island, Ohio, Connecticut, Vermont, New York, New Jersey, Maryland, District of Columbia and

Virginia. All in all, he lectured and taught in the Webb mode of the Work in these States, and Kentucky. This was confirmed in a letter he wrote to the Craft in Kentucky

He also aggressively promoted his system of work by mailing his Monitor to the known Masonic teachers in essentially every Grand Jurisdiction of his time. He personally met Benjamin Gleason on August 24, 1820, and while he found Brother Gleason to be a "great talker and not so much refined as I could wish," he convinced Gleason to use his published Monitor as an aide to the work in the lodges and Jurisdictions where Gleason worked.

All in all, Jeremy Cross would have the most widespread influence of any Masonic lecturer of his time in teaching or facilitating a uniform method of Masonic working in the United States. In addition, he clearly gave the Royal and Select Masters Degrees of the York Rite their first general acceptance in America, and he did more to facilitate the use of "pictures" as an aide to teaching the work than any previous Masonic instructor in America. He was the teacher of several of the men who would later publish Monitors of their own, namely John Dove of Virginia and Thomas Cushing of Connecticut.

But his efforts to secure a uniformity to the Masonic ritual in the United States would be halted by a few his own students, and the students of Webb's students.

It seems that every generation has its opportunists–men who want to make their own mark in their own time. With Webb and Cross leading the way, by the early 1820s, American Masonry had entered the period of the ritual publicist. Cross produced his Monitor patterned after his instructor, as did many other Masonic writers after him—Dove, Cushing, Mackey, Cornelius, Moore, Sickels, Simons, Davis, and others—and so did many Grand Lodges, who printed their own Masonic Manuals or Monitors; all based on Webb.

It is perhaps human nature for some that when they see something good, they immediately think they can improve on it. The Masonic ritual was not immune to such opportunists, who used both written and verbal methods to immortalize themselves. It would not be long before almost any Mason could acquire any one or more of a number of published lectures, supposedly pertaining to the "original" work of his own jurisdiction, or, even better, a "pure" copy of the original work of Thomas Smith Webb himself.

These published monitors were often marketed through a few innovative brethren who styled themselves as "traveling ritualists."

The "Degree Peddlers"

The last three-quarters of the nineteenth century could well be called the era of the Masonic degree peddlers. As good as Thomas Webb and his students' intentions were in regard to bringing ritual stability to the young America through standardized instruction and Grand Lodge sanction, they were not able to make their influence known in enough places to gain wide acceptance. Nor could they overcome the stubborn independence of men who seemed to relish in independence during this era. After the American states became independent, the men in the lodges seemed steadfast in maintaining what they had, or were developing for themselves. They wanted nothing that gave the appearance of English rule. For all the work Webb and his followers accomplished in the name of uniformity, they lived in a time when the thought of a uniform ritual was, in reality, offensive to many Masons. As pointed out earlier, so many diverse ritual systems found their way into the American workings that it was an extraordinary undertaking indeed to standardize the work. Men who had been taught one way were very stubborn toward the idea of "re-learning" the ritual they already knew. In every Grand Jurisdiction where the traveling ritualists worked, there was a quiet resistance to change in many of the lodges. And there were about as many ritual workings as there were lodges.

To some extent, ritual diversity between Grand Jurisdictions was actually promoted by the Grand Lodges themselves. After all, if the Grand Lodge was not able to impose a standard uniform ritual, then the next best thing was to approve brothers who were well versed in some form of ritualistic work. Thomas Webb and his students created a new method for how men learned the work in lodges. Masonic lectures were no longer delivered by way of the vision of William Preston, whereby men would learn Masonry by discussing the lessons in lodge and contemplating Masonic emblems around their own individual symbol systems. Webb and his group learned Masonry as something which was to be memorized. These early promoters of a uniform working were known and respected throughout as legitimate teachers of the work. They were professional Masons. They were the first of several generations of traveling ritualists. These men were hired to instruct lodges within a jurisdiction a certain mode of working for the purpose of standardizing the work within a Grand Lodge.

The problem, of course, was that, after the death of this first generation of ritualists, men who claimed to know Webb's work, or Barney's work, or Gleason's work, for instance, would market themselves as traveling lecturers for the purpose of profiting off the brethren they taught. And, too, individual Lodges would avail themselves of the services of traveling ritualists without the sanction of Grand Lodge. For example, in Indiana, the minutes of Webb Lodge No. 24, Richmond, record that in September, 1824, the lodge engaged one Brother Michael McLaughlin of Ohio to deliver a course of lectures covering a period of ten days, at $5 per day.[197]

By the 1840s, when Grand Lodges were unable to agree on a system of instruction and had not the finances to pay the salary of a Grand Lecturer, there were numerous instances in which lodges arranged for their own schools of instruction. Minutes of lodge after lodge indicate repeated "contracts" with men who had been hired to deliver a course of lectures for a fee plus expenses. The going rate was generally $20-25 a week, along with a vote of thanks from the lodge. The business of degree peddler as substitute Grand Lecturer was lucrative enough to enjoy an increasing following; at least for a while.

But on rare occasion, the lodges would turn against their own traveling degree peddlers.

Solemn Strikes the Funeral Chime...

There's a sad irony in the fact that the man who wrote these words sung in lodge rooms and at graves by thousands of lodges in America, was himself buried without Masonic honors.

Brother David Vinton died in Shakertown, Kentucky in July, 1833. While on his death bed at that place, the Masons of Lodge No. 73, at Bowling Green, wrote to the Grand Lodge inquiring whether David Vinton was a Mason in Good Standing. The reply was in the negative. Brother Robert Morris, in writing about the circumstances of Vinton's life in the Masonic Journal, Volume 53, 1880, eloquently said, "And so the sweet poet and Masonic songster of the period died under a cloud, and his tombstone no emblem of the Craft could have."

Very little is written about Vinton's life. He was a teacher of the Masonic ritual (primarily the York Rite) in the Southern States, having the most success in North and South Carolina. He is best known for publishing at Dedham, Massachusetts, in 1816, a volume containing a selection of Masonic, Sentimental and Humorous Songs, Duets, Glees, Canons, Rounds and Canzonets, under the title of "The Masonic Minstrel." Dedicated to the "Most Ancient and Honorable Fraternity of Free and Accepted Masons," brother Vinton sold 12,000 copies by subscription. It was in this volume that the words of the beautiful dirge used in the Third Degree are found. Known as the *Pleyel's Hymn,* the music was composed by Ignaz Joseph Pleyel, a composer who was a student of Haydn's. It is the hymn from Pleyel's "4th Quartet, op. 7," published in 1791.

The details that led to Vinton's expulsion from the Grand Lodges of South Carolina, North Carolina, Connecticut, and Virginia, have always been a bit sketchy, but apparently relate to his taking liberties as a ritual teacher and writer.

In 1821, Vinton was summoned by the Grand Chapter of Virginia to be examined on charges preferred against him by Franklin Lodge #4 of Royal Arch Masons, of which Vinton belonged. The charges were for "highly improper and unmasonic conduct." Vinton did not respond to the summons, so lost his privileges as a Mason in that Grand Chapter, and 'throughout the world.' It was publicly claimed within the craft that Vinton had made Mark Masters and Past Masters without a dispensation or a warrant. But the real reason for the charge was that Vinton was caught furnishing cipher notes of the lectures. Vinton felt that competing lecturers, among them Jeremy Cross, were simply trying to discredit his work. The incident caused some heated debate in the South.

The Grand Lodge of North Carolina followed with a public condemnation of Vinton in the Raleigh newspapers.

This action upset the Grand Lodge of Georgia, who declared that every Masonic brother ought to have his good name protected until such time as he is formally accused by a regular lodge, notified of the charges against him, and then given an opportunity to answer and stand before his accusers. In Vinton's defense, the Masons of Georgia issued a manifesto dated May 16, 1821, in which they claimed Vinton had "shown them documents which proved his moral character as a private citizen and a Mason." Apparently, his fame as a learned Mason made the matter of his offense debatable among the Grand Lodges where he had worked. He was popular in Georgia. Continuing with the manifesto, the Grand Lodge stated, "We hailed with pleasure his arrival among us, and because, by his means, we could improve ourselves in the noble and ancient art of Masonry. We have not been disappointed. His instructions have been sensibly felt. His deportment has been that of the gentleman and the Mason; and, if we are allowed to form an opinion, we will say, that the man who has thus behaved while here cannot be charged with unmasonic conduct."

The brethren of Georgia disagreed with Virginia and North Carolina that Vinton had committed a Masonic offense. According to their assessment, Vinton was simply more liberal as to the method of his communicating the lectures to the officers of lodges and chapters. To Georgia, he did not "infringe on the principles of Masonry in the least."

In fact, they revealed that Vinton's lecture ciphers had been approved by "upwards of two hundred lodges and chapters in the United States, and by some of the brightest luminaries in the galaxy of Masonry."

It turns out that Vinton's notes were far less extensive than is normally found in monitors of the present day. In fact, according to Thomas Hayward, Grand Master of Florida in 1858, who personally reviewed Vinton's lectures, his printed work would not even raise an eyebrow compared with what Pike or Mackey had published by the 1860s.

Thus, the real reason for Vinton's demise was that of conferring the Chapter degrees without authority. For this, he should have been disciplined by the Grand Chapters under which he worked. But it is hard to conclude that he actually committed any offense against the laws of Masonry. Since Webb, Cross, Dove, Barker, and others made a living by peddling degrees of the York Rite before Vinton's time, it can be argued that he was simply following the precedent set by others before him, who may have been trying to control their own market as lecturers. Although wrong in his own actions, there were no grounds for Grand Lodges to denounce him as they did. Still less, to expel him from Masonry.

Nevertheless, he was hunted down, and his last hours spent without the honor or privilege of Masonic charity. He died a broken man, a "stranger in a strange land." The kind brethren of Kentucky, who declared themselves "willing to give him funeral honors if his character were cleared up," could find no official declaration of forgiveness in his name. They could do nothing for him or his memory.

But, for tens of thousands of Masons today, David Vinton will forever be a star in the annals of Freemasonry. His simple, poetic dirge has earned him the respect of every brother who has marched the march of Solomon, or prayed the soliloquy over a fallen brother.

13 The National Quest for Ritual Uniformity

In the past two centuries there have been three organized and sanctioned national efforts to standardize the form and words of the Masonic ritual that evolved from the English workings and migrated to America. One originated in England; the others, in the United States. These are each explained here because they represent remarkable events in the history of Speculative Masonry.

The English Lodges of Promulgation and Reconciliation

When the Ancients and Moderns English Grand Lodges adopted their Act of Union in 1813, it marked the most important Masonic event in nineteenth century Masonry. It was the first attempt in the history of Freemasonry to bring the government, the authority, the workings, and the customs of some 650 Constituent Lodges in two Grand Lodges together under a single umbrella for the purpose of "standardizing" the work of Masonry to comply with the Ancient Landmarks and restore the proper officer's duties, passwords, signs, charges, etc. to the Work. In short, it was the first national movement to reconcile and adopt a uniform system of Masonic law and ritual.

And it wasn't easy.

It would take four years to define and agree on the administrative structure of such a venture. In April of 1809, the Premier Grand Lodge adopted a resolution to enjoin their lodges to revert to the Ancient Landmarks of the Society. On October 26th, the Grand Master issued a Warrant to "form the Lodge of Promulgation for the purpose of promulgating the Ancient Land Marks of the Society and instructing the Craft in all such matters and forms as may be necessary to be known by them in consequence of and obedience to the said resolution and order."[198] It was an effort by this Grand Body to bring the two English Grand Lodges, along with Ireland and Scotland, together to establish a standard Masonic system. The Premier Grand Lodge felt that, by initiating the effort, it would show good faith toward its sister jurisdictions in its desire to 'admit' that it had made changes to the laws and ceremonies of Masonry that needed to be reconciled among all of the Grand Bodies. The Ancients Grand Lodge had also appointed a committee in 1810, which agreed that such "a Masonic Union...would be expedient and advantageous to both."[199]

Most of the so-called changes were the result of the numerous exposures to the Masonic ceremonies and rituals that had been published during the period from 1730 through 1769. Some ritual changes had been made over this period from a fear of the profane gaining admission into lodges on the basis of knowledge gained from reading these exposures. Some changes were made as a matter of lodge custom; some tending to favor one form of working over another. The most significant ritual changes made by Grand Lodge action included transposing the secret words in the first and second degrees, changing the 'steps', omitting the use of Deacons as lodge officers, omitting the ceremony of installation, refusing to recognize the rite of the Holy Royal Arch as a "conclusion or perfection" of the Third Degree, and changing the ceremonies to rely chiefly on teaching the tenets of the fraternity by means of lectures rather than ceremonies.

The creation of the Lodge of Promulgation, then, was a decisive step to unify and standardize the ceremonial forms of Masonry.

This body would meet some 30 times over a two year period. It would observe the ancient and modern practices in the three degrees, and study all the forms and ceremonies of opening, closing, as well as the method in which the secrets of the art were imparted. Its last minutes were recorded on March 5, 1811, with a report to the Grand Master that the Lodge had "derived the most authentic information from the purist sources, so settled and determined a proper engagement thereof as henceforth to render all the ordinary Ceremonies of the Craft, in practice simple, in effect impressive, and in all respects strictly conformable to ancient practice..."[200] The report went on to state that "special care has been taken in every respect to prefer as concise a mode of arrangement as is consistent with a retention of the essentials; scrupulously avoiding at the same time any sacrifice to brevity at the expense of those Ancient Forms they are directed to ascertain and restore;" then follows a strong condemnation of printed communications on Masonic subjects professing to contain copious information.

However, the report also made a strong recommendation that a "degree or office of Masonic Professor of the Art and Mystery of Speculative Freemasonry" be conferred by diploma on some skilled craftsman. His task would be to select and instruct a number of assistants to teach the work to the lodges, wherever situated. He was also to draft a syllabus as an aid to lodge officers, along with a 'Pandect' comprising a comprehensive digest of everything relating to the ritual of Freemasonry. This aid was to be written in Masonic cipher and used to settle any disputes or differences which might arise from time to time in regard to the language of the several Masonic ceremonies.

The recommendation was shelved, although it would provide a "model" for what would ultimately become a popular movement in America, i.e., the Grand Lecturer system.

The ceremonies and lodge workings as agreed on by the Lodge of Promulgation were exemplified over a four year period in lodges throughout the south and north of England. Certainly, its labors paved the way for the Union of the two Grand Lodges, which took place on St. John's Day, December 27, 1813. In true English form, it was an occasion that probably worked more because it involved its royalty, than because it was "right" in the minds of the brethren of both Grand Bodies. The Prince of Wales (later George IV), had been elected as the Grand Master of the Moderns in 1790, and he also became Grand Master of Scotland in 1806. When he became the Prince Regent (heir to the Throne), he resigned his Grand Mastership; and his brother, the Duke of Sussex, was appointed to the Grand East in 1813. It was then

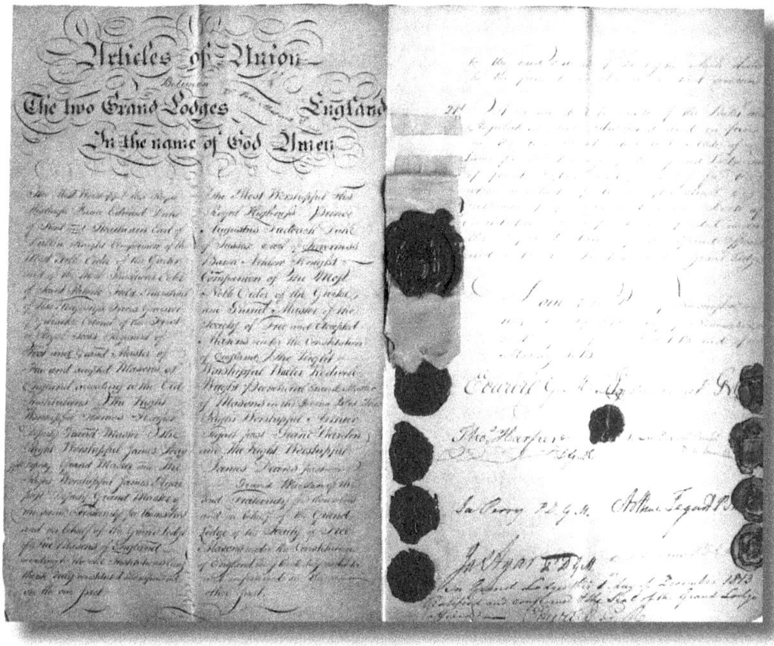

THE ARTICLES OF UNION

arranged that the Duke of Atholl should resign as Grand Master of the Grand Lodge of the Ancients so the Duke of Kent could be appointed in his place. This happened in November, 1813, and the following month, the new Grand Master of the Ancients, the Duke of Kent, proposed that the Duke of Sussex should be Grand Master of the United Grand Lodges. The deed was done, and, as these two Dukes were the sons of George III, it made the Act of Union almost a formality.

Then the new United Grand Lodge warranted what was called the Lodge of Reconciliation, made up of nine experts (and the Grand Secretary) from each of the old Grand Lodges. Its task was to get the rank and file in both of the 'old' fraternities to accept the "pure and genuine" forms for which the 'new' Grand Lodge would be bound. The process started out innocently enough. The two groups of nine met in adjoining rooms and opened their 'lodge' according to the usual practice of their respective Grand Lodge. Then they would mutually give and receive the work of both fraternities.

After meeting ten times from December 1813 until June, 1814 (and appointing some ten additional brothers along the way), a compact was signed stating that "the three Grand Lodges were perfectly in unison in all the great and essential points of the Mystery of the Craft..."[201]

As can well be imagined, the compact sounded good on paper, and probably represented the ideals of the committee. But the rank and file was not convinced. Many brethren belonging to the Grand Lodge of the Ancients were far from being satisfied, and protested against the new system. Six lodges even formed a committee to "devise measures for opposing the 'innovations' attempted to be introduced by the Lodge of Reconciliation."[202] One irritated brother, when called before the Lodge to state his objections, informed it that "the language is altogether altered and the differences are of great magnitude." Yet another crusty old brother brought forward the accusation that the Lodge of Reconciliation "had not done what they were directed by the Articles of Union, and had altered all the ceremonies and language of Masonry and not left one sentence standing!" Besides that, he figured the Lodge had no authority to "arrange anything in regard to the proceedings for working lodges."[203]

Setting aside such idle comments from the craft, the Committee held fast to their proposed workings and recommendations over the next year–even as the discontent grew. By mid-1815, the detractors had mailed a letter to the Board of General Purposes requesting that it disband the Lodge and create another. The authorities held firm, and gradually the opposition subsided.

All total, twenty-six meetings would be held from August, 1814 to March, 1815, at which the 'new' ceremonies were rehearsed. The first degree was worked twenty-two times, the second on twenty, and the third, on twelve occasions. This process would repeat itself for many years after the Union, and a lot of give and take concerning the ritual went on unofficially in London and in the Provinces up until 1825. The result was that, by 1830, the ceremonies as created by the Lodge of Promulgation (1809-11), recommended by the Lodge of Reconciliation (1813-16), and finally approved by the Grand Lodge on June 5, 1816, had been deviated from so significantly that it became difficult to ascertain what really came out of the initial effort toward ritual uniformity. Hextall concluded that what came out of the Lodge of Reconciliation was more academic than real, and amounted to much less than anticipated.

Eventually, two primary ritual centers emerged in England. One was called the Stability Lodge of Instruction, established in 1817 by brothers who wanted to keep the philosophical lectures and symbolisms made popular by the Moderns intact. This group was made up of regular attendees of the Lodge of Reconciliation and knew what that Lodge really taught. For the first fifteen years of its existence, it worked only the Lectures. It was said to have sired a number of modifications which are still in use today. Had it met at or near the Freemasons Hall, its working would have likely secured the favor of most Masons.

The other was the Emulation Lodge of Improvement, created in 1823 by nine lodges made up of members who had no close association with either the Lodge of Promulgation or the Lodge of Reconciliation. It was politically astute enough to eventually do what the Lodge of Stability failed to do. It moved its meetings to the Freemasons' Tavern adjoining the Freemasons' Hall in 1839, securing the support and influence of many Grand Lodge Officers and Provincial Grand Officers, who subsequently did their utmost to further its reputation. A well-known instructor of the period, Peter Gilkes, joined this lodge in 1825. Brother Gilkes was retired when he joined and his favorite pastime was to meet with such brethren as were disposed to meet with him every day from one o'clock until evening.

The Emulation Lodge of Improvement based all its claims for pre-eminence on the sole assumption that they derived their ritual from this known Masonic instructor, although he was not a member of the Lodges of Promulgation or Reconciliation. His method was popular because he was said to have distributed manuscript books from which his pupils could learn. Since Brother Gilkes was not a member of either the Lodge of Promulgation or the Lodge of Reconciliation, his work was presumed not to be "tainted" by the stirrings of the Union promoters. The work of the Emulation Lodge was strictly for Master Masons, and it concentrated on only the lecture sections of the degrees-claiming to take its authority from yet another group called the Grand Stewards Lodge, which was considered the custodian of the official rendering of the lectures and ceremonies–although no one seems to know as to when and under whose authority these were compiled.

Whatever the Grand Stewards Lodge might have been, there is one piece of evidence that suggests they were staunch supporters of Gilkes' lodge. The "Freemason's Quarterly Review" of September, 1836, published a short history of Emulation Lodge, as follows: "About the year 1823 several Brethren considered that the Masonic lectures were not worked in the Lodges upon a sufficiently regulated system, and that if those, whose attainments as working Masons placed them as a prominent authority, were to meet together to work efficiently, they might be the means of effecting much improvement... Some members of the Grand Stewards Lodge, hitherto the only authority for a recognized system, felt that it was necessary to watch the proceedings. Some Grand Officers, also attended... We have the authority of a Grand officer for stating that never was there so perfect an illustration of the ceremonies and lectures ever before manifested."[204] Among those best qualified to judge, it is believed the Grand Steward's Lodge was indeed the custodian of the official rendering of the Lectures, and therefore the Ceremonies.[205] It is not clear, however, if the lectures being worked in Emulation Lodge were the same as that being worked in Stability Lodge, and the same as that in the Grand Stewards Lodge. It is believed that Gilkes initially received his instruction from Dr. Samuel Hemming, who was a noted lecturer himself and who had been given the task of arranging the ceremonies and lectures for the Lodge of Reconciliation by the Grand Master in 1813. In fact, the Minutes of the Grand Lodge indicate that the ceremonies of the Lodge of Reconciliaton were rehearsed for members of the Grand Lodge on two separate occasions and were approved and adopted, and that a vote of thanks was given to Dr. Hemming for his work.[206] Hemming had presided at more than one third of the Reconciliation Lodge meetings and by 1816 he had compiled lectures on all three Degrees.

As for the lectures of the Stability Lodge of Instruction, although arranged differently, those too were chiefly compilations of the formerly delivered Hemming lectures. It is significant to note that Hemming was also an adherent of the William Preston system of working. Hemming had an astute interest in preserving what the old Lodge of Antiquity had brought to the Lodge of Reconciliation. His mastership over the Lodge of Reconciliation ended in his withdrawal from the meetings for a period of time for the reason that he could not convince the whole of the committee to agree with the Lodge of Promulgation's work. A compromise was ultimately agreed to by introducing a few changes that were new and had not previously been adopted by either of the Grand Lodges.

The lecture system of the Grand Stewards Lodge is believed to have been compiled by William Williams and William Shadbolt, who had been successive Masters between 1814 and 1818. In their younger years, both of these men had connections with the lecture system of William Finch and it is believed that it was Finch's system of lectures that were used as the base for the Grand Stewards Lodge. Henry Sadler, the first Grand Librarian of the United Grand Lodge, believed all three lecture workings—the Grand Stewards Lodge, the Emulation Lodge, and the Stability Lodge–to be Prestonian Lectures.[207]

In any event, the earliest national effort to standardize Masonic ritual practices resulted in little more than balancing lectures with ceremonies. In fact, ritual diversity seems to have ultimately taken rule over English Masonry. There are a remarkable number of different workings which are still in use today; perhaps as many as one hundred. This author has no idea as to the exact number, but in addition to the Emulation Working, there is the Oxford, the Perfect Ceremonies, the West End Ritual, the ceremonies of the Stability Lodge, the Unanimity, the Logic, the Humber, the "South London, North London, East London, and West London workings, the Metropolitan, the Bath, the Bristol, the York, the Carlile, the Exeter, the Britannia, the English, and the Taunton. Each of these rituals derived from either Modern or Ancient workings, with language adapted from Promulgation, Reconciliation, Emulation, Stability, or Grand Steward 'workings'.

It can safely be concluded, then, that the Lodge of Reconciliation decided little in the way of Masonic ritual. The English failure to create and mandate a uniform ritual system should have given their American Brothers ample warning that the brothers meeting and working week end and week out in the lodges of our ancient Craft simply won't be moved to agree on a standard means of making men Masons, or of instructing them in the tenets of the Order. As one old English Brother would exclaim in 1870, when the question of ritual arose once again in the Grand Lodge of England, it was his opinion, "that with all the good will in the world to effect a uniformity of working, it was physically impossible to effect it"[208]

Of course, he undoubtedly made his declaration, having benefited by the insight gained from two additional national attempts to establish a uniform system of Masonic workings; this time in the United States. One such movement was called "The *Baltimore Convention;"* the other, the *"Masonic Conservators."*

The Baltimore Convention

The first nineteenth century American attempt to standardize ritual practices was born in the mind of a Grand Master of the Grand Lodge of Alabama. The anti-masonic furor that had spread across the northeastern states in response to the 'Morgan Affair', and a political movement within the country to mitigate the influence of Freemasons and its institution in the affairs of private and public enterprise, had devastated Lodges and Grand Lodges. It seemed that a national voice for Freemasonry was needed more than ever. At the annual Communication held in December, 1839, John Hicks, then Grand Master, proposed a resolution, which was adopted, that all Grand Lodges in the United States elect a delegate to meet in a National Masonic Convention to be held in Washington, D.C. in March, 1842, for the purpose of determining a uniform method of work throughout all lodges of the United States.

The Convention convened on March 7, 1842, in the Central Masonic Hall at 4th and D Sts. NW in Washington, with representatives from Connecticut, Virginia, Rhode Island, Maryland, New York, South Carolina, District of Columbia, Massachusetts, Alabama, and New

Masonic Hall–Baltimore, Maryland

Hampshire in attendance. John Dove of Virginia (Dove was a student of Jerry Cross) was elected Chairman. On March 9, a committee of five, including Dove, Charles W. Moore, James Herring, William Field and Isaacs Holmes was appointed to "determine upon a Uniform Mode of Work Throughout the Lodges of the United States."[209]

The committee met and compared the ceremonies and lectures of the Three Degrees used in the lodges of their own jurisdictions. They concluded that, while there was a satisfactory degree of uniformity among them, the various modes of practices arising from the want of a fixed standard of work would inevitably, if not restrained, "fix themselves to the permanent injury of the institution."

But the men really couldn't do anything about it. There were a couple of more pressing and significant problems. First, there was not an adequate representation of Grand Lodges from the West to decide on questions of uniformity. And the Grand Lodge of Alabama, who called the convention, apparently sent a delegate who could not provide adequate information about the ritual of that Grand Lodge to effect a resolution to the chief cause of the Convention. Perhaps more significant, the Committee also wisely concluded that, even if a means were to be adopted which would check any and all digressions in the ritual and adopt a uniform method of conferring the three Degrees, then the Committee itself could do little about it. It had been given a charge which was entirely beyond its power to enforce. Even if the brethren could proceed in harmonizing a system which they could agree upon, their labor would still fail because of the failure of a means to promulgate their decisions throughout the land.

The Committee did the only reasonable thing under Masonic Jurisprudence that it could. It recommended that every Grand Lodge in the United States appoint one or more skilled brethren, to be styled Grand Lecturers, who would meet and agree upon a course of instruction necessary and proper to be imparted to the lodges and the fraternity in their several jurisdictions. The idea was that this group would then continue to meet every third year to compare their lectures and correct variations in the work.[210]

The Convention made a few other interesting recommendations before it adjourned; namely, that a Grand Representative system be adopted throughout the United States to improve communication among Grand Lodges (a practice that was already being used in some

Grand Jurisdictions), and that Certificates of Good Standing be demanded of visiting brethren when attempting to visit lodges. Dues delinquency was common among all Grand Lodges, and the committee noted there was a reprehensible practice of receiving promissory notes for the fees for conferring Degrees, rather than collect the fees before degrees were conferred. In response to a recent request to the Grand Lodges from the Grand Lodge of Missouri, it also opined that Entered Apprentices and Fellow Crafts were not members of lodges, and should therefore not be entitled to the franchises of members. It recommended that all business matters of lodges be conducted only by Master Masons working in Master's lodges. The committee also felt that uniform legislation across all States was essential to the well-being of the fraternity. The Convention agreed on an assessment of $2 per delegate to offset expenses and directed that ten copies of the proceedings be mailed to every Grand Lodge.

The National Masonic Convention adjourned until the next year, when, on Monday, May 8, 1843, the Grand Lecturers so appointed met again at the Masonic Hall on St. Paul Street in Baltimore. This time, sixteen of the then twenty-three Grand Lodges registered delegates. The most active Grand Lodges in the United States had delegates in attendance. Louisiana did not send anyone; nor did Pennsylvania or Kentucky. Louisiana was already working a French rite, and was not interested in adopting a different system. Pennsylvania was working an Irish system and also had no interest in changing to the Webb form. The remaining Grand Lodges were either in their infancy, or could not afford the expense to send a delegate.

John Dove opened the Convention with a direct admonition as to its purpose. In his Monday evening address to the delegates, Dove said, "Brethren...for the first time in the history of the United States of North America, the Craft have found it necessary and expedient to assemble by their representatives, to take into consideration the propriety of devising some uniform mode of action by which the ancient landmarks of our beloved Order may be preserved and perpetuated..."[211] While he did not specify precisely what landmarks they would be addressing, and no mention was made concerning how to resolve the problem of the first convention, that of not having an unanimous representation of the Grand Lodges present, still the Convention kicked off with high hopes and resolve to affect a standard practice in American Masonic workings.

John Dove

The objects of the Convention were two-fold: to produce a uniformity of Masonic Work in North America; and to recommend any other administrative matters found to be expedient in elevating the respect of Masonry throughout the world.

On the second day of the Convention, four standing Committees were appointed covering the work and lectures of the three Degrees, the Masonic Funeral Service, the ceremonies of Consecration and Installation, and Masonic Jurisprudence. It was also intended that the Convention would publish a Masonic Trestle Board or Manual as an aid to the degrees and ceremonies, and perhaps direct a scholarly publication outlining the origin and history of the Craft.

One of Webb's students, John Barney of Ohio, was placed on the 'Standing Committee On Work', along with John Dove, Grand Secretary of Virginia, Charles Moore, Grand Secretary of Massachusetts, S.W.B. Carnegy, a Past Grand Master of Missouri, and a fellow named Ebenezer Wadsworth, Past Grand Secretary of New York.

During the course of the next seven days, a uniform method of the work, ceremonies, and lectures in all three degrees was agreed upon and exemplified before all representatives present. The procedure for each section involved grinding out the language within the Committee and then presenting it before all the Convention delegates. For example, on Tuesday, May 10, the Committee deliberated on the lecture of the First Degree and then reported before the entire group on the following morning that the lectures on the First Degree as worked out by the committee were recommended for adoption as "the authorized work in that Degree to be recommended to the Fraternity throughout the Union."

Of course, the recommendations were not always unanimously agreed on by the full Committee. For instance, Brother Wadsworth dissented on the above recommended adoption. He was the lone dissenting vote on this particular action. Things would not go well for him in subsequent reviews. On Thursday morning, May 11, the Committee reported on the lecture of the Second Degree and recommended its adoption. This time, Brother Wadsworth moved an amendment, which was rejected. Then the Committee reported on the Opening and Closing of a Lodge in the Second Degree, which was adopted. Wadsworth, deciding that his views were not in unanimity with the Committee, requested to be excused from the Committee on Work. He was replaced by Edward Herndon of Alabama. The Committee also reported on the opening and closing ceremonies of the First Degree, which were adopted.

On Friday morning, the Convention adopted the opening of the Third Degree, along with the first section lecture. In the afternoon, the Third Degree second and third section lectures were given and adopted.

On Saturday, May 13, a committee was appointed to report on a Masonic Trestle Board, and the Committee on Work reported on another section of the work of the Third Degree. It, too, was adopted and recommended to the fraternity throughout the United States by a vote of 12 to 1; with New York again dissenting. It should be noted that Brother Wadsworth's efforts were not to be totally disregarded by the Convention. On Sunday, May 14, he reported on the Consecration, Dedication, and Installation ceremonies of Lodges. He informed the group that the Committee had compared all the various authors and systems for such ceremonies, and recommended that "the forms in the 'Monitor,' under the authorship of M.W. Thomas Smith Webb, republished in 1812, possesses the least faults of any which have been before them, and has a high claim to antiquity, and having been in general use as a standard work for nearly half a century, possesses no errors so material as to require alteration..." The Convention adopted his report with six minor amendments to the Webb working.

Then on Monday, May 15, the Funeral Service and the process of granting Grand Lodge Certificates of Good Standing as discussed a year earlier were adopted. Actually, two funeral services were adopted; one compiled by Reverend Charles Case of South Carolina, the other being the Thomas Smith Webb funeral service, which had been in use by lodges throughout the United States for many years. The Committee on Installation also referred all prayers and charges to the Committee on Funeral Service for its review. During the afternoon session, Brother Charles Moore made his report on the Masonic Trestle Board. He recommended that a committee be designated to prepare and publish a Masonic textbook, which would include the full and complete workings of the Three Degrees, together with the ceremonies of consecrations, dedications and installations; the laying of cornerstones; the funeral service, order of processions; along with the charges, prayers and selections from scripture which were appropriate for lodge work. The report was adopted.

Another interesting item of business was also brought before the convention and discussed. Recognizing the independent and sovereign nature of American Grand Lodges made any kind of unity of workings and communication difficult to achieve, two plans were devised to affect a true and permanent unity. A general Grand Lodge of the United States was proposed; and a triennial convention of all Grand Lodges was recommended. It was the feeling of some that the independence of the Grand Lodges and their infrequent intercommunication was one of the primary aspects contributing to variations in the mode of work. It seemed it would not be plausible to expect unity throughout the whole Masonic family by maintaining more than one system of polity. If the purpose of the national committee was to report on what improvement could be made in the present system of Masonic governance to promote and preserve perfect unity in the work and lectures in the Masonic rites and ceremonies, then a General Body for Masonry in the United States seemed necessary.

Apparently, the desire for State sovereignty ran deep among the delegates, as the idea of a National Grand Lodge was dropped in favor of forming a National Masonic Convention of Grand Lodge representatives. The Convention was to meet every three years to prescribe a uniform mode and form of Masonic work and ceremonies throughout the United States. The Convention would also provide a national forum for hearing differences between Grand Jurisdictions.

Unfortunately, an important section of the proposed rules would disable it from ever being an effective entity of Masonic law or jurisprudence before it even had a chance to be tested. Specifically, a sentence was added providing that the National Convention's decisions would not be binding on any Grand Lodge. This important limitation is still in existence in the rules of the North American Conference of Grand Masters today–an organization which was, in essence, sired by the Baltimore Convention. It is a nice fellowship of Masonic leaders, but it can affect nothing in the way of Masonic law.

The remaining three days were spent exemplifying and ratifying all the work of the Three Degrees. On Wednesday afternoon, a letter was prepared by the delegates, addressed to the Masonic fraternity of the United States, inviting and urging a strict adherence to the "National System" of Masonic work and ceremonies as developed and adopted by the Convention at Baltimore. Proud of their accomplishments, and buoyed up by the reasonableness of their arguments, the committee went so far as to recommend to the Grand Lodges that they send delegates to Europe with the goal of promoting an universal language within the work worldwide.

Their work complete, the Conventioneers adjourned the session on May 17, 1843 at the Merchant's Hotel, with a gala dinner, entertainment, and a grand table lodge in the best of Masonic tradition.

The work of the Baltimore Convention was performed before the Grand lodge of Maryland on May 15, 1843 (before the Convention's work was finished). Since the Convention was in town, the elected delegate from Maryland, Brother Daniel Piper, invited the Convention delegates to perform their recommended work before the Maryland Grand Lodge at its Annual Communication, which was taking place in Baltimore the same week. The Convention obliged their Maryland brothers. The work was adopted by the Grand Lodge of Maryland in full on May 23, 1843, who ordered all its subordinate lodges to practice the same.

All seemed to be moving in the right direction for a national uniform work. Everyone was excited with the results. All agreed that there was nothing that could not be recommended to the favorable consideration of the various Grand Lodges.

Then a remarkable thing happened.

The Trestle Board, or Monitor, which the Convention had ordered published, was finished in 1844. It was to be prepared by John Dove (Chairman of the Convention), Charles Moore (Secretary), and S.W.B. Carnegy. By agreement of the Committee, Moore was to draw it up, submit it to Dove for approval, publish it for a modest fee, and for his trouble, receive the profits for its sale. The actual preparation of the monitor was done by Moore, with Dove and Carnegy making recommendations along the way. And in compiling it, the Committee became divided in opinion. Apparently Moore would send a number of pages to Dove and Carnegy for their review, but would not incorporate any of their suggestions in the final draft. Dove was also opposed to retaining the usual illustrations as they were normally published in other Monitors and textbooks, and did not want them published as a part of the Baltimore Work. The other two did. Carnegy and Moore refused to consent to their omission, and when Dove refused to sign off on the document, Moore and Carnegy published it in their names.

Dove was outraged. He immediately had a circular published and mailed to every Grand Lodge, denouncing the Trestle Board, and claiming that it was not the work adopted by the convention. The circular, read in part; "I hereby announce to you that the book, published by Bro. Charles Moore, of Massachusetts, and styled the "Masonic Trestle Board," is, in no shape, entitled to the confidence of the Fraternity, as pretending to reflect the work as adopted by the Convention; a very superficial comparison of it with the printed proceedings of the said Convention will show the most flagrant departures from its substance; and the most imprudent interpolations of matter and phraseology which have ever appeared in any work professing to be authentic on the subject of Masonry."[212]

Dove also sent a letter to his own Grand Lodge, explaining in detail his objections to Moore's efforts, which included a bashing condemnation of Moore as publishing "decidedly the most offensive, ridiculous and objectionable book upon Masonry it has ever fallen to my lot to peruse..."

Dove's objective was, of course, simply to arrest any further circulation of the book. Several members of the Committee endorsed the accuracy of the Monitor. The work and lectures as presented at the Baltimore Convention were supposedly that originally compiled by Webb, with few insignificant exceptions. Benjamin Gleason himself, a direct pupil of Webb, wrote to Moore one of the recommendations that was printed inside the frontispiece of the Monitor, stating "Having examined the new "Trestleboard," prepared by you and Brother Carnegy, for the use and benefit of the United States Lodges, it is with much satisfaction that I bear testimony to its merits, and hereby cordially recommend it to the patronage of the Fraternity, wherever dispersed, as a correct and useful Manual... "[213] It should also be noted that Moore, co-author of the Monitor, had been a direct student of Benjamin Gleason himself in 1823-24, and learned the work and lectures from him. Moore had been associated with Gleason by family ties and close Masonic relations for nearly a quarter of a century, and had enjoyed all of the rare advantages of Gleason's extensive and accurate knowledge of the various rituals of the different grades of the Order. It is likely Moore knew and recognized the Webb work as well as anyone.[214]

But Dove's circular dealt a death blow to the work of the

THE

MASONIC TRESTLE-BOARD,

ADAPTED TO THE

NATIONAL SYSTEM OF WORK AND LECTURES,

AS

REVISED AND PERFECTED

BY THE

UNITED STATES MASONIC CONVENTION,

AT

BALTIMORE, MARYLAND, A. L. 5843.

BY CHARLES W. MOORE & S. W. B. CARNEGY,

MAJORITY OF THE COMMITTEE APPOINTED BY THE CONVENTION TO PREPARE THE WORK.

BOSTON:
PUBLISHED BY CHARLES W. MOORE,
21 SCHOOL STREET.
TUTTLE & DENNETT, PRINTERS.
1843.

Convention. The Grand Lodge of Virginia immediately denounced the Trestle Board, and directed that Dove and the other Grand Lecturers meet again to draw up and submit the proper published version of the Baltimore Convention. Some Grand Lodges followed suit by withdrawing their support of the National Masonic Convention. Others continued to purchase Moore's Trestle Board, even with all the opposition to it. In fact, there was a growing demand for it as reflected by the purchases made by Grand Lodges. It came to be used in nearly every state, and was even offered in Canada, New Brunswick, and Novia Scotia. Most Grand Lodges reasoned they could amend any parts which were found to be objectionable. In fact, had Dove simply left the matter alone, it may have been possible that the Baltimore Convention would have resulted in a standard uniform work across the United States. But it was not to be, although the Moore Trestle Board proved popular enough that a second addition was published in 1846, with a third edition being published in 1850. Eventually most all of the recommendations of the convention were adopted by American jurisdictions.

The great twentieth century Masonic author, Dwight Smith, Past Grand Master and Grand Secretary of Indiana, surmised that the convention, while falling short of its goal of unifying ritualistic work, made four significant contributions to the ritual workings in America. First, the due guards and signs became two distinct things. During the first century of English ritual workings, due guards and signs were used interchangeably. Due guards for both the Entered Apprentice and Fellow Craft Degrees were unknown, or at least not used. The convention agreed to a standard language for both the due guard and sign in all three craft degrees and the method in which these were given.

Second, the convention reversed the movable and immovable jewels. Under the old English system, the immovable jewels were the Rough Ashlar, the Perfect Ashlar, and the Trestle Board. The Baltimore Convention recommended these become the movable jewels and that the Square, the Level, and the Plumb be the immovable jewels. The reasoning was that these are the unchangeable jewels of a lodge, assigned to the three highest stations in the lodge, and can never be worn by officers of inferior rank except by proxy.

Third, the Convention adopted a recommendation that the business of Lodge should be conducted only in the Master Mason

Degree. Traditionally, such business was conducted in the Entered Apprentice Degree so that every member of the lodge could participate in the lodge's business. But on the tail of the 1820s anti-Masonic uprising, the conventioneers were likely proposing a defensive measure here to keep those who started but did not advance from gaining even more fodder with which the anti-Masons could use to condemn the fraternity.

Finally, and perhaps the most significant result of the Baltimore Convention, was that it urged all American Grand Lodges to eliminate a reference to the Blazing Star in the Entered Apprentice lecture as commemorative of the Star of Bethlehem. The delegates were perceptive enough to understand that Freemasonry's non-sectarianism was one of its greatest assets. Admittedly, it took a number of years for Grand Lodges to comply with this recommendation, but the universality of religion theme has proven to be a very important tenet of the Craft.[215]

When the National Masonic Convention met again in Winchester, Virginia on May 11, 1846, there were only six Grand Lodges present. Maryland, along with most of the other Grand Jurisdictions did not report. It was generally felt the Convention would not have enough representation to produce anything important to Masonry.

Thus, the most important Convention and effort concerning Masonry to be held in America or in Europe since the organization of the Grand Lodge of England at London in 1717 failed to meet its objectives to enact a uniform working for the ancient and honorable craft of Freemasonry.

The result of Moore's Trestle Board was to encourage other Masonic ritualists and writers to publish their own version of Masonic workings. As expected, John Dove published his own Monitor in 1847 and 1851, claiming it was the true workings adopted in Baltimore. Cornelius Moore published a Monitor in 1846; Z.A. Davis of Maryland published his version of the Masonic workings in 1843 and 1849. Robert McCoy added yet another in 1853.

Thus, the recommendation of the Baltimore Convention that a manual of the workings and ceremonies of Masonry be laid out in published format indeed encouraged other enterprising ritual writers to publish what they considered improved versions of the ceremonies and work. It wasn't long before any number of variations of the lectures surfaced, each claiming to be that agreed upon at Baltimore. It wasn't long before there was again 'confusion in the temple' over the Masonic ritual practiced in America.

By the eve of the Civil War, it was time for another movement.

The Masonic Conservators

The next effort to establish a national uniform ritual working was done through the auspices of a secret organization devoted to establishing and teaching the Masonic ritual within and among the Grand Lodges. Its founder was one Robert Morris, and the organization was known as *"The Masonic Conservators."*

Morris was a Past Grand Master of Kentucky, and was affectionately known as the Poet Laureate of Freemasonry. He not only was among the most prolific of Masonic poets, but he also is generally credited with having authored the ritual for the Order of Eastern Star. He was an editor and publisher of Masonic books and poems. He started a National School of Masonic Instruction. He was the first to publish an American Masonic History. He is said to have visited nearly 2,000 lodges and conferred with more than 50,000 Masons.

He initiated his scheme in June, 1860, by inviting a selected number of eminent craftsmen to join what he termed an "association of experienced and devoted Masons" under the title of "Conservators of Symbolic Masonry."[216] The idea was that there would be one *Conservator* in each lodge who could appoint a couple of trusted deputies. These men would all belong to the Association of Conservators, headed by the Chief Conservator who managed the organization nationally. A Deputy Chief could be designated for every Congressional District, and a Vice Chief for every Grand Lodge. Every elected Grand Lodge officer would be an ex-officio Vice Chief. The 'Association' would then go around the country instructing one or more intelligent Masons in the Webb work. Among its purposes was the dissemination of what Morris styled "the genuine work and lectures of the first three degrees as arranged by Preston and taught by Webb." His idea was to eliminate any changes and innovations introduced to the ritual since the death of Webb. He devised a remarkably complex cipher key to track the secret work, and he proposed a system of schools of instruction in every lodge whereby the work might be taught by Masonic lecturers trained in his system.

Robert Morris

By design, the association was to last only five years. Morris envisioned that he would have the fraternity completely won over 'to the old and original work' in this time, and that all Grand Lodges would disinherit any promulgated rituals which did not agree with that taught by the Conservators.

Morris apparently had little knowledge of human nature. In the first place, it was unreasonable to assume that all Masons would agree to think alike in matters of Masonic ritual. Secondly, by creating a secret organization and pledging everyone who joined it to secrecy in the work they were doing ran head on against some other pretty inflexible Masonic obligations. Third, many of the men he invited to join him did not believe he had any clear authority for claiming that the ritual he taught was any more original, authentic, or true than the rituals already in existence. After all, Morris was not a direct student of Webb himself. He did not even live in Webb's lifetime.

Morris, on the other hand, was intensely enthusiastic. His invitation enticed men to join by offering them a journal published for members only; by teaching them the "original Prestonian work as taught by Webb" through Morris's secret cipher; by giving them the opportunity to exemplify the degrees before their own Grand Lodge and constituent lodges. He would issue pamphlets containing the exoteric ritual of the degrees. All this for only ten dollars! Morris's strength indeed rested with his ability as a writer of Masonic ritual.

Morris even created a *"Conservator's Degree"* to more fully bind the membership together into a common organization and give it an air of a secret society (which was so much a part of the male psyche during this Masonic period). In fact, his invitation included an admonition that those entitled to be Conservators would, by necessity, be Master Masons "who appreciate the binding force of an obligation, and have already shown their ability to keep a secret."

It is evident that Morris recognized the risk he was taking in teaching a ritual which he knew would differ from that already adopted in the several Grand Jurisdictions. Perhaps he felt that by binding members to secrecy, he could avoid the possible political repercussions which were bound to emanate from those few Grand Lodges that might not endorse his work. In the first publication of his magazine to the membership (entitled *"The Conservator"* which was issued in the fall of 1860), he made a strong appeal for each member to adhere to his obligation as a Conservator. In a salutation, Morris included the following remarks; "We call your earnest attention, also to the fact that you now have underwritten pledges–the evidences of which are in the Archives, in the Chancellor's keeping–to consider every document furnished you as a member of this Association whether it may be written or printed, as between the Chief Conservator (Morris) and yourself. No persons, save those directly accredited to you by him, or whose names are published in this journal as members, can be allowed to have access to any of those documents, or to be informed of their allusions or even of their existence." He added, "This is a fundamental rule of our operations; and to it you will be held strictly responsible."

Morris was a convincing man. He knew the Masonic condition of his time; he knew there was a desire on the part of a majority of the craft for a standard system of teaching. He knew the anti-Masonic excitement of 1826-36 had broken the spirit of the American lodges. He was travelled enough to know that little or no work had been done in conferring degrees for ten years. He also knew the obligations vowed by those who enlisted in his movement would aid in cementing them into a common association of like-minded men.

Some three thousand Masons joined the movement; among them were nearly fifty Grand and Past Grand Lodge officers. There were Conservators in thirty-four states, a territory, even in England and Scotland.

The *Mnemonics,* which was Morris's method of teaching, was a complicated and difficult compilation of letters and figures in one book; along with a spelling book in which every word in the Masonic ritual was to be found. To be able to read the volume required the spelling book and an additional page of instruction. The latter told where to begin. The cipher read sometimes down, sometimes up, sometimes across; sometimes it was to be read continuously, at other times by skipping various columns. Morris intended his cipher to be unreadable by non-Masons, and it was perhaps as secret as any cipher that had been devised before (or since) his time. In the end, the complexity probably only added to the opposition which the Conservators would experience. There is no doubt his secret cipher launched a series of Grand Lodge debates over the legality of their use. Besides his 'unauthorized' organization of ritualists, Morris' Mnemonics had created another major controversy in the fraternity. Many Grand

Lodges would enact laws prohibiting the ownership of any form of "key" to the esoteric work of Masonry.

Notwithstanding, his plan went well for the first year or two. He reported in the November, 1861 issue of *"The Conservator"* that the Grand Lodges of Indiana, North Carolina, Maryland, Nebraska, Iowa, Alabama, Michigan, Wisconsin, New Hampshire, Kentucky, Tennessee, and Washington had all adopted the "Webb Work" as taught by the Conservators. By January, 1862, he predicted that every Grand Lodge except Pennsylvania would be using the Webb work before 1865. He even thought it possible that England and Scotland might come around to his way of exemplifying the work.

But it wasn't meant to be. Although attacks on his organization didn't occur for nearly two years after he launched his movement; when they did come, the fury with which the storm broke made up for any lateness in its arrival.

In October, 1862, the Grand Master of Illinois received a paper from the Conservators Association within his own State asking him to discontinue the Association. Apparently those who had been enlisted as Conservators in Illinois had met much resistance within their own lodges that the 'Conservator' work was creating much discord and confusion among the craft. The Conservators, not wanting to do battle with their own brothers, had requested the Grand Master to dissolve the Association in Illinois.

His action was swift. He required all sixty-six members to surrender rituals, pamphlets, ciphers, and all other Conservator papers in their possession to him, or otherwise dispose of these within sixty days. He apparently reported his action to other Grand Jurisdictions because it wasn't long before Missouri, Kentucky, Maine, Michigan, Colorado, Kansas, New Jersey, Vermont, and a host of other Grand Lodges ordered an investigation made into the Conservators' movement. It appears local resistance to the adopted ritual of the Conservators was ubiquitous. Some even went so far as to require that a "Renunciation Oath" be taken by every Mason in their State, vowing that they had never belonged to the so-called Conservators; that they "do not now belong"; and that they "will forever renounce and repudiate the system, and everything connected with it." Grand Lodge after Grand Lodge enacted legislation banishing the Conservators.

Still, the movement had its adherents. In almost every Grand

Lodge, there were respected and experienced ritualists who felt that uniformity was needed, and that Morris had indeed penned the true Webb work. And these feelings ran deep. Most defenders of the Morris plan considered themselves loyal to their own Grand Lodge, but they were frustrated when that same Grand Lodge enjoined on them work which they knew not to be ancient and genuine. Their intent was to abide by the law of their jurisdiction and, at the same time, learn the "real" work so that they might, over time, convince the powers to be of the wisdom of the Conservator's plan. And, in some instances, Masonic toleration was at stake. Some simply felt that a Mason had the inalienable right to join whatever association he wanted, and a Grand Lodge was wrong in dictating against this freewill of association. Of course, Morris was leading the cause of his own defense through his own adherents. In one of the pronouncements he mailed to all members, he stated that no law of Masonry could affect the right of an individual to "learn whatever system or sort of Masonry that he pleases." And as one can well imagine, there were plenty of Grand Lodges who set out to prove him wrong in his contention.

One problem that Morris repeatedly encountered, and ultimately could not overcome, was his own failure to prove that he was actually using the truest Webb form of ritual. Two of his strongest critics were New Hampshire and Vermont; both of whom used the Barney work from a cipher that Vermont had developed with John Barney himself. It must be remembered that Barney learned the work directly from Webb and Gleason. Morris claimed to have copied the cipher from the Grand Lecturer of Vermont. But Samuel Willson reported the cipher Morris received from him was not the original and contained mistakes. To make matters worse, Willson stated that Morris made several more mistakes in copying the cipher and misread many passages.[217] Of course, when this word got out to other Grand Lodges, Morris strongly and eloquently refuted Willson (and Vermont's) claim. But the damage had been done. The word rapidly spread that Morris's form was not Webb; nor was it the Baltimore Convention work.

A claim was also falsely disseminated that Morris had created his movement primarily to enrich himself. Although in actuality, he hardly had the funds to travel to each Grand Lodge, and he died a poverty-stricken man, Grand Lodge after Grand Lodge passed condemnatory resolutions, laws, and edicts, denouncing the Conservator's movement.

There was much fear that, by introducing into the various Grand Jurisdictions a system of ritual and lectures foreign to that prescribed by them, the Conservators would, in the end, destroy the very fabric of Masonry itself.

Over the last three years of the movement, essentially every Grand Lodge had enacted Morris and his Conservators out of business. Morris spent these years primarily defending the purposes of the Conservators and responding to the attacks made on him personally. And, too, the Civil War was in progress, cutting off the Southern States; and the North had no sympathy for the man or his actions.

Morris, while forced to spend great amounts of his time and energy responding to the most vicious of attacks, still remained undeterred in his overall purpose. On July 6, 1863, he issued a lengthy circular to the Grand Lodge of Michigan in response to a particularly harassing circular which was being widely circulated among Grand Lodges by one James Fenton, who claimed to be a Grand Secretary. In it, Morris confirmed how he came to acquire the Webb work, and how he believed that every experiment after Webb was a 'bastard' form to one degree or another. He assailed Webb's students, claiming for example that Barney adapted the Webb work in every State where the Grand Master required it. Morris claimed that Barney "adapted his Work to the views and wishes of the Brethren of the different states." He also asserted that the "Gleason Key," while similar to the Webb Work, was not faithful to it, and where it differed, "was un-authoritative." He even proclaimed the Baltimore Convention to be "a humbug of the largest dimensions. It was a bladder promptly pricked." Morris asserted that, in many instances, the delegates at Baltimore returned home claiming the Convention taught the work they had previously been teaching, with only a few new things added. It is not hard to envision that Masonic egos might well have got in the way of the bigger picture in all of these instances.[218]

Try as he may, Morris was unable to neutralize his critics. The Conservators, as an organized movement, was destined to die without accomplishing its mission. True to his word, when the five years had run its course, Morris dissolved the Conservators Association by closing out its books. He bid an official farewell by publishing a letter in *"The Voice of Masonry"* (which had become the official organ of the association). In it, he steadfastly maintained that, "Whatever he (personally) may have failed in, we (the association) have accomplished more in five years than all other agencies combined have done in forty..."

And indeed, the movement was not a total loss. It called national attention to the fact there was an old system of ancient rituals extant, and that these terminated with the Webb-Preston rituals; that everything created after that were modern innovations to the pure work. It assured the craft that the ritual taught by the Conservators was so very close to the Webb form that differences lie only in a few minor adaptations. The movement also exposed to the fraternity that dangerous powers lie in the hands of Grand Secretaries (alluding to the personal attacks of many Secretaries against the association). And the ritual it taught left its impression, and was in fact absorbed into the work of a number of Grand Lodges whose work today follows very closely the ritual of the *Mnemonics*. It can safely be said that, after the Civil War, many Grand Lodges practiced a closer uniformity than existed prior to the 1860 era. Morris concluded that his movement resulted in a "national uniformity of work to a degree ten times greater than has been experienced since the revival of Freemasonry."

And it should be pointed out that Morris, for all the attacks made against him, really had the best of intentions. He was a lifelong student of Masonry; he was widely known and respected as the best ritualist of his time; he was widely traveled, and had an excellent reputation as both a Mason and lecturer. He was kind-hearted, as his poetry would reveal. And he would not profit from the promotion or sale of his work.

History should be kind to this man, who sincerely believed in his heart that ritual uniformity was in the best interest of Freemasonry. He truly felt that he was preserving the integrity of Masonic practice through the labors of his movement.

As it turns out, the Conservators movement was the last organized effort in the United States to establish a national system of uniformity in the practice of Masonic ritual.

During the whole of the nineteenth century, the Grand Lecturer system slowly evolved, and eventually became deeply entrenched within each Grand Lodge. Efforts shifted from a national goal of uniformity to that of uniformity within.

And that is another story.

14 The Masonic Ritual Today

Any Mason who has examined a visitor from another state or who travels beyond his own jurisdiction soon learns that the ritual and ceremonies of Symbolic Masonry practiced in a neighboring jurisdiction are different from those he witnessed or learned when he became a member of the Craft. If one could visit the over fifteen thousand lodges in the fifty American Grand Jurisdictions, he is likely to find that Masonic practice has been altered in many ways by time, regional influence, customs, ideas, and beginnings. It can safely be said that, just as sons and daughters from the same mother and father are never exactly alike, so Masonry, formed from the same source, is not exactly the same anywhere.

But even with these subtle differences, ritual practices between nearly every Grand Jurisdiction are remarkably similar. The fact is that, while there are many variations in the ritual words spoken in lodges today, the nation is still united in substance of Masonic teachings. It has been said by many a brother who reports to his lodge after a visit to another Grand Jurisdiction that "they don't use the same words we do, but somehow they get the same message across." Even when one visits Pennsylvania, a Grand Lodge that is unique in its ritual practice, using an old Irish form, he will still find the teachings and fundamentals are the same in the essentials. And to the traveling Mason, the differences we encounter when witnessing the work of other Grand Lodges perhaps makes us all the more appreciative of the beauty, genius, and interest which is so uniquely ours in Freemasonry.

It can be surmised the reasons all these local differences have not changed the overall lodge patterns Masons are familiar with today are due to the three primary influences in ritual development that have been outlined herein. First, there is no question that printed Monitors have had a profoundly stabilizing influence on preserving the main themes of the Masonic ritual. Although adapted and modified by many different individuals over the years, a review of each makes it apparent these ritual teachers have all attempted to conform to the basic Preston-Webb form. In most instances, the authors of printed ritual Monitors since Webb have claimed their work was the true Webb teaching. Webb and his students had a profound effect in unifying Masonic ceremonies and workings in the United States. There is no question the early roving ritualists influenced the standardizing force of the Grand Lecturer system in America.

And there is no doubt that both the Baltimore Convention and Morris's Conservator Movement had great influences on standardizing the work. The ritualists who participated in both of these programs undoubtedly taught the work they learned. And again, for the most part it was workings they were already acquainted with in the major essentials.

The balance of the tendency toward ritual uniformity can be attributed to the Grand Lecturer system which is now almost universally employed by Grand Lodges.

We have clearly seen that the Grand Lecturer has historically been the thread that both weaves the similarity we find in ritual practices and promotes its differences.

Throughout the history of Masonry, the ritual has migrated more by word of mouth, or mouth to ear, than by any other means. When men such as Smith, Dunckerly, Calcott, and Preston taught what they knew to their English brethren, they did it in the form of verbal instruction. Thomas Smith Webb carried his adaptation of Preston's work to every State in which he traveled, and transferred it to others by his own words. The students he personally instructed, including Snow, Barney, Gleason, Fowle, and Cross; all served as Grand Lecturers to Grand Lodges; all teaching the Webb form to anyone who would take the time to learn it; and all delivering by word of mouth what they knew of Masonry. Barney served as the Grand Lecturer of Illinois and Ohio; Snow served as Grand Lecturer for Ohio. Gleason served as the Lecturer for Massachusetts; Cross was the Grand Lecturer of Connecticut; Fowle of New York. And what was not directly influenced by these men was carried out by those who claimed to be taught by them.

In Grand Lodge after Grand Lodge, its ritual workings have been formally adopted as the result of the employment (for a fee) of a Grand Lecturer or traveling lecturer who was well skilled in the work; or as the result of a committee being selected to review the work of the traveling lecturer, or a Grand Lecturer hired to teach the work. The "professional" Grand Lecturer was very much in vogue for the first three-quarters of the nineteenth century. In the case of New Hampshire, for instance, Thomas Thompson, Grand Master from 1801 to 1808, wrote to the Grand Master of Massachusetts, inviting him to meet and confer on the subject of ritual uniformity. A Committee was established consisting of George Richards (who was the editor of Preston's "Illustrations of Masonry"), Lyman Spaulding, Grand Secretary of New Hampshire, and John Harris, High Priest of the second chapter of the York Rite in New Hampshire. This group of New Hampshire men met with Henry Fowle, Benjamin Gleason, and a fellow named Stephen Bean, all of Massachusetts. The joint Committee voted unanimously that the work of Fowle and Gleason was "as correct as can possibly be expected" and the same was adopted by both Grand Jurisdictions. The Grand Lodge of Massachusetts later (1810) employed Gleason to teach the work in that Jurisdiction, and he was employed in that position for many years.

The era of the professional Grand Lecturer was destined to be short-lived, however, as brethren in local lodges learned the work and became proficient in it. They began teaching it to their own lodge members. Once a particular form of the ritual became fairly widely known and practiced, there was no reason to pay for ritual instruction. It didn't take long for a Grand Lodge to see that the employment of a Grand Lecturer was an unnecessary expense to the Grand Lodge (or to the local lodges).

By the turn of the twentieth century, almost every Grand Jurisdiction had thus gone to a system where the most learned ritualists taught the work of the degrees as a volunteer service to the fraternity.

The Grand Lodge Lecturer system primarily exists today to keep whatever ritual form that has been adopted in a particular jurisdiction standard to that Grand Body. The primary duty of the Lecturer is not only to instruct the brethren in a particular ritual form, but to keep differences from "sneaking into" the adopted work.

Today, Grand Lecturers are generally either appointed by the Grand Master or elected by Grand Lodge. The title varies among jurisdictions. Some are called Grand Instructors (as in Delaware and New Jersey). Wyoming has a Chief Instructor; Nevada a Master of Instruction; Pennsylvania an Instructor of the Ritualistic Work. Some are styled Grand Examiners (Illinois); still others are called Custodians of the Work, or Grand Custodians (Iowa, Minnesota, Nebraska, South Dakota). In Nevada, the brother is known as the Worshipful Master of Instruction. Texas, Georgia, and Florida utilize a Grand Lodge Committee on Work.[219]

By whatever name given him, the Grand Lecturer exercises complete supervision over ritual. He presides over all matters relating to ritual and instructs the men chosen to assist him in teaching the work within his Grand Jurisdiction. In many jurisdictions, the Lecturer is assisted by a Committee on Work; all of whom are responsible for keeping the adopted work of their particular jurisdiction in a pure form. The system is also often accented by a group of district lecturers who make themselves available to instruct brethren in their geographic areas through local or area schools of instruction. In Connecticut, Ohio, and South Carolina, the responsibility of ritual instruction is placed in the hands of the District Deputy Grand Masters.

In most Grand Jurisdictions, there is an established examination procedure whereby one is "certified" to instruct the work in his area. Local Brethren who teach the catechisms to candidates, or instruct their brothers in the language of lodge, often have an annual opportunity to review the language, or to check themselves as to their own proficiency. In today's system of American Masonry, more time, effort, and emphasis is placed on teaching and preserving the adopted ritual work than on any other aspect of the fraternity. The Grand Lodge ritual instruction system is deeply entrenched within each Grand Lodge.

It can be concluded that the old emphasis of searching for ritual uniformity has, during the present century, shifted from a national goal of standardization to that of uniformity within. The ritual energy in our own time has focused on preserving whatever internal form exists within the boundaries of our own Grand Lodges. The 20th Century has been marked with a stubborn intolerance for introducing any modifications, revisions, or innovations into that established internal ritual form.

Ciphers

As strong and resilient as the Grand Lecturer system has been to the American lodge experience over the past century, it, too, is currently being upstaged by a combination of printed ritual exposures, adopted (and spurious) ritual ciphers, and digital ritual exposures. The brother who wants to learn the ritual workings of his jurisdiction today has several tools available to him in addition to oral instruction.

Of course, printed ritual ciphers have been around since Brown's *Master Key* and Morris's *Mnemonics.* William Preston even printed his lectures in cipher form. But the old system of coded ciphers which were un-readable by the non-initiated has gone the way of the ringer washing machine. Modern ritual cipher books are made on the principle of first letters only, or two letter codes, the idea being that one must be familiar with the ritual to de-cipher it. The Redding Masonic Supply Company of New York began publishing such ciphers at the turn of the twentieth century. Each book was coded for the workings of a particular Grand Lodge. How the company acquired the workings is not known, but these ciphers became a popular way for men in lodges to keep the work in their minds. By 1928, these "unauthorized" versions of ritual workings were so common place that Grand Masters were questioning whether or not they could be legally stopped. The question was discussed at the Grand Master's Conference held in Washington, DC that year. The consensus seemed to be that legal sanctions against publishing houses managed by non-Masons would be futile and the likely publicity might stir additional controversy from others outside the fraternity.[220]

The arguments in favor of Grand Lodge adopted and sanctioned ciphers are the same today as were promoted by Robert Morris a century ago. They provide an accurate key to the adopted work of a jurisdiction and therefore result in greater accuracy and uniformity among the lodges. They save time, prevent the cost of travelling officers, and they facilitate the learning of the ritual in areas where ritual instructors are not available. They are popular among lodge officers, degree participants, and candidates engaged in proficiency work involving memorization. Those who support the use of ritual ciphers claim the work in their lodges to be better because of their use.

Arguments against ciphers are that they violate Masonic obligations and jeopardize the secrecy of Masonry. They eliminate the 'mouth to ear' instruction and therefore rob the candidate of the opportunity to spend valuable one-on-one time with a lodge mentor. The ciphers are said to reduce ritual learning to a mere mechanical act.

The more complex question regarding the legal use of ciphers, purchasing pirated ritual workings, or downloading published exposures direct from the Internet, is whether or not the ritual workings of Freemasonry indeed any longer represent the secrets of the fraternity. After three hundred years of ritual exposures, it is a bit trite to assume that the language of Freemasonry is still a secret. The fraternal obligations taken to discourage the so-called 'secrets' from being written down or delineated can hardly be said to be binding so long as there are different standards regarding what is considered monitorial and what is considered esoteric language among the workings of our Grand jurisdictions. The Degree obligations themselves are published in some Grand Lodge ritual Monitors. What is considered sacred to one jurisdiction is public to another. Perhaps it can be said that the only true secrets of Freemasonry are those which are not visible; that is, those which cannot be known by the profane, or even to the Mason who is not 'duly and truly prepared' to discover them. Perhaps the secrets of Freemasonry lie in the communication of the spirit, the bond that exists between initiated men, the insights which appear only when conversations and instruction touch the deepest part of our inner nature; that repository of the sacred breast which can never be breached by decoding a cipher or reading an exposure of a Masonic ritual. As Joseph Fort Newton, editor of *The Builder* wrote a century ago; "the truths of Freemasonry are passed silently, mystically, from soul to soul."

Today, there are only five Grand Lodges in the United States who do not have adopted ritual ciphers as aides to the memory work.

Ritual Variations

The result of standardizing the ritual from within is that there are many variations in how the degrees and ceremonies of Masonry are practiced today. When one looks at these actual differences, it is surprising how numerous and striking they seem to be. And there is no single source which can explain all of them. Some are simply the result of a particular individual's personal method of instruction, or his interpretation of that which was never written down in his Grand Jurisdiction; and which later became the adopted mode of work. Some variations are the obvious result in how floor work and customs have migrated from the original ritual source, i.e., the Ancients Grand Lodge, the Moderns, Reconciliation, etc. Others are from the legacies left by the traveling ritualists like Webb, Cross, Moore, Dove, etc. But whatever has influenced the diversity, it is interesting to note some of the ways in which Grand Lodges carry out its ritual functions.

To cite a few general examples without revealing the work of any particular Grand Lodge, one Grand Jurisdiction will syllable a word in which another letters it; one will hold as private grand honors what are given as public grand honors in another (grand honors are forms of recognition given to highly respected officers, such as the Grand Master and are sometimes given in private ceremonies; at other times in public); while still others deny there is such a thing as public grand honors. Ritual work which is published as monitorial in some Grand Lodges is regarded as secret in others. In an interesting article on ritual diversity published by California's Committee on Masonic Education during the 1920s, it was revealed that one of the most conspicuous points of difference is in the placing of the lesser lights in the lodge room. Eleven different methods are used in various Grand Jurisdictions of the United States, as graphically shown in a diagram accompanying this page. The most common form is to have the lights in an equilateral triangular form along the south, east, and west sides of the altar. However, a surprising number of Grand Lodges place the lights in a right triangular fashion on the altar, which significantly changes the symbolic meaning.

Some Grand Lodges permit the use of ciphers or keys to the esoteric work as aides to the memory work; others consider it a severe Masonic offense to possess any such ritual key beyond the published ritual Monitor outlining the degree lectures. The Grand Jurisdictions that presently permit ritual ciphers include Alaska, Arizona, California, Colorado, Connecticut, Delaware, District of Colombia, Florida, Georgia, Hawaii, Idaho, Illinois, Indiana, Iowa, Kansas, Kentucky, Louisiana, Maine, Massachusetts, Michigan, Minnesota, Montana,

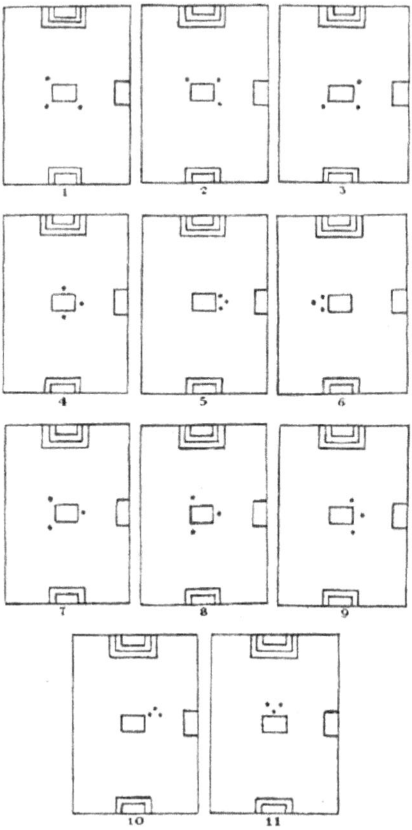

Fig. 1–
Alabama
Pennsylvania
Wyoming

Fig. 2–
Connecticut
South Dakota
Wyoming

Fig. 3–
Georgia

Fig. 4–
Arkansas

Fig. 5–
Arizona
California
Idaho
Illinois
Kentucky
Nebraska
Missouri
Nevada
Utah
Vermont
Wisconsin

Fig. 6–
Iowa
Kansas
Minnesota

Fig. 7–
Colorado
Michigan
Ohio

Fig. 8–
District of Columbia

Fig. 9–
Indiana

Fig. 10–
Massachusetts

Fig. 11–
Maryland

Nebraska, Nevada, New Hampshire, New Jersey, New Mexico, New York, North Carolina, North Dakota, Ohio, Oklahoma, Oregon, Rhode Island, South Carolina, South Dakota, Texas, Utah, Vermont, Washington, Wisconsin, and Wyoming. In some jurisdictions, ciphers are made available to any Master Mason who desires one. In at least one Grand Lodge, a copy is given to the candidates. Many Grand Lodges make ciphers available to their constituent lodges only, and brethren may use them to check their language. Most ritual ciphers are one, two, or three letter keys which are easy to de-code if one is already familiar with the language.

In several Grand Jurisdictions, spurious sections have been added to the ritual as the result of adopting work written by individuals who were not necessarily attached to the Grand Lodge in any official way; not unlike the creative traditions of Preston or Webb. Occasionally a brother will pen language that seems to "fit" with the surrounding broader themes. In Oklahoma, for example, a lengthy and dramatic "J-b-m Soliloquy" is given following the tragedy. It is among the most beautiful segments of the Third Degree drama presented in the Oklahoma working; and profoundly reinforces an understanding of the tragic hero metaphor in Greek mythology. This author has not researched how many other Grand Jurisdictions have adopted this poignant soliloquy. It was written by Eugene S. Elliott, who served as Grand Master of Wisconsin in 1886-87. The soliloquy in its entirety was published in the January 1921 issue of the *"Quarterly Bulletin"* of the Iowa Masonic Library.

In addition, Georgia and Oklahoma (and perhaps others) include a heart rendering "Eulogy on Mother" immediately preceding the Pillars and Globes lecture at the porch of the Middle Chamber. Oklahoma's version is the lengthier of the two Jurisdictions. The authorship remains a mystery, but it appears in the Oklahoma ritual for the first time in 1918. Two years later a young man named J.B. Saunders was serving as the Master Councilor of his DeMolay Chapter and used a version of it to honor Chapter Mothers. His Chapter Dad was impressed enough to suggest he send it to the DeMolay headquarters in Kansas City. It became the "Flower Talk" for the Order of DeMolay. It was delivered for the first time on July 20, 1920. The eulogy given in the Fellowcraft degree closely parallels the DeMolay working. It is likely that almost every Grand Lodge has a similar story involving the work of one of their own beloved brothers whose creativity and efforts seemed too good to pass by.

In many Grand Jurisdictions, a single ballot elects for all three degrees. In others, a ballot must be had on each candidate before each degree, and in an increasing number of Grand Lodges, more than one ballot is required to deny a man membership in the fraternity. Many jurisdictions adhere to the ancient custom of examination of Entered Apprentices and Fellowcrafts in open lodge before permitting advancement; in others, the Master accepts the avouchment of an instructor that the candidate(s) have attained a suitable proficiency to entitle them for the next degree. The number of candidates who can be initiated in the same ceremony varies from one to five among jurisdictions.

Most lodges exemplifying the 'Middle Chamber' lecture use a floor carpet with a rude representation of a flight of winding stairs. Others possess an actual set of winding stairs which either lead from the lodge room to a room or gallery above, or from an ante-room to a middle chamber on an upper level.

The gavel with which the Master rules the craft is of all shapes and sizes. The mallet is the common form, but a wedge-shaped instrument is also employed, often with a square handle. In some Grand Lodges, a setting maul is used by the Master. The Past Master's Jewel is usually a compass open sixty degrees upon a quadrant. In some Jurisdictions, the points of the compasses are above a square, surrounded partially by a quadrant. In Pennsylvania, the Past Master's Jewel is the Forty-seventh Problem of Euclid, as it is in many workings in England.

Most, but not all, Grand Jurisdictions display the square and compasses on the altar. Some refuse to display it upon the Volume of Sacred Law. Some do not call it the compasses, but rather use a mariner's instrument–the compass. Both have the same meaning in Masonry, that of inscribing a circle or boundary. Indeed, both words have been used as long as anyone can remember–appearing both ways in the old English exposures.

Aprons are worn in one jurisdiction in a certain way as a Fellowcraft; in another, as a Master Mason. What is correct for a Fellowcraft in one state is often right only for a Master Mason in another. And, of course, both jurisdictions will claim that theirs is the right way. Grand Lodge aprons differ greatly among the jurisdictions. Some permit heavy embroidery, with rosettes and tassels, emblems and decorations; others permit no emblems or decorations at all. Some are blue, others are purple; still others must be white. The same is true with Grand Lodge dress. In the northeast, most Grand Lodge officers are correctly dressed only when they wear evening clothes, with a black tie and gloves. In others, any sort of dress is acceptable. In some, top hats for the Grand Master are essential; most allow the Grand Master to choose his own headpiece. In the southwest, it is not uncommon for Grand Masters to wear cowboy hats, or Stetsons.

In some Lodges, business can only be conducted in a lodge open in the Master Mason Degree. Others require that business be done in the Entered Apprentice Degree only. Some Jurisdictions require that lodges be opened in every degree for which there is to be any work. Others require only that the lodge be open in the highest degree in which there is work. Still others allow the lodge Master to decide for himself what degree should be open on any given evening. Some allow movement between degrees in a single evening; others consider it unmasonic to 'resume' work in any degree once the lodge has moved away from that degree.

During the degrees, Jurisdictions differ on the number of knocks required at the door, or in open lodge. In some, the number is the same in all three degrees; others have a different knock for each degree. Some require the candidate to give his own best effort on how many knocks are required of him to gain admission; in others, a brother does all the knocks for him. The number of circumambulations also differ among jurisdictions; the number varying depending on the degree being worked. In some, the circumambulations are the same, regardless of which degree is being worked. Many Grand Lodges require all corners to be 'squared' during floor movements; while others allow officers and candidates to move about the lodge room in a very informal manner. There appears to be uniformity in ritual grips or handshakes, although some Jurisdictions require that these always be covered when given so that they will not be recognized by a "profane" when passed between two brothers.

The scripture references used in the three degrees are also not uniform. The bible openings for the First Degree are customarily at Psalm cxxxiii; in the Second Degree at Amos vii; and in the Third Degree at Ecclesiastes xii. However, in some workings, the First Degree reference is Ruth ii; in the Second, Judges xii; and in the Third, Genesis iv. There is at least one working where II Peter is referenced in the First Degree; Judges xii, the Second; and I Kings vii in the Third. In some Grand Lodges, the scripture reference used throughout is II Chronicles ii; and, in another, the Gospel of St. John is used. Some lodges display the volumes of sacred law of the five major world religions on the altar at every meeting; some only the bible. Some Grand Lodge laws require that any brother who desires to address the Master of the lodge, must first give the proper due guards and/or signs before he can be recognized to speak; in some instances, the sign must be held during the whole time the brother is addressing the Master. In several Jurisdictions, every brother in lodge must display a certain sign and hold it during the lodge prayers, as well as any time degree obligations are given.

In almost every Grand Jurisdiction, it is customarily expected that a visiting brother conform to the customs and practices of that jurisdiction. The reason relates to a certain admonition promised in most obligations; but it also contributes to the uniformity and decorum of the work being presented. The tendency is to do only that for which we have been personally taught; however, out of respect for jurisdictional authority, one should comply with local laws to the extent he is made aware of them, or observes them in practice.

Masonic funerals also differ widely among the states. In some the Master conducts the whole service; in others, the Wardens take part. Some lodges deposit only the sprig of acacia; in others, the scroll is also deposited. Still in others, the apron and a white glove is laid on the grave. Some services require that a shovel full of earth be deposited in the grave. Some jurisdictions have only one service; others have as many as six different services. Some are extraordinarily long, and gloomy in both language and decorum; others are short, and very comforting to the bereaved.

The above illustrations clearly show that there is no one "right" way to perform Masonic ritual practices; that all workings derive from different men, different minds, different methods; different States, different ideas–but still wholly at one in the essentials. Masonry continues to be universal in its philosophy, in its fundamentals, in its teachings–and in its method of teaching–which makes it something uniquely different from any other joining process found anywhere in the world. It is one of the great tributes to the genius of the system and to the adaptability of Masons, that it can be so at variance in unimportant details, but so wholly united in all that is important and essential to the ancient craft.

Current Challenges in Masonic Ritual Practices

After nearly three centuries of ritual practice in the American Masonic institution, one would think that we have finally come to an agreement, at least within our own states, that what was good enough for our forefathers is good enough for us. Regardless of what we might surmise, standardizing Masonic ritual remains an elusive thing. In fact, the future of Masonic ritual, long the staple and principle landmark of the craft, may be more uncertain today than at any other time in history. The tenacious emphasis (almost reverence) that has always been placed on the exactness and completeness of the American ritual is under broad attack and critical scrutiny today; both from within and without the fraternity. And when this current upheaval has played itself out in Grand Lodges across the United States, the result may well be only a remnant of what is now practiced. We may even see a different form than that currently practiced in lodge.

Ritual change is already occurring and is currently being influenced by several important sources today.

First, outside influences are having their effect on Masons and Grand Lodge decisions regarding ritual. The anti-Masonic movement has once again raised its banner of intolerance against the fraternity–this time with more enthusiasm and a larger public audience than at any other time in history. A new wave of protestant fundamentalism is sweeping the country, and the leaders of a growing extreme within this movement want Freemasonry destroyed. Although their charge that Masonry is an anti-Christian religion is absurd and has been answered a thousand times, their pervasive methods of twisting truth to satisfy their own personal or political agendas will likely not give the fraternity any peace as long as there is extremism and intolerance among men and women of faith.

The movement is particularly unsettling to many Masonic leaders. In too many Grand Lodges, the leadership is painfully aware that a high percentage of their membership is not well enough informed about the meanings and symbols of Masonry to respond to many of the claims, or even to know whether or not allegations made against the fraternity are factual. Ironically, this seemingly corporate ignorance which pervades the rank and file is the direct result of several consecutive generations of Masons being taught only ritual language. Over the past 70 years, very little has been presented to American Masons in the way of Masonic education during their process of joining and becoming 'proficient.' Very little knowledge beyond the language of the ritual has been passed down from one generation to the next.

Of course, the anti-Masonic movement is not all bad for Freemasonry. It can be debated that the publicity which the fraternity gleans from those who are visibly opposed to it may actually be encouraging an increase in interest and membership in lodge. Fortunately, most main-line Americans see anti-Masonic propaganda as promoting a theme of hatred, usually in the name of Christianity. Many tolerant Christians find this type of 'group-bashing' offensive (if not un-Christian), especially when it originates from a so-called Christian group. In fact, many thoughtful people see the anti-Masonic movement as a scheme more to satisfy some political or private agenda than in adhering to any legitimate ideology. To the extent that Masonry and Masons are perceived as innocent victims of these thoughtless attacks, the result may be an increased interest and empathy toward the fraternity. Religious intolerance is increasingly moving people from the faith of their forefathers.

But the bashing has indeed caused some problems. Many Masons don't personally know how to respond to their critics. In too many cases these critics are church friends and social acquaintances. It is easy to understand the feelings of embarrassment and confusion members experience when such people repeatedly inform them that Masons are "satan-worshipers," and hand them pamphlets that appear to document these claims. To counter this tension, some members simply drop out. They quietly let their dues lapse and are removed from the rolls of their lodge.

Others are bringing pressure to bear on their Grand Lodges to "do something about it." One such example was in Oklahoma during the 1992 Southern Baptist Convention. In response to a perceived threat against Freemasonry by the largest protestant denomination in America, along with a call to action by lodge members, the Grand Master sent a delegation of Masons to the Convention held in Houston to respond to the media in the event the Baptist leadership took a formal stand to prevent Baptist men from joining the fraternity. The convention had been studying Freemasonry through its Home Mission Board–a group established by the SBC to study world religions, cults, and other non-Christian organizations. The SBC concluded that Freemasonry was not incompatible with religion. Freemasonry became a household word during this conflict, with followers lining up on both sides to engage in the rightness of their ideologies.

And, too, when public criticism is aimed at an area which can be attributed to the language of Masonic ritual; to some Masons, the attack can be easily mitigated by simply changing the language. Negative claims and propaganda espoused by religious groups have fueled some Grand Lodges to enact changes in the ritual language itself. One of the most notable examples is the action by the United Grand Lodge of England as a result of a recommendation of the Faith and Order Committee of the Methodist Church of England to the General Conference of Methodists in 1985 that concluded Methodists should not be Masons. The Conference adopted the recommendation. The following year, the Grand Lodge removed the symbolic penalties from the ritual obligations. At issue was the church's concern that such penalties were gruesome and bloody in nature and no man should be required to swear to them before God or on the Holy Writ. The British Grand Lodge, without regard for the symbolic solemnity with which Masons are required to think about their obligations, and without informing the craft from whence the penalties came or how they are to be internally processed by the candidates, removed all references of them from the obligations taken by their candidates in all three degrees. Even though the penalties were retained elsewhere in the ritual (and it can well be argued such action is justified on the basis that, in the early workings, the penalties were not initially part of the obligations); still, the Grand Lodge changed a custom that had been in existence in England since 1730.

In reaction to similar forays of public opinion in the United States, several Grand Lodges have adopted additions to actual ritual language which explains that the penalties for violating one's Masonic obligations are symbolic and were never meant to be interpreted literally. The penalties symbolically refer only to the pain and horror any honest man should feel at the thought that he had violated his sworn word. The penalties are not and were never intended to be afflicted on another Mason, as is often alleged in anti-Masonic propaganda.

Of course, there is nothing wrong with making constructive changes in Masonic ritual which helps explain and teach the meaning behind the words. It is clearly within the power and authority of any Grand Lodge to give directions on matters of ritual. But it is important that such changes be made only in response to inquiries made from within the fraternity, and after careful study; not as a reaction to idle remarks heard from individuals or groups outside of Masonry who do not understand even the most elementary of Masonic concepts.

After all, if every word was removed from Masonic ritual that has at one time or another invoked some anti-Masonic sentiment, there would be no obligations in Masonry; neither would there be a Volume of Sacred Law upon which to base Masonic teachings or commitment (yet both the oath and the holy book can be traced all the way back to the Regius Poem–the oldest of Masonic documents). There would therefore be nothing to bind Masons to each other. In such a world, this author perceives that Masonry would no longer be Masonry. And it would not be long before the ritual no longer mattered.

Another hotly debated issue in anti-Masonic circles today is the claim that Masonry denies Jesus Christ as our Lord and Savior because it refuses to allow its members to use the name of Christ in Masonic prayers. Grand Lodges are reacting to this "anti-Christian" allegation by debating whether or not ritual prayers should be altered to give a Christian "slant" to the spiritual admonition given in lodge. More and more, lodge chaplains are adding their own Christian reference to prayers given in lodge without regard for the reasons the ritual specifies it otherwise. Almost every ritual prayer in Masonry is written in such a way so as not to offend the sensitivities of any man's personal faith or creed. The idea is that the Jewish, Hindu, or Muslim brother each has inherent rights as Masons equal to those of their Christian brothers in preserving the universality of spirit which Freemasonry teaches. The true Mason who is also a Christian cannot be less a Christian in deeds of fraternalism, charity and education because of his union with brothers of a different faith. Nor can the believer in Judaism, Islam, Hinduism or any other religion be less a man of his own faith because he prefers to tolerate his neighbor's beliefs. If Freemasonry had a creed, it might be: Do not kill nor harm your brother for refusing to believe in your idea of

God, nor refuse him physical, mental or spiritual aid because he does not agree with you in your opinions on the high themes of theology and philosophy.

It is not a matter of being un-Christian. The fraternity clearly evolved from a Christian base. The informed Mason knows that the eighteenth Century English Masonic ritual was sprinkled throughout with references to the Christian faith. As we have seen, for years the Apprentice's Prayer, for instance, ended with the words, "....grant that this, our new Brother, may dedicate his life to thy service and be a true and faithful Brother among us, endue him with Divine Wisdom, that he may, with the Secrets of Masonry, be able to unfold the Mysteries of Godliness and Christianity. This we humbly beg in the Name and for the Sake of Jesus Christ our lord and Savior. Amen." As was mentioned earlier, the Masonic lecturers and authors Dunckerly and Hutchinson both added much Christian phraseology to their work, the words of which were adopted by essentially every lodge in England for the better part of the eighteenth century.

The work was slowly "de-Christianized" during the period from about 1760 through the Union (1813-16). This was done not to discard Christianity, but to insure that the practice of brotherly love in Masonry discarded all forms of bigotry, dogmatism, and intolerance. Both English Grand Lodges prior to the Union, and the United Grand Lodge after, wanted to preserve the important Masonic principle that Masons honor all moral systems which strive to better mankind. Again, informed Masons understand why Christian ritual prayers are not given in lodge. Christian Masons are not threatened by it. They go to church to worship God and pray for a blessed immortality. They pray in lodge to seek guidance in their Masonic labors and to acknowledge to the Grand Architect that the principles taught in Masonry are sublimely inspired.

However, those who have never been taught this important distinction in Masonry will continue to wonder why Masonic ritual does not acknowledge the Word made Flesh. Unfortunately, it is these brothers who are the most prone to fall prey to the predatory anti-Masonic mandate that seeks to either destroy Masonry, or force it to conform to a different system of morality–one based on dogmatic intolerance.

The second major influence challenging Masonic ritual today

comes from within. Frankly stated, there are fewer Masons; therefore, there is less language. The era of the 'certified' lecturer is quickly vanishing in lodges across North America. As late as twenty years ago, one could find in almost every lodge a ritualist who knew all the adopted memory work of his Grand Jurisdiction. Today, it is difficult to find one such brother in an entire county or region. The lodge ritualist is literally dying off in the fraternity. And he is not being replaced by enough younger men willing to make memorizing and teaching the same priority in lodge.

The result is that, in many lodges, the lecture sections of the degrees are no longer being communicated. Candidates are no longer becoming acquainted with important concepts such as the forms of lodge, the furniture, the ornaments, lights, jewels, tenets; the symbolism of the building of the Temple, the nine classes of emblems; the meaning of the Third Degree. When the emblems and symbols of Masonry are not taught as the candidate progresses through the degrees, it is difficult to expect the newly raised Mason to learn how to think symbolically in the process. And, in Masonry, if one does not learn to think symbolically, he has little chance of ever learning the real secrets or genius which is woven within the language and allegories of Freemasonry. There is some evidence that the lapse rate is beginning to rise in Masonry for the first time in this century. This may partially be due to the 'shortened' form of ritual practice. Freemasonry has historically had the lowest suspension rate of any organization in the world. Masonic scholars are generally in agreement that the reason the drop out rate has historically been so low is because of the uniqueness of the joining process.

Nonetheless, to the extent that the adopted ritual in its complete form is no longer being performed as a required ritual function of lodge, it can be concluded that the ritual practice is slowly being revised from that known by Masons of only two generations past. In the typical lodge of the new century, there is simply less language presented today than in the past.

There is yet another pressure which is causing ritual alterations today–and it also has to do with the mortality rate. The average age of Masons in the United States is sixty-four. In most Grand Jurisdictions, slightly more than fifty percent of the membership is older than sixty-five years. This means that more members are dying each year, and this death rate is likely to increase significantly over the next few years.

Actuarial studies have shown that the fraternity will lose more than forty percent of its membership over the next decade. To offset this decline, the rate of admissions must turn around significantly.

Largely due to baby boomers not following their fathers into the fraternity, the overall mortality rate in Masonry, coupled with an almost universal policy which prohibits new member solicitation, has resulted in fifty-four consecutive years of declining membership nationally. The fraternity has lost over sixty-five percent of its strength in numbers over this span of time.

The result is that Grand Lodges are increasingly moving toward the adoption of policies aimed at reversing the declining trend by "jump-starting" their membership numbers. As of this writing twelve Grand Lodges have adopted (or authorized by Grand Master dispensation) the shortening of the categorical lectures historically required of each candidate for advancement. Some have eliminated almost all memory work previously associated with the joining process. Others offer alternative forms of proficiency, allowing candidates to present written or oral reports in lodge as a test of their knowledge of things Masonic. If this trend continues, the catechism, which represents the oldest ritual form known to Masonry, is likely to be eliminated in most Grand Jurisdictions (except for occasional demonstration purposes) within the next few decades.

The panic to replace member losses due to death, coupled with the perception that men no longer have time to participate in the Masonic joining process in the traditional way, have driven a number of Grand Jurisdictions to adopt an occasional "One Day Class." With this approach, a man who has been elected for membership in a lodge can opt to get all three of the symbolic degrees of Masonry in a single day. There is no required memory work, no personal experience in joining, and no time spent "one-on-one" in meaningful dialogue with a well-informed brother.

There are several advantages to this approach. In the one day class, the work is usually performed by the best ritual team in the State or area. And typically, nothing in ritual language is omitted on these special degree days. A candidate can expect to see everything in the way of ritual that has been adopted by his Grand Lodge. The other obvious benefit of the one day class is the opportunity it gives many lodges to bring business and professional leadership to Masonry. It is usually the 'white collar' professional who perceives he has no time to participate in a lengthy joining process. Further, perhaps another reason the one day class is not meeting with a lot of opposition where it has been permitted is that many older Masons may privately see it as an opportunity to convince their sons, or grandsons, whom they have long quietly wanted to have as brothers in lodge, to join. Finally, for lodges that can no longer perform the work, the classes enable them to add to their ranks of new members in the hope the new men will take on ritual parts to fill the lodge's degree deficiencies.

The disadvantage may well be that the process of joining, being shortened in time and personal commitment, may not be internalized within the candidate to the same degree that is normally the case in the slower, more lengthy (traditional) joining process. The newly raised brother may not have the same sense of "ownership" toward his particular lodge if special attention is not immediately given him to become an active participant.

It is increasingly likely he will not continue his membership for long if the culture of his lodge does not meet his needs. This is of critical importance to the fraternity. If the "new leadership" which is being encouraged to come into Masonry gets a bad first impression in lodge, it could have disastrous implications for the lodge's future chances of survival. A lodge that has been "disbarred" from connection with its community because of what the Masons who have left the lodge have told their friends about it will indeed be in for a rough time. Such a lodge is unlikely to survive. This author knows of one example where a brother blackballed the CEO of the largest employer in his town (the 'nay' voter was a disgruntled ex-employee). The lodge did not raise another Master Mason for ten years! A similar result is possible when the word gets out among the community's professional circles that there is nothing in Masonry that is relevant. A lodge can simply be 'overlooked' out of existence.

Of course, the judgment is still out on whether or not one day classes will have any long term effect on Masons or Masonry. But if these opportunities become routinely available to lodges on an area-wide basis, they will undoubtedly change or alter ritual proficiency at the local level. When men are either "held back" for a one day opportunity, or opt to wait until they can become Masons in such a setting; and the ritual is therefore not performed regularly by lodge members, it may not be long until its accuracy is lost to the lodge. When lodges lose their ritual proficiency, experience shows they no longer attract men to the fraternity.

There are vast areas in rural America where not even one Master Mason has been raised in the last five years. For those lodges that are already to the point they no longer can perform the ritual work (and there are many of these in every Grand Jurisdiction); and who see the one day class as the only way they can acquire new members, the practice of Masonry as it has traditionally been known, will be permanently lost to many of them. A lodge simply cannot re-create outside its ritual environs what it can within; no more than a Mason can have the same personal experience when he is watching a degree as he had when it was being performed on him for the first time.

15 The Rebirth of Masonry and Masonic Ritual

The American Masonic experience is very much in transition today. It is the proverbial good news/bad news situation. The bad news is that the fraternity will not be able to grow without making a number of strategic changes. It simply will not be able to overcome its increasing mortality rate by using traditional approaches to attract men to it. Men no longer follow their fathers into Masonry. And they haven't for several generations. Grand Lodge policies holding to the "no-ask" rule will most assuredly mark a death blow for the fraternity in their State or Province. Furthermore, new strategies must be quickly implemented in several important areas simultaneously or Freemasonry may indeed fall below the critical mass required to sustain it as a twenty-first century institution.

Grand Lodges that have undertaken actuarial studies already know membership at the State level is at a critical level. It is safe to say that a majority of lodges do not have enough able members to operate any community or benevolent programs. Few have enough active men to open and conduct business at regular monthly meetings. Charters are being forfeited by more and more lodges each year. In fact, if Grand

Lodges would enforce current mandates regarding that which is required for lodges to keep charters, we could expect to lose over fifty percent of the lodges which are now holding charters.

Masonry is literally dying too fast to sustain its present structure. But it doesn't have to die. It simply has to change.

If the fraternity in America is to survive, it can no longer do what it has been doing for the past half century. The dynamics must change. The way Masonry is practiced must change. How it is understood by those who are already Masons (and those who are not yet Masons) must change. This does not imply the kind of change which alters its basic fabric, that is, what the organization is, what it stands for, and so forth. Clearly, the ritual process of becoming a Mason is a fundamental that should not change. What is needed is the kind of change that will ultimately cause Freemasonry to become a relevant twenty-first century organization that meets the needs of its current and future members and addresses important needs of society in such a manner that Masonry might again become what it once was; the organization of excellence noted for making a difference in the world.

At the corporate level, the day of the Grand Master's program, designed to address only one problem at a time, is quickly reaching its zenith. Masonic leaders and members alike know the problems facing the fraternity. Those that have been paying attention realize that throwing State mandated programs at lodges will not solve the issues which must be solved. Masonry can no longer afford the time required to test one Grand Lodge program this year; and, if it doesn't work, try another next year. It is futile to toss around what limited volunteer energy is still available as if members were a school of fish, darting one direction and then another. The pomp and ceremony of Grand Lodge visitations, conducted solely for the purpose of meeting and greeting the Grand Master, while nice, are not enough. In a culture that thrives on sound bites and visual aids in almost every aspect of life, the focus of Masonic leadership must be disciplined enough to literally turn heads (minds) in a different direction; a direction that is so uniquely different that it attracts attention.

The challenge of contemporary Freemasonry is in determining how to direct thinking in the ancient wisdom traditions, using the formats of information transfer available to today's aspirant; kind of a new model of instruction that embraces old school ideas. There is a formula available through the fraternity which will compel each individual to want to get in touch with what leading a life with meaning means; to ascertain how one goes about finding the truth for oneself, and to rediscover how one becomes transformed by the path of his own life. How the message is communicated must change, but the medium for it remains unchanged. It is still about instruction and education, knowledge and vision.

The man who desires to join the fraternity today has a different vision. He has received his perceptions about Freemasonry from a virtual warehouse of information and knowledge available to him every day in the digital world of instant information and processing. He has seen or read the very best of what has been written or spoken about Masonry. He has also surfed through the very worst about us from those who are driven by intolerance, hatred, or illusions of conspiracy. What is important for today's Masonic leaders to understand is that, if what this man has seen or read about us has compelled him to join, his expectations of us will be quite high.

We need only to deliver on the promises of our words for him to find in us a match for his hopes and aspirations. But to do so will require strategic thinking. In this regard, Freemasonry would be well served if we could do some things as if we had a national presence. For instance, it would be very strategic for Grand Lodges to seek out and cultivate viable private and public partners to enhance their presence, visibility, and credibility in the world. Much ambassadorship can be gained from such partnerships. More significantly, the Grand Lodges of North America should begin to meet and confer on how best to collectively accomplish the Mission of Freemasonry (a statement that has already been adopted by that consortium of State Bodies). American Masonry should choose a national approach around which it might pool its intellectual and member resources to solve its most pressing issues. While a national Grand Lodge is not suggested here, an organization is sorely needed which can make strategic policy recommendations and decisions on behalf of all Grand Lodges aimed at the restoration and renewal of the fraternity. This body should be given the authority to conduct studies and raise funds on behalf of the fraternity to implement strategies for Masonic restoration and renewal, including member assessments directed toward this important goal.

At the local lodge level, governance and effectiveness must vastly improve; emphasis on ritual and internal lodge operations must be balanced with broad programs of social and community involvement for members. Optimism should replace pessimism as the driving force for change. Local lodge dynamics should find ways to get members to visualize their own role in the change process. Time, convenience, and quality must be at the core of the renewed lodge's strategy. Lodge officer selection should be based on proven leadership ability and experience, rather than on ritual proficiency. This might establish the right balance of leadership in the lodge; allowing the ritualists to confer the degrees and the lodge officers to direct the progress of the fraternity.

Indeed, a number of important factors are at issue if the organization is to realize a renaissance. Sweeping changes must be made in how Masonry is introduced to males who may be interested in joining, and how it is also introduced to their families. Further, programs in lodge must relate to the interests of men. A high priority must be given to how the local Masonic organization creates a presence and respect in its community through its public involvement and charities. Internally, attention must be given to how degrees are conferred on men by its rituals, how Masonry is taught to men through its internal education programs, how its ritual forms and symbol associations become internalized in the male psyche; and, thus, open the window of transformation in men; how Masonry is practiced in daily life by the actions of its members.

Of course, it is not the purpose of this book to suggest strategies for resolving all of these issues (many excellent strategies have been developed and recommended to Grand Lodges through the work of the Masonic Renewal Committee–a standing committee of the North American Grand Master's Conference), but there are equally important strategic considerations which need to be addressed with the ritual itself.

If Masonry is to expect to keep its archaic ritual language (and this author believes that it should), then a mechanism must be established whereby the history and intent of the ritual is explained and made known to every Mason who experiences it. There is an increasing pressure being placed on Grand Lecturers today to update or modernize the language of the degrees. It is felt that somehow, if the language is made more contemporary, Freemasonry will be more appealing. This author would warn against such temptations for several reasons.

First, much of the genius of Masonry is in the language; the words are fundamental to its allegorical form, and the transformation process in men. Many of the lessons in Masonry are allegorical; that is, the instruction can only be discovered by intuition and insight. In many instances, the language facilitates this process of discovery. It can also hide that for which a man has not yet prepared himself by his own life experience to discover. Yet, when sentences or paragraphs are omitted or restructured, it is possible to forever destroy that which has been purposely hidden behind the allegories. The explanation of the liberal arts and sciences covered earlier in this book is one example: It would be easy to suggest the commentary in the Middle Chamber lecture regarding the arts and sciences is not relevant in today's world of extraordinary scientific technology and our contemporary "speed of light" information transfer capability. But what is hidden behind the arts and sciences allegory makes a difference in the way men understand their own spiritual nature and perceive their journey to mature masculinity. Men must be awakened to the sacred within them. This is the fundamental purpose of initiation. The journey to the Middle Chamber shows the path. But the path is hidden within the allegory of the words. Its meaning must be interpreted to be understood. The words must all be in place in order for the seeker to unlock the mystery of their hidden meaning.

Secondly, all ritual language has its tradition. When considering actions to remove or revise language, the weighty question becomes what language should be altered or removed? How does a Grand Lodge go about enacting such changes? Who should decide questions regarding alterations in ritual language? Do most Grand Lodges have men who have made a study of Masonic ritual and are qualified to consult on language changes? Would we want to alter, for instance, the language given in the Entered Apprentice's prayer, that begins with the words, "Vouchsafe Thine aid, almighty Father of the Universe, to this our present convention, and grant that this candidate for Masonry may devote his life to thy service and become a true and faithful brother among us..." when this language can be traced as far back as Pennell's Constitution of 1730, and likely taken from an older source? Surely, no Grand Lodge would remove language that has been preserved in Masonic ritual throughout the whole of its history!

Third, there is an inherent veneration for Masonic language that is now adopted in each Grand Lodge. With all the efforts that have been made to establish a uniform working in the United States, and with all the attention that has been given the ritual over the past 200 years, it has seen few substantive changes within any given Grand Lodge. It remains substantially intact as a landmark of the fraternity. To adopt significant changes now is to literally risk turning Freemasonry into a different organization. There are many different esoteric systems being practiced in the United States today. Each is defined largely by its ritual. The ritual of Freemasonry is uniquely its own. Part of its genius is that every culture and every generation has adapted to it. Yet it is still transforming in its impact. It is not necessary that it be adapted to meet the needs of a 'modern' culture. It already meets the needs of men within a deeper psychological and cosmological framework.

In this author's view, it is not the ritual that needs alteration in American Masonry. The "Masonic script" is fine. The experience of the last three hundred years has given us ample evidence to conclude that we are happy in all the essentials with the words we have adopted within our own jurisdictions. Our words may not be the same as our Masonic neighbor's words. But they are our words. And we are proud of them.

However, there are other related challenges within our current culture that should be given attention. The first, and most significant is that, in too many lodges, how the ritual is presented does not make the best (or worse, the right) impression. The production value of rote memorization is not adequate to hold and keep the attention of lodge members. It appeals only to the five percent who are the lodge ritualists; the presenters of the words, and the few others who want to be like them. The American lodge experience has long overlooked its most important asset; the larger majority of its members. Participation in lodge should not be a passive activity. Ritual words (and phrases) alone, without the attending accoutrements essential to creating and preserving the sacred ritual space;[221] ceremonial acts performed without explanation; and inadequate venues for sharing information, knowledge, education, and dialogue in interpreting the allegories, symbolism, and secrets; these shortcomings do not stimulate the mind to think, or open the heart to insight, or raise the mind, body, and spirit of the candidate or member to higher aspirations; intellectually, spiritually or psychologically.

Unfortunately, unless this interactive process occurs, there is no magic. There is no basis for transformation. And Freemasonry then fails in its mission to take good men and make them better (it is the actual transformation of the individual that ratifies this mission.)

One thing is therefore certain. The presentation of ritual and member learning opportunities in lodges must dramatically improve if Masonry can hope to engage men in this century. Again, we know that a digitally connected society will have high expectations of the organizations it embraces. And in a world whose pace is not likely to slow down, men will simply discard any organization which fails to meet these expectations. The decision a lodge makes then, as to how it chooses to present its ritual and education to the next generation of Masons, may well determine its own future.

The New Experience of Masonic Ritual

If there is a universal in Masonry, it has been that the fraternity has always made the essential adaptations to meet the needs of the male culture in every generation. That is, it did so up until the last seventy years. And while we have a lot of catching up to do to connect ourselves once again with today's (and tomorrow's) culture of men, it is not too late to begin the process.

As regards the ritual, not only must we give its presentation to men whose talents and gifts center on effective communication (when the ritual is being narrated); and to those with special skills in dramatic technique (for the enactment of the third degree drama section). We must also understand that a new means of visualization and reality can now be tapped because of recent advancements in technology. Utilizing these resources can do much to improve the craft today.

To begin with, Grand Lodges who have not already done so should consider converting all lecture sections of the degrees to a digital format. When the lectures are narrations, these should be recorded using men trained in professional communication. When images are included, these should be guided by men skilled in visual techniques to give the most effective overall impact to the candidate. For those jurisdictions that include esoteric language within the body of their lectures, these words, sentences, or phrases should either be adopted as monitorial or moved so the digitally produced words can be uploaded in flash drives, placed on home computers and portable devices; or made digitally available in encrypted areas of Grand Lodge websites for protected review by members. Some consideration might also be given to adding contemporary visual images to the Hiram myth explanations, using contemporary images in parallel with the old lantern slide images; thereby giving men an easier means to integrate the truths represented by the ancient drama through their familiarity with contemporary cultural icons.

Grand Jurisdictions should move toward providing all members with comprehensive Masonic Education programs in both audio and visual format. This would begin with materials that can be given to prospective members as an introduction to Masonry; along with digital files which outline the concepts of initiation, why Masonry uses ritual as its teaching form; along with information delineating the major themes or lessons intended in each degree. These can be given to each candidate as he progresses through the degrees. There is also much to be gained by developing a set of audio files which cover every aspect of Masonry not specifically covered in the ritual language, including history, symbolism, philanthropy, biographies, and governance; all delivered as an application on portable devices. Again, the informed Mason is the very best ambassador of Freemasonry.

Finally, the availability of computer generated graphics, and new motion and sound technology now makes the conveyance of Masonic information accessible to literally everyone in the world. This provides a couple of significant opportunities. CD-ROMS can be developed that enables the Masonic story to be dramatically communicated through a combination of visuals, music and narrative. A "guided tour" of Masonry can literally be accessed by any home computer.

More significantly, "Virtual Reality" is a computer resource which is just beginning to be explored and is expected to receive wide use in the corporate world over the next decade. Virtual Reality is essentially an 'artificial world' that is generated by integrating computer graphics, animation, music and motion with the mind of the user. Currently, for instance, it is possible to create a virtual lodge room with stations and places on one's home computer. Each member of the lodge can also create a computer avatar representing himself to be placed within this virtual space. He then communicates via his home computer through his avatar in lodge to all those networked with him with their own avatars in the same virtual space. Ritual instruction and floor work can literally be taught with every member sitting in his living room. Masonic knowledge can be delivered and discussed through the voices and actions of the avatars. In an even more advanced technology, the players utilize head-mounted displays and tactical gloves which "direct movement' through a world of un-reality, very much like stepping into a television set and experiencing the same surroundings as the film has produced. The technology gives one the ability to artificially explore abstract concepts through mental modeling. In other words, one is transformed to a computer created world that immerses him into a multi-sensory experience.

As this concept sees further development and becomes economically affordable, the candidate progressing through the degrees in Masonry will have at his fingertips a true learning-by-doing model. It will be possible for him to 'migrate" to the actual world of Hiram, for instance, and experience much of the same sensation one would have experienced had he actually "been there." Virtual Reality duplicates a three-dimensional, real world experience. In addition, there is a multi-sensory communication which is inherent in this technology. In other words, one not only sees and hears what is being presented, but he "feels the invisible,", that is, his emotions and behaviors are affected by the objects he confronts on his journey. Thus, we will be able to give the new Mason the same transforming experience in his own home that the ritual subliminally provides for him in lodge. Imagine the impact a candidate will realize if he is the "Hiram" of the Masonic allegory in a simulated computer world!

Of course, this doesn't imply that the degrees should be presented at home rather than in the lodge. Nothing can replace the overall fraternal experience of a lodge setting. But 'virtual' venues allow the fraternity to duplicate or reinforce that experience in a multidimensional simulation that will not only teach, but will motivate men to learn much more about what being a Mason actually means than has been possible in the past.

Finally, technology is being developed today that may allow the use of interactive holograms as "props" to enhance the actual lodge ritual experience. With this capability, the lodge room might be turned into a projection-based quarry, hillside, or sea coast where the scenes and symbols encountered would actually be positioned in a three-dimensional environment. The candidate and the lodge members would all experience the stones, the tools, and the craftsmen of King Solomon's era come to "life." The lodge would again become the true temple of Masonry!

Of course, we are not there yet. But one possible solution to bringing Masonry to a renaissance in the next century is to begin the planning and visioning today to be on the cutting edge of what is technically possible in the future. This is great work for a committee of young men.

The goal of Masonry is the same as it has always been–to make the Masonry of tomorrow meet the needs of men in their own time–as in all times.

The New Experience in Lodge

The dynamics of the American lodge experience is also very much in flux as we begin the second decade of the twenty-first century. It is important that we understand that the Masonic experience was always intended to be, first and foremost, a fraternal experience that engages the well-being of men in multi-generational settings which are comprised of elders, peers, and subordinates.

The human need for ritualization has not diminished in our society. What has diminished is the availability of knowledgeable ritual elders who understand the archetypal human need for ritualization in all stages of a man's life. What is needed are competent and effective ritual elders who provide positive images of mature masculinity for the younger men in lodge. Development into mature manhood does not happen automatically. Men are social animals. We need a lot of software to go with our biological hardware. Our initiatory rites and the conversations we have within the private settings of our lodge is the software which channels and contains our man energies toward powerful and responsible outcomes. Young men should not be thrown to their own devices in seeking the mature masculine soul. They should have help from other men who understand by their own life experience how the path is to be forged. Here is a great secret we should all cherish in our Masonic Order:

> Freemasonry is a rite of manhood that connects young males to the collective masculine soul; to the spirit of being a man; and to the community of men. It is the traditional organizational venue for male role modeling and male to male communication.[222]

Being a good role model is the best vehicle men have to establish in the minds and souls of those who follow them that they too belong. They are welcome. They have the magic of manhood. There is a place by the fire for them. Freemasonry is designed to facilitate this level of deep fellow feeling among men.

Fraternal association serves more than a mundane purpose. The life of our society is very much the product of our ongoing activities with each other and our symbolic interpretation of the meaning these activities have to us internally. This is the reason all of us possess the inherent ability to yield positive influence on human behavior. It is the reason the quality we invest in our lodge experience is so critically important. We get out of Masonry what we qualitatively put into it. Social interaction is the process that feeds our behavior. Even if we don't consciously realize it, we take into account what others are doing, or are preparing to do, and we accept or abandon their action based on our own interpretation of the rightness of it. And there is an important distinction to be made that is perhaps obvious. When we are just going along with the group and displaying trivial or perfunctory behavior without assigning meaning to it, we are not engaged in symbolic interaction. We are simply being guys. It has been shown in this study that the tradition of the festive board, the history of Masonic feasts, and the jocularity of the tavern experience in our own fraternal past are a reflection of the importance males place on just being guys. There is a guy in every man that is less serious and more aggressive than his more manly aspects. Therein is the duality which we spend half our lives trying to reconcile.

But I can also assure the reader that we attend and participate in the function of lodge because we assign symbolic meaning to it. As men, we inherently know that symbolic interaction is far more significant to us in the long run of our life experience. We ultimately want to live a responsible life and be accountable to the duties we owe our gender; because to not do so has too many consequences.

Whenever, we, as individuals, act outside the positive and productive norms of society, then we miss the whole point of taking on the mature masculine. In such circumstances, we only contribute to an already clouded definition of manhood. And then we wonder and lament over why society bashes our gender. Yet, when we give the worst side of our humanness a public face, that is, when we are dishonest, greedy, abusive, selfish, anti-social, anti-cultural or perverse, then we contribute to society's stereotyping of male behavior. The result is that we all sacrifice how we want to be defined as men. Such stereotyping has a dramatic impact on the integrity of our gender and our self-esteem as males.

One objective of Masonic teaching is to combat this stereotyping. Our lessons empower us to take on a healthy image of manhood by assigning unto ourselves the practice of interpreting what has symbolic meaning for us in ways that will bring us health, happiness, virtue, status, and harmony in our life. When we are successful, not only have we enhanced our gender, we have achieved symbolic integration between ourselves and the higher principles of virtue and morality within us. We are then truly acting on the square of virtue and morality.

In fact, in Freemasonry, we often announce our quest for symbolic integration through naming the higher principle involved. In Craft rituals, we circumambulate about the lodge in the name of Wisdom, Strength, and Beauty; in the Royal Arch, we pass through the Veils in the name of Peace, Love, and Unity; in the Knights Templar, we make our pilgrimage in the name of *In Hoc Signo Vinces;* in the Ancient and Accepted Scottish Rite, we quest in the name of Liberty, Equality, and Fraternity; in the Rosicrucian Order, we journey in the name of *INRI.* And we do the same in life. We discipline our lives in the name of family, work, and social obligations. We pray and worship in the name of God, Jehovah, Allah, or some other symbolic icon of the Great I Am. We go to our deaths in the name of God, country, ideology, or a way of life.

And all these symbolic interactions, taken together, define who we are and determine our social status. Our Masonic symbol system, then, serves a social purpose, as well as ordering our behavior. Thus, it is in the name of status that we uphold our styles of life in the drama of hierarchy in which we live. And the way in which status (or if you prefer to call it social honor) is distributed in a fraternity of men, is through the status of those who belong.

This means that, above all else, a specific style of life should be expected from those who wish to belong to our inner circle and wear the title of Master Mason. It is our personal and organizational expression of how we choose to define ourselves as men; how we are going to act and be perceived by those who are watching. And, it does not matter who we are, there is someone watching. And he is watching us to determine if our example has a symbolic meaning to him that he will desire to emulate.

As Masons, it is essential that we understand why we have so many honorific names and titles in our different Masonic Degrees and Orders. Honorific names give us symbolic power to endow our actions with dignity, glory, and integrity. Freemasons are to be men of great dignity because dignity is the alchemical dew which falls down upon the head of individuals of social honor. When we understand this symbolism correctly, then we must recognize that honor becomes the demand which a positively privileged status group raises for the deportment of its own members.

Freemasonry is all about status. Our symbol system, then, creates and sustains our belief that our ways of acting actually function as a brand, or name, that directs how we live, and governs how others perceive us, and therefore distinguishes us from the rest of the community. The sociological function of Masonic ritual and the male bonding it facilitates for us is no less than a dramatic construct for individual and social improvement. The path to enlightenment, honor, and status is always an upward way. Through our organization, we are about the business of communicating and sustaining status in the lives of our members. If we do any less, we stop short of fulfilling our promise that we improve ourselves in Freemasonry because personal improvement implies moving to a higher state of grace.

This understanding of the importance of social honor is a key also to perceiving why we must not bring the character of the profane world into the tyled recesses of the lodge. A lodge leader has status to a new member if that new member perceives the lodge leader to be of a higher class, or has an elevated dignity, or a better image than the new member. This was the model of the lodges in our formative years. The lodge offered a popular conduit for status seekers who wanted to be in the same group with the men of social honor; that is, the younger members who wanted to emulate the men of status in the community. Unfortunately, as the organization grew in popularity over the centuries, it too often overlooked the old agreement it had with its members regarding expectations of quality. Discounting the built in restrictions regarding investigations of prospects, and succumbing to the pressure of creating an organization that was available to every man, lodges began attracting men who did not understand the dignity associated with social honor. When social honor is not preserved, it becomes much more challenging to attract men with values that are expected in an organization that has social status. As this necessary tenet of fraternal association was set aside in a majority of lodges over a sustained period of time, men in lodge eventually lost their motivation to belong because they saw no increased value in being a member. Over time, it becomes extraordinarily difficult to attract men of social honor into the ranks because such men generally care nothing about an organization they perceive will not improve their status. We have created, very subtly over time, an organization which has little perceived value to men interested in social honor.

There are only two ways out of this dilemma. We can sanction the creation of new lodges where the vision is social honor and hand pick men of status to join (which is highly recommended); or we can change the cultural paradigm of our existing lodges by educating our members about the Masonic importance of status. This is a much more difficult remedy than creating new lodges, but it can be done. The key to keeping status in an existing lodge at a high enough level to sustain perceived value over time is if the upper level (older) men become mentors to the lower level (younger) men and the upper level men are consciously aware that the subject of mentoring is social honor, which can only be taught through life experience and symbolic interaction. This is the reason multi-generational lodges are so important.

One thing we can gain from this historical review of the men who grew our fraternity in the past, is that all of them had mentors they looked up to in promoting and embellishing progress in the fraternity. Mentoring is a status feeder! It feels good and does wonderful things to the ego of the mentor; and it feels special to be mentored. Mentoring is a form of service. Men will join organizations in which they can both give and receive service. This is why role modeling, and the right kind of role modeling, is critically important. Our experienced members need to understand how to mentor our younger members and our younger members need to perceive they are receiving valuable attention from our older members in the ways of social honor. I believe this to be the organizational formula for our future success in American Masonry.

In the journeys of our Degrees and the regular enactments of our ceremonies and rituals, in the processionals and regalia of our titled men and the songs we sing in veneration of our traditions; in the private conversations we have as Brethren where knowledge is shared and wisdom is passed along, we are creating and re-creating the meaning and purpose of our lives. In this honored and eccentric engagement, we develop a deep sense of brotherhood and community because we are acting out in the presence of each other the roles we believe necessary to life itself. The staging of the roles in the dramatic theatres of our fraternity is, then, a staging, or presentation of ourselves to our own private audience whose approval gives us our sense of identity and belonging.

Within the sacred space of lodge, we lead our younger Brethren to the ethical and spiritual traditions which will facilitate their own transformation into manhood. We are supposed to be the moral compass for them. Our task as elders is to focus our old fraternal purpose of teaching and mentoring them—of helping them find the mature masculine within themselves, and participate themselves in the raising of the next generation of elders; of producing men who will have status, honor and integrity in their time.

This is our extraordinary purpose. Through the ordering principles of our rituals and symbols, we create in the new member a state of mind wherein he truly believes that moral integrity and social honor is also important to him—that it can define his manhood like he believes it has defined ours.

We are his guidepost. If we do our job right, we will bond him to us by our powerful and compelling dramas, by the meaning of our words, by the ordering structure of the men in our lodge; and by our own examples of what it means to live a consciously awakened life—a life that is manly, caring, responsible, joyful, uplifting and filled with meaning and purpose; a life where patriarchy embraces its own wisdom and is happy to freely give it away to a worthy subordinate, to share what it has learned; and ultimately, as Brothers, to communicate status to those who will replace us—those who crave also to become real men.

16 Conclusions

If we can draw an important conclusion and direction from this book, I believe we must focus on the two men who had the greatest impact on what has evolved as the Masonic ritual practices we inherited from their singular visions and efforts—*William Preston and Thomas Smith Webb*. Both, in different ways, have given us a sound and reliable template for the promulgation and perpetuation of our art.

It is also insightful to review what we can draw from the development and evolution of the forms and practices which have been the focus of this study, the rituals which we as Masons of the present century have inherited from our forefathers. I will begin with the ritual itself because it will quickly take us to Preston's remarkable significance, and his underlying trust in the nature of our engagements as Masons regularly meeting together in the private assemblies of lodge.

It is clear from our review of the early ritual exposures that the late seventeenth and early eighteenth century Masons defined the nature of fraternal association quite differently than the brothers of the late eighteenth and early nineteenth centuries. During the pre-Grand Lodge era, the ritual practices were simple and primitive, with very short making ceremonies and a heavy reliance on the Old Charges of the operative masons for moral instruction. In the earliest known catechisms which dated from 1696 to 1730, the ritual practices focused almost exclusively on questions and answers which related to the actual ceremonies conducted inside the lodge room, along with a few rudimentary questions about the symbols represented in the furnishings of the lodge. There were no more than thirty-seven distinct questions and answers, and, in their entirety, summarized what Freemasons believed in and were expected to know and practice, both in and out of lodge. In the later versions of these, we find some added questions relating to those qualified to be fellow crafts, and procedures for applying for financial aid and for mutually recognizing other Masons.

Prichard's *Masonry Dissected* (1730) gave us the first definitive acknowledgement that Craft Masonry had evolved into a three degree system. The ceremonies were still presented in a catechism format, but the explanations were considerably longer than a decade earlier. It was easy to see that the moralizing associated with symbols was taking on more significance as the number of lodges grew and the conversations in lodge became more focused on learning and less on conviviality. The ritual exposures of the 1760s revealed the structure of the ritual itself had become the central and stabilizing infrastructure of Freemasonry during the thirty year period after Prichard's popular exposure. There were formal opening and closing ceremonies, different methods of preparing the lodge and the candidates in each degree, separate obligations for each, different passwords, formal apron presentations, and different arrangements for wearing an apron for each degree. A long elaboration on the Hiramic legend and the traditional history of the third degree was in place; and the ceremonies of the Ancients and Moderns Lodges took on more similarities.

But we also find that one important essential was conspicuously absent in all of the ritual exposures of the first fifty years of Grand Lodge ritual development. The lectures which explain the particulars of King Solomon's Temple, the explanations of the many hieroglyphical emblems of Masonry, and the valuable and useful lessons regarding the symbolism of the Degrees were not yet there. In fact, with the exception of a lecture on the history of the Grand Lodge, there was not a single lecture presented in any exposure that was similar to the present day third section lectures we routinely deliver in lodge. And this brings us to Preston, his private lectures, and what I believe to be his most important contribution and prophecy to the ultimate success of Freemasonry.

Preston's *Lectures and Syllabus* clearly represented the most brilliant and elaborate expansion of Masonic knowledge in the eighteenth century. His themes were the typical themes of the English Enlightenment: God as Grand Architect of the Universe and Grand Geometrician; the recurring images of Deity as a Design Principle; not as a Descartian self-contained First Principle, but as a kind of benevolent Supreme Guide directing human affairs in accordance with fixed laws. The universe was an ordered phenomena and man was a part of the ordering structure of the cosmos. The influence of scientific knowledge to the application of reason; the measurements and quantifying principles of mathematics, geometry and physics as a function of magnitude, expansion, and proportions; the obsession with symmetry and the patterning of opposites as applied to moral and ethical conditions, ideas and principles, and as a unifying replication of God in man. The assumption that moral and ethical behavior and codes could create harmony within and between individuals, and that Freemasons could be enabled to actually live in a kind of utopia within the tyled, or sacred spaces, and associations of their lodges.[223] These were new and profound concepts which had not before been included in ritual structure. These ideas launched Freemasonry in an entirely new philosophical direction.

How did Preston and his contemporaries get from the ceremonial forms presented in what we think of as our first degree ceremonies and the first section rituals of the Fellowcraft and Master Mason degrees as suggested in the 1760s exposures, to the fully developed themes and courses of study provided to the rest of the Masonic world by the end of the eighteenth century? The answer was given us in a superb and groundbreaking lecture delivered by Trevor Stewart, Past Master of Quatuor Coronati Lodge No. 2076, as the Prestonian Lecture of 2004.[224] It is essential that we develop an understanding of how this gap was closed in order to draw some important conclusions in regard to what we have (and have not) brought forward from that eighteenth century model to our own contemporary lodge culture.

It should be pointed out that Preston's lectures were not the result of a creative moment he had with the guys over a few weekends of conversation ruminating over Masonic symbolism. Rather, these were the product of the extended culture in which he lived and experienced Masonry. Preston was a member of eight Masonic lodges. He was conveniently placed at the center of London's Masonic life because he served as the clerk to two Grand Secretaries over a period of a dozen years. This put him in a position to establish many valuable contacts on a daily basis with the most prominent and intellectually active Masons then in London. As much as he was a mentor to others in illustrating his ideas and lectures, he was also a collator of the opinions of a vast number of other intelligent men with whom he wrote and conversed. He found that the culture of London Freemasons was steeped in customarily discussing the content of their ceremonies, the meaning of its themes, along with a host of other topics.

Preston came to understand the gentlemen who had been attracted to membership in lodges were attracted at least in part by the promise of engaging in regular stimulating conversations over a vast range of subjects. Such men would not have been attracted to a society which merely pursued the re-enactment of medieval builders' trade rites. There had to be sufficient intellectual stimulus in the conversations held in lodge or such men as Elias Ashmole would not have retained their interest or membership—as he did for more than three decades.

Stewart reminds us of the art of eighteenth century conversation. He states; "Theirs was the era that urged its educated gentlemen to participate regularly and willingly in polite conversation. One of the key indicators of whether a man was educated and a gentleman was if he could participate fluently in rational discourse with his peers. It was a basic assumption then that through polite discourse, a corporate interchange which could be simultaneously challenging, stimulating and pleasing to the intellect, something like 'self-improvement' could be achieved."[225] Having regular, stimulating conversation with one's peers was one of the morally enhancing goals that Freemasons both espoused and emphasized in printed discourses and in their regulations.

Another important facet of the eighteenth century lodge culture was that many of the active Freemasons were also known to be club men. It is well known that the Royal Society had a significant number of Freemasons within its membership over the whole of the eighteenth century. There were also other clubs meeting regularly in London taverns which were not Masonic but which included Masons in their membership. These clubs may have had formal and/or semi-formal meeting structures, but they offered programs and discussions covering a broad range of topics; sometimes controversial, often scientific, and frequently antiquarian in their interests. All of them were cosmopolitan and energetic. The unifying and leveling factors that held things together for them was the fluency of their discussions; the idea that impartial and informed debate on literally any topic was worthwhile; that anyone with sufficient intellect and ability to express himself could join in. The sheer excitement of making and reporting new discoveries was a compelling reason to attend and participate in club life.

Preston lived in a world of informed conversation. He thus provided, in his lectures, a syllabus of the topics and conversations that had been routinely held in lodges from the founding of Grand Lodge to the time his work was published. He and his co-authors were intimately connected with association life in and around London and his lectures reflect the societal and intellectual aspirations espoused and engendered by those who lived in the main urban centers in eighteenth century Britain. The frequency of these discussions and the fact that they continued over a number of decades tells us a lot about the character and interest of these Brethren.

It also says something about what they regarded as the legitimate activity of lodge. Stewart informs us that the formulation of Freemasonry by Preston could only have been created by him because there existed already in print a whole series of scientific and exegetical works which propagated the notions that found their way to his Syllabus. Many of these publications had been penned by Freemasons. Moreover, there existed a vibrant willingness and an ability to explore such ideas in London Lodges using practical demonstrations and regular discussions. Preston had a built-in propensity of speculating in the Lodges upon which he was an active participant. And he was a visitor of many others. The rapid and complete adoption of his published works throughout the English Craft meant that the subjects and the grand morals associated with them became the norm upon which skilled Freemasons sought mastery in things Masonic, and by which all subsequent attempts at developing Masonic symbology was measured. There is no doubt that his thoughts on the symbols of the Craft and how they should be arranged represent the most significant contribution by any one man to the practice of Freemasonry.

What Preston left his Masonic heirs to contemplate is the profound significance that knowledge, education, and a shared discourse plays in the success of Freemasonry. The conclusion we can draw from his efforts is he taught us that investigating the vast range of possible meanings in Freemasonry is an active process. Listening to someone else deliver only the words of the ritual is not. Freemasonry will never come to mean much to its members unless we find a better way of ensuring that the process of self-improvement is owned by them. Everything that Preston taught us suggests that the heart and soul of Freemasonry is something much more dynamic, much less restrictive, and much broader in vision than our current practices offer.

Perhaps it is time to recreate in our own time the indispensable intellectual component of Masonic dialogue which enabled the completion of Masonic philosophy by the end of the eighteenth century.

American Freemasons have identified far more readily with Thomas Webb than William Preston, and this explains at lot as to how our lodge practices came to be so one-dimensional in our own culture. Webb was first and foremost a publisher of books. His greatest contribution to the American Craft Lodge is that he produced a volume pertaining to Freemasonry. As far as anyone knows, Webb never actually spent any time in England poring over the words of Masonic ritual with William Preston. It is true that he became a close friend and Masonic associate of the Englishman John Hanmer, who claimed that he learned the work directly from Preston and taught it to Webb. But there is no certificate authenticated by Preston that he taught the work to Thomas Smith Webb.

If one was a bookseller, it seems far more likely that he would be just as interested in buying Preston's books as memorizing Preston's work. There is no doubt that Webb conceived the notion of publishing his own work from Preston's good example. *Illustrations of Masonry* was advertised for sale in July, 1796 at the Albany book store of Barber & Southwick. Webb would have certainly acquired a copy of Preston's volume as soon as it was available in the city. Webb's study of Preston's *Illustrations* was presumably the principle factor which moved him to prepare and publish a similar book for American Masons.[226]

Webb's *Monitor* was an instant hit, and became the standard work in the American lodge room. Whether he conversed with Preston or read Preston, there is no question he understood the philosophy of Freemasonry and duplicated much of what Preston had published. More significantly, the materials for the lessons, symbol explanations, and lectures he gathered from Preston, he re-organized (and in some cases, added to) in a much easier and continuous format than was available in Preston's *Illustrations.* The structure of the *Monitor* is so remarkably different from the *Illustrations* that one can easily conclude Webb drew his ideas for the organization of his own book from other sources. So much different, in fact, that Webb's work may well have been just as heavily influenced by the 1760s exposures, *Jachin and Boaz* and *Three Distinct Knocks.* The catechisms published in these sources, taken together, are in many cases word for word with Webb's *Monitor.* He appeared to like the organization of these later exposures and blended their form with Preston's philosophical genius.

Regardless of lineage, Webb's *Monitor* was almost the only book of rituals known to the American craft after 1797. His concern for stabilizing the ritual practices in the United States into one cohesive and harmonious working, and his passion for instruction by means of rote learning in lodges and to his students, had the effect that, even after two hundred years, there remain few old Masons who have not been trained in the art of Masonic memory by way of Webb's published or spoken words.

The principal difference between Preston and Webb, then, is that Preston's goal was the regular and persistent communication of knowledge; to advance the enlightenment of the individual Mason and the status of the whole fraternity through the individual and group processes of learning. His was a vision of brothers coming together weekly in private conclaves of male association with an attitude of pragmatic worldliness. Their purpose is to be bound by the mystic ties of their ceremonial forms, yet be engaged in open-ended conversation in a sacred place for transcendence in human thinking and the transformation of the human spirit.

Webb, on the other hand, saw the formal ceremony as the structure of Masonry itself. Masonic ritual provided a form of ordered service in which the symbols and lessons conveyed presented positive reinforcement to the human psyche week end and week out. By communication of the proper and well-chosen 'Words of the Mason,' the instructive tongue meets the attentive ear and the beauties of virtuousness are inculcated upon the faithful breast. To him, the ritual enabled the collective well-being of the society of Masons. The ritual bound the young man to his elders and peers to peers. It cemented the world of nature with the human spirit and facilitated the discovery of one's self and his self-worth. Webb's vision was that the Masonic ritual was the ultimate science of action, possessing its own logic, structure and order. It alone can 'initiate' one into a higher level of awareness of himself and the world in which he lives. The ritual is empowerment itself. No wonder, then, that Webb was driven to perfect what our seventeenth and eighteenth century fore-bearers created for us; and then teach it to others in what he sincerely believed to be its purest form.

What Webb left for his heirs to contemplate was the profound significance of the Masonic ritual itself; and the necessity of always ensuring that it be left pure in form, tied to its eighteenth century beginnings, and available to every generation in its manufactured fullness, un-tampered by ignorance and innovation.

Thus, it would seem the wisest conclusion of this present work is that we acknowledge it is essential for every generation of fraternal men to hold firm to the substance of the adopted work in whatever jurisdiction they reside. The 'Mason's Words' are the skeleton of the society of Freemasons. They are our history. They are our lineage. They are the bridge that unites us as a society of friends and brothers in our own time with all generations of Freemasons that have gone before us; and will come after us.

Yet, equally important, the knowledge, intelligence, wisdom, and experience of Brothers meeting together in private conclaves of studied men, sharing what they know, and learning from each other in open and stimulating conversations week end and week out, month after month, year after year; is the fabric of our society of Freemasons. We reflect the history of ideas in man's quest to interpret the meaning of life.

It is essential that both the skeleton and the fabric be in place in order for the lodges and its members to be clothed in the light of Masonry.

If all we can aspire to ourselves, and offer to our newcomers, is to learn the Preston-Webb ritual by heart and then regard that as the peak of their Masonic accomplishment; and conversely, if all we can aspire to ourselves, and to offer our newcomers, is shallow and perfunctory conversation of little substance, meaning, or merit—then what chance of further possibility of future growth will these things offer to them?

Such a restrictive vision of the 'Grand Design' does not match that of Preston's shared dialogue with the learned men in lodge, or that of Webb's philosophical journey of the *Words*. Such a limiting vision does not begin to match modern life as it is experienced by young men.[227] This is what we must now know.

ENDNOTES

[1] Carpenter, Audrey T., *John Theopholis Desaguliers:A natural Philosopher, Engineer and Freemason in Newtonian England,* London, The Continuum International Publishing Group, 2011, pp. 88-89

[2] Heiron, Arthur, *The Craft in the 18th Century, Old Time Manners and Customs and Reminiscences of a Bi-Centenary Lodge,* Transactions of the Quatuor Coronati Lodge, London, Vol. 37, Part 1, January, 1924, pp. 53

[3] In practice, the mop and pail were used for ceremonial purposes only in lodge halls that used chalk in making the floor drawings. Many lodges had floor cloths made for ritual workings. The mop and pail was far more frequently used for the more practical purpose of cleaning the lodge room. Unless a lodge owned the premises, it is unlikely they had any cleaning responsibilities.

[4] Heiron, pp. 60

[5] Ibid, pp. 60

[6] Ibid, pp. 75

[7] Ibid, pp. 80

[8] Clark, Peter, *The English Alehouses: A Social History, 1200-1830,* London, Longman Group, Ltd., 1983, pp. 9

[9] Ibid, pp. 10

[10] Ibid, pp. 11

[11] Ibid, pp. 13

[12] Ibid, pp. 13

[13] Ibid, pp. 230

[14] Frere, *Grand Lodge, 1717-1767, pp. 48*

[15] Jones, *Freemason's Guide,* pp. 170

[16] Clark, pp. 306-07

[17] Drake, Samuel Adam, *Old Boston Taverns and Tavern Clubs,* W.A. Butterfield, 1917, pp. 38-39

[18] Ibid, pp. 17

[19] Knoop, Douglas; Jones, G.P., and Hamer, Douglas, *The Early Masonic Catechisms,* Second Edition edited by Harry Carr, for the Quatuor Coronati Lodge No. 2076, Manchester University Press, London, 1963, pp. 31

[20] Stevenson, David, *The Origins of Freemasonry, Scotland's Century, 1590-1710,*Cambridge University Press, New York, 1990, pp. 136

[21] Stevenson, *Origins,* pp. 130,

[22] Carr, Harry, *The Early French Exposures, 1737-1751,* The Quatuor Coronati Lodge, No.2076, London, 1971, pp. viii, ix

[23] Stevenson, David, *The Origins of Freemasonry, Scotland's Century, 1590-1710,* Cambridge University Press, New York, 1990, pp. 13

[24] The word "charge" is rarely used today, but in the context of the manuscript constitutions of the guilds, a "charge" meant a precept, order, or injunction. In Masonry, a charge is often given as an address to the candidate near the close of each of the degrees. These charges recite the duties which reaching a particular level of membership has imposed on him. There are also charges given by the lodge Master to his lodge brethren during the opening or closing of regular lodge meetings; and a charge is given the Master himself during his installation as the presiding officer of the lodge. Charges describe the rules that are to be followed by those who call themselves Masons; thus their placement with the constitutional documents of the Craft.

[25] Berman, Ric, *The Foundations of Modern Freemasonry,* Sussex Academic Press, Portland, 2012, pp. 11

[26] Carr, Harry, *600 Years of Craft Ritual,* Transactions of the Quatuor Coronati Lodge, London,Vol. 82, June, 1968, pp. 154

[27] Ibid, pp. 154

[28] Stevenson, *Origins,* pp. 16

[29] Carr, pp. 156

[30] Frere, A.S., *Grand Lodge, 1717-1967,* printed for the United Grand Lodge of England at the University Press, Oxford, Great Britain, 1967, pp. 12-13

[31] Dobb, Maurice, *Studies in the Development of Capitalism,* London, 1946, pp. 89-90

[32] Berman, pp. 11

[33] Kebell, Peter, *The Changing Face of Freemasonry, 1640-1740,* University of Bristol, unpublished PhD dissertation, 2009, pp. 13-15

[34] Carpenter, pp. 83

[35] Desaguliers, J.T., *A Course of Experimental Philosophy,* 2 vols., London, 1763, pp. x

[36] Carptenter, *John Theophilus Desaguliers,* pp 101

[37] Blackmer, Rollin, *The Lodge and the Craft,* The Standard Masonic

Publishing Co., St. Louis, MO, 1923, pp. 34

[38] Bullock Steven C., *Revolutionary Brotherhood:Freemasonry and the Transformation of the American Social Order, 1730-1840,* Institute of Early American History and Culture, University of North Carolina Press, 1966, pp.42-43

[39] Anderson, James, *The New Book of Constitutions of the Antient and Honourable Fraternity of Free and accepted Masons,* London, 1738, pp. 110

[40] Prescott, Andrew, "The Earliest Use of the Word Freemason", *Yearbook of the Grand Lodge of Scotlan, 2004,* Edinburgh: www.freemasons-Freemasonry.com/prescott02.html

[41] Berman, pp. 18

[42] Brown, William Moseley, *From Operative to Speculative,* The Masonic Service Association, Washington, DC, 1958. See also Stevenson, *Origins,* pp. 63

[43] Frere, *Grand Lodge,* pp. 27

[44] Ibid, pp. 28

[45] French, G.H.T., *Guilds Versus Lodges,* Transactions of Quatuor Coronati Lodge, London, Vol. 95, pp 185

[46] Wells, Roy A., *Freemasonry in London from 1785,* Lewis Masonic, Terminal House, Middlesex, 1984, pp. 32

[47] Examples of ritual texts in this section all come from Knoop, Jones, and Hamer's *Catechisms.* Rather than cite each reference separately each time ritual text is presented or explained, the source only is given.

[48] Knoop, Jones, and Hamer, *Catechisms,* pp. 31-32

[49] Knoop, et al, pp. 33

[50] Knoop, et al, pp. 36

[51] Knoop, et al, pp. 48-49

[52] Knoop, et al, pp. 52-53

[53] Holme, Randle III, *An Academie of Armorie, or, A Storehouse of Armory and Blason,* Chester, 1688, pp. 46

[54] Pease, Raymond Burnett, *Masonic Parallels in Shakespeare,* The Masonic Service Association, Maryland, 1952, pp. 26

[55] Poole, Herbert, *Masonic Ritual and Secrets Before 1717,* Transactions of the Quatuor Coronati Lodge, London, Vol. 37, Part 1, January, 1924, pp. 5

[56] Knoop, et al, pp. 160-161

[57] Ibid, pp. 161

[58] There are three kinds of cubits: the King's cubit, which is the English measure of three feet; the holy cubit, which is one foot, six inches; and the common cubit, which is one foot, nine inches. Since the biblical cubit is one foot, six inches, this is the length referred to in Masonic ritual.

[59] Harvey, James M., *Initiation Two Hundred Years Ago,* The Supplement—Micsellanea Latomorum, Quatuor Coronati Lodge, London, 1953, pp. 213
[60] Harvey, *Initiation,* pp. 213-214

[61] Jackson, A.C.F., *English Masonic Exposures, 1760-1769,* Lewis Masonic, Terminal House, Middlesex, 1986, pp. 22

[62] Jackson, pp. 30

[63] Harvey, Initiation, pp. 214

[64] Ibid, pp. 214

[65] Jackson, *Exposures,* pp. 69

[66] Jackson, A.C.F., *Masonic Passwords, Their Development and Use in the Early 18th Century,* Transactions of Quatuor Coronati Lodge, London, Vol. 88, pp. 106.

[67] Ibid, pp. 108

[68] The Fundamental Constitutions and Orders of the Society entitled *Philo-Musice et Architecturae Societas Apollini.* British Museum, Addl. Ms. 23203

[69] De le Tierce, in 1742, produced one of the first translations of the 1738 Constitutions for the use of his lodge in Frankfurt. His book included Chevalier Ramsay's Oration. It was titled *Histoire, Obligations et Status de la Tr. Ven. Confraternite des Francs-Mascons, traduit par le Fr. De la Tierce.* Frankfort, 1742

[70] Jones, Bernard E., *Freemason's Guide and Compendium,* HARRAP, Ltd, London, 1950, pp. 195

[71] Allan, Mason J., "Our Ritual: A Study in its Development," an article taken from *Masons and Masonry,* a compilation of essays published in the Grand Lodge of Scotland Year Books, 1953-72, Lewis Masonic, Terminal House, Middlesex, 1983, pp. 181-82

[72] Rylands, J.R., *The Masonic Penalties,* Transactions of the Quatuor Coronati Lodge, London, Vol. 77, January, 1964, pp. 26

[73] Jones, *Guide and Compendium,* pp. 279

[74] Rylands, *Penalties,* pp. 25

[75] Hogan, Timothy, *The Alchemical Keys to Masonic Ritual,* Denver, CO,

2007, pp. 16

[76] Allan, Timothey; Hutchens, Rex; and Sintetos, Miles, *A Discussion of the Symbolic Penalties in Freemasonry,* undated manuscript prepared for the Arizona Lodge of Research

[77] Ibid, pp. 6

[78] Conder, Edward, *The Miracle Play,* Transactions of the Quatour Coronati Lodge, London, Vol. 14, Part 1, January, 1901, pp. 61

[79] Ibid, pp. 61

[80] Buckness, Peter A., *Entertainment and Ritual, 600-1600,* Stainer and Bell, Ltd., London, 1979, pp. 72

[81] Ibid, pp. 62

[82] Ibid, pp. 84

[83] Ibid, pp. 115

[84] Knoop. Et al, *Catechisms,* pp. 89. The description of the Noah story summarized in the text is described in detail in the manuscript, which can be found on pp. 92-93. It has been suggested by authorities at the British Museum that the dating of the Graham MS may be 1672 rather than 1726.

[85] Knoop, Jones, and Hamer, *Early Masonic Pamphlets,* pp. 122

[86] See Samuel Lee's *Orbis Miraculum,* 1659 and John Bunyan's, *Solomon's Temple Spiritualized,* 1688. There had been a long tradition in Europe of attempted reconstructive descriptions of Solomon's Temple and symbolic meanings attached to it. Exhibitions of constructed models of the temple were on public display in London during the founding era.

[87] Jones, *Guide and Compendium,* pp. 317-18

[88] Hogan, Tim, *Entering the Chain of Union, An Explanation of Esoteric Traditions and What Unites Them,* 2012, pp. 59

[89] Hughan, William James, *The Three Degrees of Freemasonry,* Transactions of the Quatour Coronati Lodge, London, Vol. 10. Part 2, 1897, pp. 133

[90] Berman, Ric, *The Foundations of Modern Freemasonry,* Sussex Academic Press, Portland, Oregon, 2012, pp. 71

[91] Jones, *Guide and Compendium,* pp. 240

[92] Johnson, Melvin M., *The Beginnings of Freemasonry in America,* Volume 14, The Masonic Book Club, , Bloomington, Ill, 1983, pp. 376-77

[93] Frere, *Grand Lodge,* pp. 88

[94] Rebold, Emmanuel, *A General History of Free-Masonry in Europe,* translated

by J. Fletcher Brennan, Editor of the American Freemason's Magazine, American Masonic Publishing Association, Cincinnati, 1868, pp. 80-81

[95] Carr, Harry, *The Early French Exposures, 1737-1751,* published by The Quatuor Coronati Lodge No. 2076, London, 1971, pp. xii

[96] Ibid, pp. 6-8

[97] Ibid, pp. 34

[98] Ibid, pp. 143

[99] *Ahiman Rezon,* 1764, p. xxx

[100] James, P.R., *The Lectures of English Craft Masonry,* Transactions of the Quatour Coronati Lodge, London, Vol. 79, Nov. 1966, pp. 142

[101] McCleod, Wallace, in his preliminary remarks to a facsimile reprint of the first English edition of Wellins Calcott's *"A Candid Disquisition of the Principles and Practices of the Most Ancient and Honourable Society of Free and Accepted Masons,"* published by The Masonic Book Club, Boomington, Illinois, 1989, pp. 1

[102] Mackey, Albert G. and McClenachan, Charles T., *Encyclopedia of Freemasonry,* Revised edition by Hawkins and Hughan, The Masonic History Company, Chicago, 1924, pp. 342-43

[103] Hutchinson, William, *The Spirit Of Masonry,* a new edition edited by George Oliver, 1775, Bell Publishing Co., Crown Publishers, 1982, pp. 124

[104] Ibid, pp. 329-30

[105] Ibid, pp. 343

[106] *William Hutchinson and HIS SPIRIT OF MASONRY,* an article written by the editor of *The New Age,* official organ of the Ancient and Accepted Scottish Rite, SJ, Vol 1, June, 1904

[107] McCleod, *A Candid Disquisition,* The Masonic Book Club, pp. 14-15. All ritual and language citings and references in this chapter are taken from this facsimile reprint of Calcott's work.

[108] Ibid, pp. 16

[109] Ibid, pp. 199

[110] Knoop and Jones, *The Genesis of Freemasonry,* pp. 7

[111] Alex Horne, *Preston as Preceptor and Ritualist,* Transactions, AQC, May, 1968, pp. 141

[112] Hills, Gordon P.G., *Brother William Preston: An Illustration of the Man, His Methods and His Work,* The Prestonian Lecture of 1927, from "The

Collected Prestonian Lectures, 1925-1960, " Lewis Masonic, Terminal House, Shepperton, Middlesex, 1974, pp. 2

113 This sketch of Preston's early life is attributed to Stephen Jones and was originally published under the title of the *Memoirs of Mr. William Preston, Past Master of the Lodge of Antiquity No. 1,* The Freemason's Magazine, January, 1795, pp. 2-5

114 Ibid, pp. 6

115 Preston, William, *Illustrations of Freemasonry,* Masonic Classic Series, The Aquarian Press, Wellingborough, Great Brittain, 1986, pp. xxvi

116 Preston included in his First Edition of the *Illustrations of Freemasonry* a complete description and record of the Gala itself, which was held at the *Crown and Anchor* Tavern on the Strand. The account cited is from pp. 19

117 James, P.R., *The Lectures of English Craft Masonry,* Transactions of the Quatuor Coronati Lodge, Vol. 79, Nov., 1965, pp. 142

118 Cartwright, E.H. described the whole of *Browne's Master-Key* in Transactions of Quatour Coronati, XLV, pp. 90.

119 Richard, F.M., *William Finch,* Transactions, A.Q.C., Vol LV, pp 188.

120 Dyer, Colin, *William Preston and His Work,* Lewis Masonic, Terminal House, Shepperton, Middlesex, 1987, pp. 31

121 Hills, pp. 11

122 Hills, pp. 12

123 Hills, pp. 13

124 The Grand Lodge of All England had been in existence for many years prior to the creation of the 1717 Grand Lodge and was centered in the city of York in the north of England. It is purported by Mackey to have held an annual assembly for all lodges within and outside of London for centuries. It was the recognized authority of all masons prior to 1567, when a Grand Master was elected to serve the *South* of England. Its regulations formed the basis for Anderson's Constitutions of 1723. Sir Christopher Wren served as its Grand Master in 1666. The formation of the 1717 Grand Lodge was said to be a result of the persistent inactivity of the older Grand Lodge. Preston believed the later Grand Lodge was motivated primarily by London Masons to give a more public and popular face to the old private institution. See Hyneman, *History of Freemasonry in England from 1567 to 1813,*Worthington, NY, 1878

125 Hills, pp. 13

126 Dyer, pp. 160

[127] James, pp. 143

[128] See C.W. Firebrace, *Records of the Lodge of Antiquity,* Vol II, London, 1926. Firebrace notes that at a meeting of Preston's Lodge of Antiquity dated 21 March, 1787, there is an entry stating that "the first three sections in the Lecture of the First Degree were delivered from the Chair, and ably illustrated by the Officers and Brethren present." pp. 55-56

[129] James, P.R., *William Preston's Third Lecture of Freemasonry,* AQC, Vol. 85, pp. 73

[130] See Dyer's notes in his Appendix of *William Preston and His Work* regarding the dating of various printed manuscripts of the *Syllabus Books*

[131] All of the sections and clauses from the *Syllabus Books* presented in this chapter were taken from P.R. James "Lectures of William Preston," published in the Transactions of the Quatour Coronati Lodge in Volumes 82, 83, and 85, and written in 1969, 1970, and 1972

[132] In a later reprint of the *Illustrations* by Dr. George Oliver in 1855, an alternative form of the First Degree Charge was given, and is said to have been recommended by Samuel Hemming, who was Master of the Lodge of Reconciliation during the time of the 1813 Hemming's ritual forms all came from the Ancients workings, whereas Preston's were of the ritual forms of the Moderns.

[133] See Horne, Alex, *Our Craft Monitor: Its Origin and Development,* published by the Masonic Service Association, Silver Springs, Maryland, 1980.

[134] Dyer, *Preston and his Work,* pp. 150-151

[135] Pike, Albert, *Morals and Dogma of the Ancient and Accepted Scottish Rite of Freemasonry,* House of the Temple, Washington, DC 1871, pp. 107-08

[136] Wood, Gordon S., *Radicalism of the American Revolution,* Vintage Books, New York, 1993, pp. 13

[137] Ibid, pp. 60-61

[138] Ibid, pp. 82

[139] Bailyn, Bernard, *The Origins of American Politics,* New York, 1968, pp. 72-73

[140] Wood, pp. 85

[141] Ibid, pp. 109

[142] Ibid, pp. 125

[143] Ibid, pp. 129

[144] Ibid, pp. 223

[145] Ibid, pp. 224

[146] *Colonial Freemasonry,* Transactions of the Missouri Lodge of Research, edited by Lewis C. Wes Cook, Vol. 30, 1973-74, pp. 5

[147] Ibid, pp. 107

[148] Haywood, H.L., *Studies of Masonry in the United States, Part VII., The Provincial Grand Lodge System,* The Builder, March, 1925, pp. 85

[149] The Builder, 1925, pp. 85

[150] *Colonial Freemasonry,* pp. 6

[151] Ibid, pp. 6

[152] Drake, Samuel Adams, *Old Boston Taverns and Tavern Clubs,* W.A. Butterfield, 1917, pp. 34-35

[153] Drake, pp. 103

[154] See Tatsch, Hugo J., *Freemasonry in the Thirteen Colonies,* Macoy Publishing and Masonic Supply Co., New York, 1929; and Cook's, *Colonial Freemasonry,* Missouri Lodge of Research, 1973-74

[155] Warren was raised in St. Andrews Lodge on November 26, 1761. He was elected Master in 1768 and became Grand Master in 1769. On March 3, 1773, he was given a commission by the Grand Master of Scotland to be Grand Master of Masons on the Continent of North America.

[156] Denslow, William R., *Freemasonry and the American Indian,* 1956, pp. 118

[157] Ibid, pp. 125

[158] Bizzack, John, *Discovering Freemasonry in Context,* unpublished manuscript, Draft 11, Lexington, Kentucky, March 2012, pp. 91

[159] Martin, Clarence, *Traveling Military Lodges,* paper presented at the Conference of Grand Masters in Washington, DC, February 23-24, 1943

[160] Milborne, A.J.B., *Transactions of the American Lodge of Research,* Vol. X, pp. 22-85, 1966. Milborne gives a detailed description of each of the known lodges, along with an excellent bibliography for persons interested in this particular line of inquiry.

[161] *Colonial Freemasonry,* pp. 88

[162] Tatsch, *Masonry in the Thirteen Colonies,* pp. 209.

[163] The six causes of ritual diversity given by Brother Pounds were widely published in Masonic magazines and Grand Lodge bulletins across the country. I encountered the list no less than four times in publications distributed between 1915 and 1922.

[164] Clark, George B., *Genealogy of Masonry in the Colonies,* 1939. Also see Wallace Mcleod, *Causes of Ritual Divergence,* "The Grand Design," Anchor Communications, Virginia, 1991, pp 93-96

[165] Bollock, *Revolutionary Brotherhood,* pp. 221

[166] Leyland, Herbert T., *Thomas Smith Webb, Freemason, Musician, Entrepreneur,* The Otterbein Press, Dayton, Ohio, 1965. Most of the material penned in this chapter was taken from this definitive biography of Webb.

[167] Ibid, pp. 31

[168] Ibid, pp. 53

[169] *Temple Lodge #14, MS By-Laws Book, Condensed History of the Lodge, Albany, NY, 1893, Taylor and Hawley, pp. 4*

[170] *Webb, Thomas Smith, The Freemason's Monitor; Or Illustrations of Masonry; In Two Parts,* 1797, Albany, Spencer and Webb, pp. A

[171] Chapman, Alfred F., *St. Andrew's Royal Arch Chapter of Boston, Massachusetts,* Boston, 1883, pp 30-31

[172] Leyland, pp. 76

[173] Horne, Alex, *Sources of Masonic Symbolism,* Transactions, Victoria Lodge of Education and Research, Victoria, B.C. 1977

[174] Horne, Alex, *Our Craft Monitor, Its Origin and Development,* The Masonic Service Association, Maryland, 1980, pp 14

[175] Ibid, pp. 24-25

[176] A detailed description of the services and processional was published in the *Rhode Island American,* November 8, 1819. The hymn sung at the funeral services was from Handel's chorale, "The Dead March," from the Oratorio *Saul.* The words and music appear on pp. 219-219 of the 1826 edition of Jeremy Cross's *True Masonic Chart,* under the title of 'funeral hymn'. Leyland thought this hymn was the predecessor of the Pleyel Hymn (funeral dirge) now in general Masonic use.

[177] Freemason's Repository, *Thomas Smith Webb, No. 33,* pp. 141, Grand Lodge of Rhode Island. The Grand Lodge published a biographical series on Webb which ran in its monthly bulletin, beginning in 1871 and ending June, 1874.

[178] Mount Vernon Lodge Records, Providence, R.I., as provided by the Grand Secretary

[179] Notice of Authorization to John Snow by Franklin County Court of Common Pleas as Administrator of T.S. Webb's estate dated Aug. 2, 1819

[180] Letter from Snow to a Companion Z. Hood in Granville, OH, dated Aug. 10, 1819; in the possession of Richard D. Snow who included the contents in a biographical sketch he penned for the Ohio Grand Lodge. The author received a copy of the publication but failed to get the date the article was written.

[181] Ohio Grand Lodge Proceedings, 1848

[182] Spargo, John, *John Barney, Freemason Extraordinary,* Address delivered at the 161st. Annual Communication of the Grand Lodge of Vermont, F. & A.M., June 9, 1954.

[183] Spargo, pp. 4

[184] Joseph Cerneau was a charlatan who at one time may have received a legitimate patent to confer degrees in the Lodge of Perfection of the Scottish Rite, but, ignoring his limited authority, created his own Grand Consistory and Grand Encampment and began operating a degree mill for the higher degrees. Conferring his own degrees on Masons in a number of states and outside the legitimate and recognized Bodies, Grand Lodges often took action requiring their members either to withdraw from this clandestine Scottish or York Rite organization or face expulsion. This created divisions of loyalty among Masons and added to the anti-masonry fervor already prevalent in many states between 1826 and 1850.

[185] Charles W. Moore was the Editor of the *Freemason's Monthly Magazine.* These remarks appeared as a quote made by Moore and reported in the June 1, 1880 edition of the *Magazine.*

[186] Leyland, Herbert, *Thomas Smith Webb,* pp. 112

[187] *Freemason's Monthly Magazine, 1860,* pp 228, a reprint of Phillip Tucker's allocution as Grand Master of Vermont in his address to his Grand lodge at its annual communication, 1859.

[188] *The Lecturer of Sixty Years Since,* "The Voice of Masonry and Tidings from the Craft, A Monthly Magazine Devoted to Masonic Science, Harmony and Uniformity, Volume II," Rob Morris, LL.D., Editor in Chief, John C. W. Bailey, Publisher and Printer, Chicago, Ill., 1864, pp. 205

[189] *The Diary of (Rev.) William Bentley,* Volume IV., Salem, Mass., 1811-1819, pp. 308

[190] *Freemason's Monthly Magazine,* 1865, Volume XXIV, pp. 205, Charles W. Moore, Editor, Boston, Hugh and Tuttle

[191] Kilmer, David H., *The Autobiography of Henry Fowle of Boston (1766-1837),* Heritage Books, Maryland, 1991, pp. x-xi.

[192] "Jeremy L. Cross, *Voice of Masonry, Volume I,* 1862, Rob Morris Editor, pp. 269

[193] Cross, *Voice of America,* pp. 274-

[194] *Drummond's Comments on the Activities of Jeremy L. Cross,* History of the Cryptic Rite, Volume II, pp. 1299

[195] A History of the Cryptic Rite, Volume II, *A Diary Kept by Jeremy L. Cross from August 17, 1817, to April 3, 1820,* published by the General Grand Council, R. & S. M. of the United States, pp. 1271

[196] "The Broken Column," *Short Talk Bulletin, Vol. 34,* February 1956, Masonic Service Association, Silver Springs, MA

[197] *The Indiana Freemason,* May, 1967

[198] Hextall, W.B., *The Special Lodge of Promulgation, 1809-1811,* A.Q.C. Transactions, Vol. 23, 1910, pp. 37-38

[199] Gould's "History of Freemasonry," Vol. II. pp. 498

[200] Hextall, pp. 55

[201] Chetwode-Crawley, W.J., *The International Compact,* AQC, Vol. 28, p. 144

[202] Hextall, pp. 235

[203] Ibid, pp. 247, 243

[204] *Freemason's Quarterly Review,* 1836, p. 322, as cited by Hiram Hallett, in *A Short Account of the Lodges of Promulgation, Reconciliation, Stability and Emulation,* Parrett, Ltd., 1932, pp. 31

[205] Hallet, Hiram, *A Short Account of the Lodges of Promulgation, Reconciliation, Stability and Emulation,* ,citing Henry Sadler, p. 9

[206] Hallet, pp 39

[207] Sadler, Henry, *Illustrated History of the Emulation Lodge of Improvement No. 256, 1823-1903,* Spencer, 1904, London, pp. 115

[208] Hallet, pp. 43

[209] *The National Masonic Conventions: The Birth and Places of Celebration, 1842-1843-1846,* Committee on History, Grand Lodge of Maryland, 1943, a text of the proceedings published in commemoration of the one hundredth anniversary of the National Masonic Convention held in Baltimore, Maryland, May 8, 1843

[210] Ibid, pp. 30

[211] Ibid, pp. 50

[212] Ibid, pp. 103-04

[213] *The Masonic Trestle-Board, adapted to the National System of Work and Lectures, as Revised and Perfected by the National Masonic Convention, at Baltimore, Maryland, A.L 5843 by Charles W. Moore & S.W.B. Carnegy,* Boston, 1843, pp. 3

[214] Shepherd, Silas H., "The Ritual in the 19th Century", an article appearing in the *Masonic Tidings,* Grand Lodge of Wisconsin, July, 1918, Masonic Committee on Masonic Research, pp. 5. See also "Notes on the Ritual," Wisconsin Grand Lodge Committee on Masonic Research, Research Pamphlet No. 19, March 1, 1924

[215] *Trestle-Board, a facsimile reprint of the original Trestle-Board published by the Baltimore Convention of 1843,* with a foreword by Dwight Smith, Grand Secretary, Grand Lodge of Indiana, Volume 8, The Masonic Book club, Bloomington, ILL, 1978, pp. xiv, xv.

[216] "The Masonic Conservators," *Short Talk Bulletin, Volume XXIV, No. 1,* Masonic Service Association of the United States, Washington, DC, January, 1946, pp. 3

[217] Denslow, Ray V., *The Masonic Conservator,* The Masonic Service Association of Missouri, published by the Grand Lodge, Ancient, Free and Accepted Masons of the State of Missouri, 1931, pp. 46-47

[218] Ibid, pp. 87-95

[219] *Instruction and Inspection of Ritualistic Work in United States Grand Lodges,* Masonic Service Association, Silver Spring, Maryland, May, 1974

[220] *Ritual Ciphers,* undated manuscript published by the Masonic Service Association, Silver Springs, Maryland, pp. 1-2.

[221] The Traditional Observance lodge model is an excellent example of how ritual space can effectively be created to enhance "setting a world apart" from the profane experience. Following French lodge traditions, features include a dress code for members, chambers of reflection for candidates, candle lit lodges, darkened rooms, contemplative music, periods of meditation, the singing of Masonic odes, and circles of union at closing.

[222] Davis, Robert G., *Understanding Manhood in America: Freemasonry's Enduring Path to the Mature Masculine.* Anchor Communication, Lancaster, VA, 2005. See pp. 108-110 on symbolic interaction; also much of the information in this Chapter was taken from Chapter 12

[223] See James, P.R., *The First Lecture of Freemasonry by William Preston,* AQC, Vol. 82, pp. 104-155*; and William Preston's Second Lecture of Freemasonry,* AQC, Vo. 83, pp. 193-247, and *William Preston's Third Lecture*

of Freemasonry, AQC, Vol 85, pp. 69-123.

[224] Stewart Trevor, *English Speculative Freemasonry: Some Possible Origins, Themes and Developments,* Prestonian Lecture, 2004, United Grand Lodge of England

[225] Stewart, pp. 14

[226] Leyland, Herbert, *Thomas Smith Webb,* pp. 74

[227] I purposefully ended this study with essentially the same admonition Brother Stewart delivered to his English Brothers in the Prestonian Lecture in 2004. It is a message that should be delivered and heard throughout the world.

INDEX

C

D

G

H

Q

R

S

T

Y

www.ingramcontent.com/pod-product-compliance
Lightning Source LLC
Chambersburg PA
CBHW062156270326
41930CB00009B/1551
* 9 7 8 0 6 1 5 8 5 3 8 2 6 *